This book is to be
the last date

**aker**
The Anthony Gell School, Wirksworth

▶ **Paul Hogan**
Fulwood High School, Preston

▶ **Barbara Job**
Christleton County High School, Chester

▶ **Renie Verity**
Pensby High School for Girls, Heswall

**Stanley Thornes (Publishers) Ltd**

# Contents

## Acknowledgements

The publishers thank the following for permission
to reproduce copyright material:
Aerofilms, p. 147; Ancient Art & Architecture
p. 239 (both – Ronald Sheridan); ED142018
The Thinker, Bronze by Rodin (front view)
Musee Rodin, Paris/Bridgeman Art Library,
London, p. 201; British Broadcasting Corporation,
p. 52; British Mensa Ltd, p. 337; Central Statistical
Office, p. 285; Channel Four Television, p. 52;
Collections, pp. 296 (Brian Shuel); Derbyshire
County Council & Derbyshire Constabulary,
p. 186; The Hulton Deutsch Collection, p. 51;
Independent Television, p. 52; Kraft Jacobs
Suchard, pp. 308, 313; Milepost $9\frac{1}{2}$, p. 142;
National Savings, p. 159; The National Blood
Service, p. 295; Reproduced from the Ordance
Survey mapping with permission of The
Controller of Her Majesty's Stationery Office
© Crown copyright (07000U), pp. 225, 241, 243,
262; Sky Television, p. 52; Sporting Pictures (UK)
Ltd, pp. 166, 249; Tony Stone Images, pp. 43
(Simon Jauncey), 92 (John Lawrence), 237 (Dale
Durfee), 251 (Tim Davis), 268 (Kevin Kelley),
304 (David Sutherland), 314 (Art Wolfe); York
City Archives, p. 250.
All other photographs by Martyn F. Chillmaid.

The publishers have made every effort to contact
copyright holders but apologise if any have been
overlooked.

First published in 1996 by
Stanley Thornes (Publishers) Ltd
Ellenborough House
Wellington Street
CHELTENHAM   GL50 1YW

98  99  00  /  10  9  8  7  6  5  4

A catalogue record for this book is available from
the British Library.

ISBN 0–7487–2459–1

Original design concept by Studio Dorel
Cover design by John Christopher, Design Works
Cover photographs: Roger Howard/Ace Photo
Agency (front); Chris Fairclough Colour Library
(spine); Baron Wolman/Tony Stone Images (back)
Artwork by Maltings Partnership, Eric Apsey,
David Oliver
Cartoons by Clinton Banbury
Typeset by Tech Set Ltd
Printed and bound in Spain by Mateu Cromo

# 1 Graphs

QUESTIONS

EXTENSION

SUMMARY

TEST YOURSELF

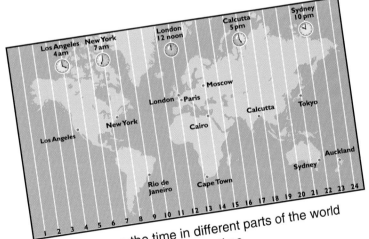

The map shows the time in different parts of the world when it is 12 noon in UK winter time.

Do you have any relations in New Zealand?
Be careful if you telephone them.
It is nearly 12 midnight in New Zealand when it is 12 noon in the UK!

Look in a world atlas to find out:
- how continents such as Africa arrange time zones to fit countries' borders
- what happens when a traveller crosses the International Date Line.

# C O R E

## 1 Conversion graphs

Class 8J are in Paris on an exchange visit. They are buying presents for their friends.
They want to convert the prices from francs to pounds.
They have a conversion graph.

### Exercise 1:1

This is the graph that 8J are using:

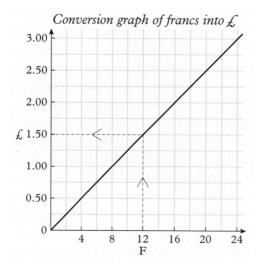

1   Anne is buying a model of the Eiffel Tower. It costs 12F.
    Find 12F on the bottom scale of the graph.
    Follow the red line to the graph.
    Read off the price in £ from the side scale.

2   Ned is buying a picture of Paris. It costs 8F.
    Convert this into £.

**3** Danielle is buying two pens. They cost 4F each.
   **a** Find the cost of a pen in £.
   **b** Find the total cost in francs and £ of 2 pens, 2 notebooks and a poster.

**4** Terry has £12 which he wants to convert to francs.
   How many francs will he get?

---

| **Conversion graph** | We use a **conversion graph** to change from one unit to another. Conversion graphs are always straight lines. | 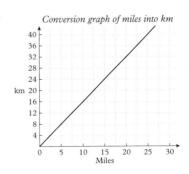 |
|---|---|---|

---

## Exercise 1:2

**1** Here is a conversion graph for US dollars ($) into £.

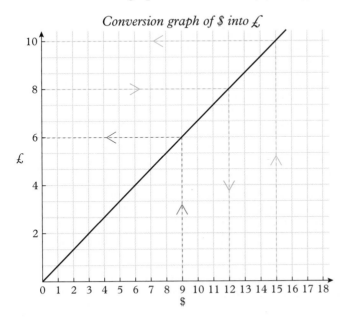

*Conversion graph of $ into £*

   **a** Convert $9 into £ (red line).
   **b** Convert $15 into £ (blue line).
   **c** Convert £8 into $ (green line).
   **d** Convert £9 into $ (to the nearest dollar).

3

**2**  This graph converts miles into kilometres.
It can also convert kilometres into miles.

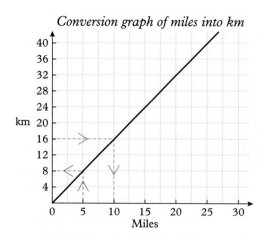

*Conversion graph of miles into km*

**a**  Convert 5 miles to km (red line).
**b**  Convert 15 miles to km.
**c**  Convert 16 **km to miles** (blue line).
**d**  Convert 30 km to miles.

**3**  This graph converts kilograms into pounds (lbs).

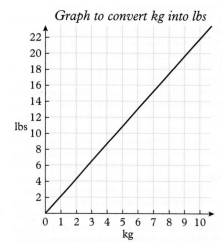

*Graph to convert kg into lbs*

**a**  A bag of sugar weighs 1 kg.
About how many pounds is this?
**b**  A large bag of potatoes weighs 5 lbs.
About how many kilograms is this?

**4**  Will all conversion graphs start at (0, 0)?
Explain your answer.

# 2 Graphs and rules

### *Exercise 1:3*

**1** Ben is taking part in the school sponsored walk.
He is being sponsored £2.35 per mile by his family. The further he
walks the more money he will collect.
He works out the amount in a table.

| Number of miles | 1 | 2 | 3 | 4 | 5 |
|---|---|---|---|---|---|
| Amount £ | | | | | |

  **a** Copy the table and fill it in.
  **b** Draw a graph of this information.
     Put the miles on the horizontal axis scaled from 0 to 5.
     Put the amount on the vertical axis scaled from 0 to 21.
  **c** Extend your graph to work out how much Ben will collect if he
     walks 7 miles.

**2** Josh is also doing the sponsored walk.
He is being sponsored £2.85 per mile.
  **a** Copy the table for Josh. Fill it in.

| Number of miles | 1 | 2 | 3 | 4 | 5 |
|---|---|---|---|---|---|
| Amount £ | | | | | |

  **b** Draw a graph for Josh.
     Put it on the same diagram as Ben's.
  **c** How much will Josh get if he walks 7 miles?
  **d** How much will he get if he walks $4\frac{1}{2}$ miles?
  **e** About how far would Josh have to walk to get £20?
  **f** How much will he get if he walks 15 miles?
     (This is not shown on the graph but you can work it out. How?)

**3** Yasmin is being sponsored £1.50 per mile.
  **a** Make a table to show the amount Yasmin will get.
  **b** Draw a graph for Yasmin on the same diagram as Ben's and Josh's.
  **c** Use your graph to work out how much Yasmin will get if she walks $3\frac{1}{2}$ miles.
  **d** How far would Yasmin need to walk to get £10.50?
  **e** Compare all three graphs.
     What happens to the graph as the sponsor money increases?
  **f** Write down where you think the line would be for these amounts of money per mile:
     (1) £5
     (2) £1
     (3) 50 p

**4** Lee is being sponsored £2.50 per mile.
  **a** Work out how much he will get for walking 5 miles.
  **b** Plot this point on a graph.
  **c** You only need two points to draw a straight line graph. Join this point to (0, 0) to get a graph for Lee.
  **d** Use your graph to work out how much Lee will get if he walks $3\frac{1}{2}$ miles.

**5** Three friends have been sponsored to enter a swimming gala. Alice is getting 40 p per length, Bob is getting 65 p per length and Camilla is getting 72 p per length.
  **a** Draw a rough sketch of all three graphs on the same diagram to show how you think they will look.
  **b** Make tables for each of the swimmers.
     Go up to 50 lengths in multiples of 10 lengths.
  **c** Plot accurate graphs from your tables on the same diagram.
  **d** Compare your graphs with your sketch.
     Write down any differences.
  **e** Describe what happens to the graph as the amount of sponsorship per length increases.

## ◄◄REPLAY►

| **Formula** | A rule written out in algebra is known as a **formula**. |
|---|---|
| *Example* | Josh is being sponsored £3 per mile. The *total* he collects equals £3 × number of *miles*. In short form this is: $t = 3 \times m$ |
| | Remember that we do not write × signs in algebra. This means that the rule should be written $t = 3m$ |

## Exercise 1:4

Write down the short form of these rules.
Use the red letters and numbers.

**1** The *total* amount raised in a sponsored walk at £2 for each *mile*.

**2** The *total* amount raised in a sponsored swim at £6 for each *length*.

**3** The *wages* earned by someone earning £4 per *hour*.

**4** The *height* of a plant which grows at **3** cm per *month*.

**5** The *distance* covered by a car travelling at **30** miles per *hour*.

**6** The *amount* of money Joanna saves if she saves **£6** per *month*.

**7** The amount Andy earns is calculated using the formula $w = 4h$
$w$ is his wages and $h$ is the number of hours he works.

Work out Andy's wages if he works for:
**a** 5 hours
**b** 7 hours
**c** $3\frac{1}{2}$ hours
**d** $6\frac{1}{4}$ hours

Sometimes it is useful to draw a graph of a rule.

*Example*

Manish has a part-time job as a waiter.
He earns £2.95 per hour that he works.
He works out a table to show how much he can earn.

| Number of hours | 1 | 2 | 3 | 4 | 5 |
|---|---|---|---|---|---|
| Wages £ | 2.95 | 5.90 | 8.85 | 11.80 | 14.75 |

His rule is: *wages* equals £2.95 × number of *hours* worked.
In algebra this is:     $w = 2.95h$

Manish draws a graph of his table:

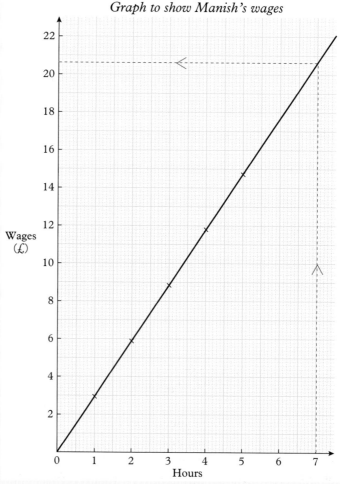

*Graph to show Manish's wages*

He can now see how much he would earn for 7 hours' work.
Follow the red line.

## Exercise 1:5

**1** Joel and Lianne are jogging together. Lianne soon gets ahead of Joel.
Lianne jogs at 4 metres per second (m/s).
Joel jogs at 3 metres per second.
They each work out a rule for the distance they jog.

   **a** Write Lianne's rule in algebra using the letters $d$ and $s$.
   **b** Copy this table for Lianne's rule.
     Use your formula to fill it in.

| Number of seconds | 10 | 20 | 30 | 40 | 50 |
|---|---|---|---|---|---|
| Distance | | | | | |

   **c** Draw a graph for this table.
   **d** Write Joel's rule in algebra.
   **e** Make a table for Joel's distances.
     Draw the graph on the same diagram as Lianne's.
   **f** Describe the differences between the two graphs.
     Explain why the graphs are different.

**2** At Stanthorne High the pupils hire lockers.
There is a deposit of £3 for the year and a charge of 75 p per half term.
   **a** Copy this table and fill it in.

| Number of half terms | 1 | 2 | 3 |
|---|---|---|---|
| Cost £ | | | |

   **b** Draw axes for a graph.
     Put the number of half terms from 0 to 6 on the horizontal axis.
     Put the cost from £0 to £10 on the vertical axis.
   **c** Plot the points from your table.
     Join them with a straight line.
     Continue the line to the edge of the graph.
   **d** From your graph, work out the cost for hiring lockers for:
     (1) 4 half terms
     (2) 6 half terms
   **e** Explain why the graph does not start at (0, 0).

**3** Three friends are running a race.
Sherene runs at a steady
speed of 5 m/s.
Kelly can only run at 4 m/s so she
gets a 3 m start.
Alix can run at 6 m/s so she starts
from 4 m behind the line!

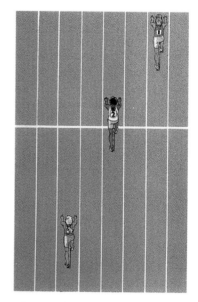

The formula for Kelly is
$d = 4t + 3$

**a** Write down a formula for
Sherene.

**b** Write down a formula for Alix.

**c** Copy and complete this table.
It shows the distance past the
starting line for the first
6 seconds of the race.

| Time (secs) | 0 | 1 | 2 | 3 | 4 | 5 | 6 |
|---|---|---|---|---|---|---|---|
| Distance Kelly | 3 | | | | | | |
| Distance Sherene | 0 | | | | | | |
| Distance Alix | −4 | | | | | | |

**d** Draw a rough sketch of what you think the graphs will look like.

**e** Predict who you think will be in the lead after 6 seconds.

**f** Draw axes from 0 to 6 horizontally and −4 to 32 vertically.

**g** Draw graphs for the three girls.

**h** Write down the times when one person overtakes another.

**i** Write down the order of the runners after six seconds.

**j** Who will be in the lead after 10 seconds?
Who will be last?

# 3 Time

The time is 7.55 am.
Stan's bus journey to school takes 47 minutes.
He wants to know if he will be at school by 8.45 am.

---

At 7.55 am it is 5 minutes to the next hour.
$47 - 5 = 42$
The bus arrives at 8.42 am.

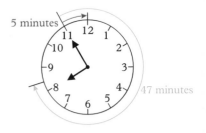

5 minutes

47 minutes

---

### Exercise 1:6

**1** Work out the times when these buses arrive.
   **a** Bus leaves at 7.50 am and takes 45 minutes.
   **b** Bus leaves at 3.35 pm and takes 50 minutes.
   **c** Bus leaves at 7.25 am and takes 36 minutes.
   **d** Bus leaves at 10.17 am and takes 52 minutes.

| am | **am** stands for ante meridian. | This means before noon. |
| pm | **pm** stands for post meridian. | This means after noon. |

7.55 am is in the morning.    3.04 pm is in the afternoon.

Timetables for buses and trains use the 24-hour clock.

*Examples*

*We always have four figures.*
7.55 am is the same as **07 55**
3.04 pm is the same as **15 04**
Midnight is 00 00
Midday is 12 00

---

**2**  Work out the times when these buses arrive.
Use the 24-hour clock.
   **a**  Bus leaves at 15 52 and takes 14 minutes.
   **b**  Bus leaves at 08 05 and takes 39 minutes.
   **c**  Bus leaves at 14 19 and takes 55 minutes.
   **d**  Bus leaves at 21 43 and takes 26 minutes.

---

*Example*

A train leaves at 08 36.
The journey takes 2 hours 45 minutes.
When does the train arrive?

*Work out the minutes first.*
At 08 36 it is 24 minutes to the next hour.
$45 - 24 = 21$
A train taking just 45 minutes would arrive at 09 21.
A train taking 2 hours 45 minutes would arrive at 11 21.

---

**3**  Work out the times when these trains arrive.
Use the 24-hour clock.
   **a**  Train leaves at 12 44 and takes 1 hour 37 minutes.
   **b**  Train leaves at 08 52 and takes 3 hours 18 minutes.
   **c**  Train leaves at 18 25 and takes 2 hours 19 minutes.
   **d**  Train leaves at 15 38 and takes 4 hours 26 minutes.

**4**  Ms Davies has an important meeting.
She needs to be in Manchester at 9.45 am.
Her train leaves at 7.52 and takes 1 hour 34 minutes.
Will Ms Davies be early or late and by how many minutes?

**5** A film lasts 112 minutes.
   **a** How long does it last in hours and minutes?
   **b** If the film starts at 8.15 pm, when will it finish?

· · · · · · · · · · · · · · · · · · · · · · · · · · · · · · · · · · · · · · · · · · · · · · · · · · · · · · · · · ·

---

*Example*    How long is it from 8.35 am to
9.12 am?

From 8.35 to 9.00 is 25 minutes.
From 9.00 to 9.12 is 12 minutes.
25 + 12 = 37
Answer: 37 min

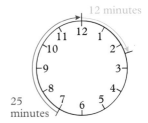

---

## Exercise 1:7

**1** How long is it between these times?
   **a** 7.25 am to 8.17 am
   **b** 09 34 to 10 28
   **c** 6.48 pm to 7.15 pm
   **d** 16 25 to 17 33

---

*Example*        How long is it from 8.35 pm to 11.42 pm?

8.35 to 9.00 is 25 min                          11.00 to 11.42 is 42 min

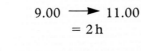

9.00 ⟶ 11.00
     = 2 h

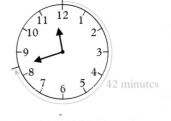

25 + 42 = 67 min
         = 1 h 7 min
2 h + 1 h 7 min = 3 h 7 min

---

13

**2** How long is it between these times?

   **a** 5.15 pm to 7.37 pm        **d** 9.05 am to 3.54 pm

   **b** 19 29 to 21 08             **e** 17 28 to 21 43

   **c** 09 20 to 13 46             **f** 16 42 to 23 15

**3** Sian's school day starts at 8.50 am and finishes at 3.35 pm.

   **a** How long is Sian at school?

   **b** Morning break is 15 minutes and lunch is 1 hour.
      How long is Sian with her class?

You can use a calculator with a `° ' "` key to do calculations with time.
The symbols stand for degrees, minutes, seconds. They are meant for calculating angles.
You can use them for time.
If your calculator has a **DMS** key ask your teacher for help.

---

*Examples* **1**  Enter 9 h 30 min on the calculator.

     Key in:    `9` `° ' "` `3` `0` `° ' "` gives a display   $9.5$

     Key in:    **SHIFT** `° ' "` gives a display   $9°30°0$

     $9°30°0$  means 9 hours 30 minutes and 0 seconds.

    **2**  Enter the time 15 25 on the calculator.

     Key in:    `1` `5` `° ' "` `2` `5` `° ' "` gives a display   $15.4166...$

     Key in:    **SHIFT** `° ' "` gives a display   $15°25°0$

     $15°25°0$ means 15 hours 25 minutes 0 seconds.

---

## Exercise 1:8

**1**  Copy this table and fill it in.

| Time | Decimal display | h min display |
|------|-----------------|---------------|
| **a**  6 h 30 min | | |

   Enter these in your table:

   **b** 8 h 15 min    **c** 15 45    **d** 18 20    **e** 23 35    **f** 12 midday

*Example*    How long is it from 9.40 am to 1.08 pm?

> 1.08 pm is 13 08
> The calculation is    13 08 − 09 40
> Key in:

> [ 1 ] [ 3 ] [ °, ,, ] [ 0 ] [ 8 ] [ °, ,, ]

> [ − ] [ 9 ] [ °, ,, ] [ 4 ] [ 0 ] [ °, ,, ] [ = ] [ SHIFT ] [ °, ,, ]

> Answer: 3 h 28 min

**2**  Use a calculator to find how long it is between these times.
   **a**  9.25 am to 11.37 am          **d**  6.23 pm to 8.49 pm
   **b**  10 05 to 15 38               **e**  10.04 am to 3.52 pm
   **c**  9.36 pm to midnight          **f**  8.45 pm to 11.19 pm

Your calculator may not have a special key for time calculations.
You can still use it to calculate times.

*Examples* **1**  Convert 9 h 20 min to a decimal.

> Do the minutes first:    $20 \div 60 = 0.333...$
> Now add the hours:    $0.333... + 9 =$

> Answer: 9.333... h

**2**  Convert the decimal time 15.3745 h to hours and minutes.

> Subtract the hours: $15.3745 − 15 = 0.3745$
> Change to minutes: $0.3745 \times 60 = 22.47$ min
> 22.47 min is 22 min to the nearest minute.

> Answer: 15 h 22 min

**3**  Convert these times to decimals.
   **a**  8 h 30 min   **b**  14 h 20 min   **c**  30 h 8 min   **d**  50 min

**4**  Convert these to hours and minutes correct to the nearest minute.
   **a**  6.5 h   **b**  0.75 h   **c**  7.256 h   **d**  8.675 h   **e**  17.666 666... h

## Exercise 1:9

| Liverpool Lime Street | 0600 | —    | 0710 | 0745 | —    | 0845 | 0945 |
|-----------------------|------|------|------|------|------|------|------|
| Runcorn               | 0617 | —    | 0727 | 0802 | —    | 0902 | 1002 |
| Hartford              | —    | 0648 | —    | —    | 0856 | —    | 1013 |
| Crewe                 | 0639 | 0702 | 0753 | —    | 0914 | 0925 | 1025 |
| Stafford              | 0700 | —    | —    | 0837 | 0935 | 0944 | 1047 |
| Tamworth              | 0720 | —    | —    | —    | —    | —    | —    |
| Nuneaton              | 0735 | —    | —    | —    | —    | 1008 | —    |
| Rugby                 | —    | 0802 | —    | —    | —    | 1023 | 1125 |
| Milton Keynes Central | —    | —    | —    | 0933 | 1031 | 1049 | —    |
| Watford Junction      | —    | —    | 0930 | —    | —    | —    | 1214 |
| London Euston         | 0853 | 0912 | 0953 | 1020 | 1117 | 1136 | 1237 |

The timetable shows some trains from Liverpool to London.

**1**  **a**  What time is the earliest train from Runcorn that stops at Watford Junction?
   **b**  How long does the train take to get from Runcorn to Watford Junction?

**2**  Donna has an important appointment in Milton Keynes at 10 45. Which train should she get from Liverpool?

**3**  **a**  What time does the 10 13 from Hartford get to Rugby?
   **b**  How long does this train take to get from Hartford to Rugby?

**4**  I have just missed the 06 39 from Crewe to London Euston.
   **a**  How long will I have to wait for the next train?
   **b**  What time will I arrive in London?
   **c**  How much later will I arrive than if I had caught the 06 39?

**5**  There are five trains on this timetable that go from Liverpool to London Euston.
   **a**  Work out the time each train takes to get from Liverpool to London Euston.
   **b**  What time does the fastest train leave Liverpool?
   **c**  What time does the slowest train leave Liverpool?
   **d**  Look carefully at the timetable.
      Why do you think some trains take longer than others?

# 4  Travel graphs

Carl and Sian enjoy train spotting.
They know that express trains
travel very fast.
Other trains go more slowly.

### Exercise 1:10

Copy these axes on to squared paper.
Use them for all the questions in this exercise.

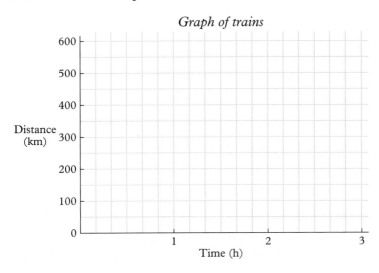

*Graph of trains*

**1  a**  Copy the table for an express train travelling at an
average speed of 200 km/h.
Fill it in.

| Time from start (h) | 0 | 1 | 2 | 3 |
|---|---|---|---|---|
| Distance travelled (km) | 0 | 200 | | |

**b**  Plot the points from the table.
Join them to get a straight line.
Label your line 'express train'.

17

**2** **a** A goods train travels at an average speed of 100 km/h.
Make a table for this train like the one in question **1**.
  **b** Plot the points from the table.
Join them to get a straight line.
Label your line 'goods train'.

**3** A cross-country train travels at an average speed of 150 km/h.
  **a** Describe where the line for this train will go on your graph.
  **b** Make a table for the cross-country train.
  **c** Plot the points from the table.
Join them to get a straight line.
Label your line 'cross-country train'.

**4** **a** Describe how the speed of a train affects its graph.
  **b** Describe the graph of a train that is not moving.

**5** The axes you have used for this exercise use six divisions for one hour.
How many minutes does one division represent?

**6** How many minutes does one division represent on these scales?

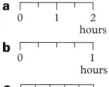

**7** What are the times shown on these scales?

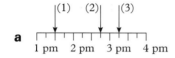

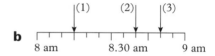

## *Exercise 1:11*

**1**

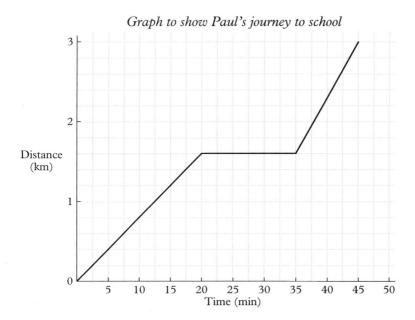

*Graph to show Paul's journey to school*

The graph shows Paul's journey from home to school.
**a** Paul started by walking.
How long did he walk?
**b** Paul stopped at a shop to buy a pen.
(1) How does this show on the graph?
(2) How long did Paul stop?
**c** Paul was late and started to run.
How long did he run?
**d** How long did Paul's journey take altogether?
**e** If he left home at 8.05 am, what time did Paul arrive at school?
**f** How far does Paul travel to school?
**g** How far is the shop from Paul's school?

**2** Copy the axes from question **1**.
Draw a graph of Anne's journey from home to school.
**a** Anne walks 1 km in 15 minutes from home to the bus stop.
Draw a line to show this on your graph.
**b** Ann waits 10 minutes for a bus.
Draw a horizontal line to show this on your graph.
**c** The bus travels 2 km in 15 minutes to get to Anne's school.
(1) How far has Ann travelled altogether?
(2) How many minutes does Ann take to get from home to school?
(3) Use your answers to (1) and (2) to help you complete your graph.

**3** Copy the axes on to squared paper.

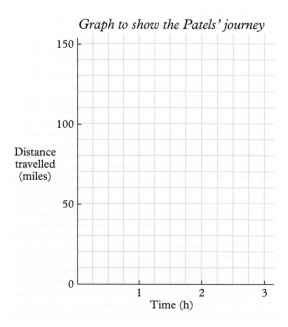

*Graph to show the Patels' journey*

The Patel family are travelling on the motorway in their car.

**a** They travel at 60 miles/h.
   How far do they travel in one hour?
   Plot this point on your graph.

**b** They continue at 60 miles/h for another 30 minutes.
   (1) How far do they travel in 30 minutes?
   (2) How far have they travelled altogether?
   (3) Plot this point on your graph.
   (4) Draw the line for the first part of the journey.

**c** The Patels stop for coffee for 30 minutes.
   Draw this on your graph.

**d** They continue for one more hour.
   They are now 120 miles from home.
   (1) Plot the point they have reached on your graph.
   (2) Draw a line for this part of the journey.

**e** At what speed did they travel after coffee?

**f** The average speed for the whole journey

$$= \frac{\text{total distance travelled}}{\text{total time taken}}$$

   Find the average speed of the Patels' journey.

**4**  Copy the axes on to squared paper.

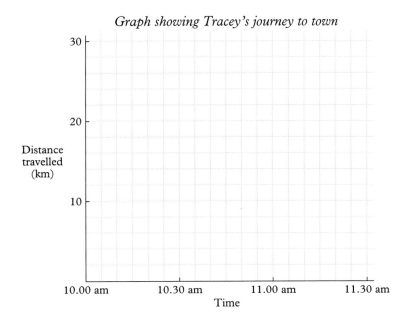

*Graph showing Tracey's journey to town*

Tracey goes out on her bicycle on Saturday morning.
She leaves home at 10 o'clock.

**a**  Tracey starts cycling at 32 km/h.
  (1) How far does she cycle in 30 minutes?
  (2) Plot this point on your graph.
  (3) Draw the line for the first part of Tracey's journey.
**b**  Tracey spends 20 minutes in the library.
   Draw this on your graph.
**c**  Tracey leaves the library with a friend.
   She walks 2 km pushing her bike. This takes 20 minutes.
   Draw Tracey's walk on your graph.
**d**  Tracey rides 8 km into town in 20 minutes.
   Draw this on your graph.
**e**  How far does Tracey travel altogether?
**f**  At what time does Tracey arrive in town?

**1** This graph converts inches into centimetres.

  **a** A ruler is 6 inches long.
About how many centimetres is this?

  **b** A book measures 4 inches by 8 inches.
What is the size of the book in centimetres?

  **c** A television has a 67 cm screen.
What is this in inches?

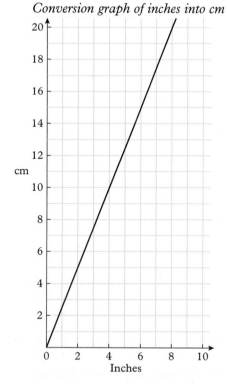

*Conversion graph of inches into cm*

**2** Keeping a cat costs about £4 per week.
  **a** Plot a graph of the cost.
  **b** How much does it cost to keep a cat for 6 weeks?

Keeping a large dog costs about £7 per week.
  **c** Plot the cost of keeping a dog on your diagram.
  **d** Why is the dog graph steeper?

**3** The school play is due to start at 7.30 pm. It starts seven minutes late.
There is an interval of 15 minutes. The play finishes at 9.44 pm.
How long is the play?

**4** Jaswinder is revising for GCSE.
He wants to do three hours' revision each night.
Jaswinder starts at 4.25 pm.
He breaks for tea which takes 45 minutes.
At 7.40 pm he stops to watch television.
  **a** How long has Jaswinder worked?
  **b** The television programme ends at 8.35 pm. Jaswinder starts his revision again.
When will he finish his three hours?

**5** Luke goes into town after school. He leaves at 4 pm.
Copy the axes.
Draw a travel graph of Luke's trip.

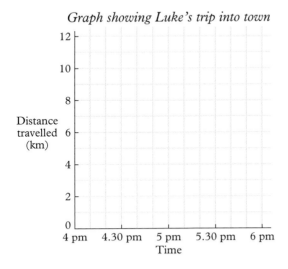

*Graph showing Luke's trip into town*

|  | Distance | Time taken |
|---|---|---|
| walk to library | 4 km | 40 min |
| choose books | – | 30 min |
| bus to town | 5 km | 20 min |
| walk through town | 2 km | 30 min |

**a** (1) When was Luke travelling the fastest?
  (2) How can you tell this from the graph?
**b** How far did he travel altogether?
**c** What was Luke's average speed for the whole trip?

**6** How long is it between these times?
Give your answers in hours and minutes.
**a** 11.24 am to 2.15 pm
**b** 08 45 to 11 37
**c** 4.26 pm to 7.55 pm
**d** 8.51 pm to 10.44 pm
**e** 00 43 to 05 28
**f** 6.21 am to 2.42 pm

23

**1** This table shows the exchange rate for Spanish pesetas and £.

| £ | 1 | 2 | 3 | 4 |
|---|---|---|---|---|
| Spanish pesetas | 200 | 400 | 600 | 800 |

**a** Draw a conversion graph. Use these scales.

**b** Continue your graph to the edge of the scale.

**c** Use your graph to work out the cost of these items in £:
(1) A toy donkey costing 1000 pesetas
(2) A picture of Madrid costing 700 pesetas

**d** How many pesetas would you get for £50?

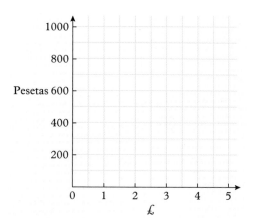

**2** Draw a horizontal axis from 0 to 3 hours and a vertical axis from 0 to 150 miles.
On your axes draw a graph of Mr Brown's car journey.

Mr Brown drove for 30 minutes at 70 miles/h.
He stopped for lunch for 30 minutes.
After lunch Mr Brown drove for 45 minutes at 60 miles/h.
During the last hour of his journey he slowed to 40 miles/h.
**a** How far did Mr Brown travel altogether?
**b** What was Mr Brown's average speed for his whole journey?

**3** Work out the average speeds of these journeys in miles/h or km/h.
**a** 75 miles in 1 h 30 min
**b** 36 km in 20 min
**c** 24 miles in 18 minutes
**d** 68 miles in 17 minutes
**e** 48 km in 25 minutes
**f** 125 km in 50 minutes
**g** 460 miles in 3 h 50 min
**h** 121 km in 2 h 45 min

**4** A bird flies 100 metres in 50 seconds.
**a** What is its speed in metres/second?
**b** Convert its speed to kilometres/hour.

# SUMMARY

- ## Conversion graph

  We use a **conversion graph** to change from
  one unit to another.
  Conversion graphs are always straight lines.

  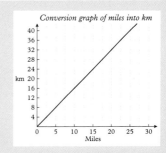

- ## Graphs and formulas

  Nicky is being sponsored £3 per mile
  The *total* he collects equals £3 × number of *miles*.
  In algebra this is $t = 3 \times m$
  We write $t = 3m$

  To draw a graph of a formula first fill in a table:

  | Number of miles | 1 | 2 | 3 | 4 | 5 |
  |---|---|---|---|---|---|
  | Amount £ | 3 | 6 | 9 | 12 | 15 |

  Then draw the graph.

  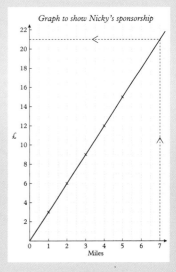

- ## Time

  **am** stands for ante meridian. This means before noon.
  **pm** stands for post meridian. This means after noon.

  24-hour clock times always have four figures.
  6.35 am is the same as 06 35
  5.25 pm is the same as 17 25

  You can enter times in your calculator using the **DMS** or ° ' '' keys.

- ## Travel graphs

  Time is always shown along
  the horizontal axis.
  Distance is always shown on
  the vertical axis.

  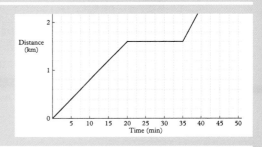

1   This is a conversion graph for
    German marks (DM) into £.
    **a** Convert DM10 into £.
    **b** Convert DM13 into £.
    **c** Find £3.50 to the nearest DM.

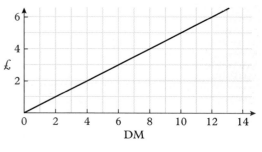

2   Alison earns £5 per hour as a waitress.
    **a** Copy this table and fill it in.

| Number of hours | 1 | 2 | 3 | 4 | 5 |
|---|---|---|---|---|---|
| Wages £ | | | | | |

   **b** Draw a graph of Alison's wages.

3   Amy took part in a sponsored fast for charity.
    She stopped eating at 19 30 on Tuesday.
    She had her first meal at 16 48 on Wednesday.
    How long did her fast last?

4   The graph shows Mohammed's journey to work.

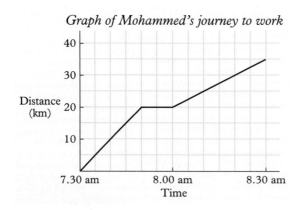

*Graph of Mohammed's journey to work*

   **a** On the way he stopped at the paper shop. How long did he stop for?
   **b** How far was Mohammed's journey to work altogether?
   **c** Mohammed travelled at different speeds before and after stopping.
      (1) Which part of the journey was faster?
      (2) Explain how the graph shows this.
   **d** Write down Mohammed's speed for the second part of the journey.

# 2 Estimating your mental power

The number $10^{100}$ is called a googol.

This is a 1 and one hundred zeros.

$10^{100} =$ 10 000 000 000 000 000 000 000 000 000 000 000 000 000 000 000 000 000 000 000 000 000 000 000 000 000 000 000 000 000 000 000 000 000 000 000 000 000

It takes Kerry $\frac{1}{4}$ second to write a zero and $\frac{1}{5}$ second to write the 1.
How long does it take her to write a googol?

# 1 Powers and roots

This number pattern is special.

The dots always form a square.

◀◀ **REPLAY** ▶

$$1 \times 1 = 1 \qquad 2 \times 2 = 4 \qquad 3 \times 3 = 9$$

For $1 \times 1$ we write $1^2$ (one squared).
For $2 \times 2$ we write $2^2$ (two squared).
For $3 \times 3$ we write $3^2$ (three squared).

---

**Square numbers**

The **square numbers** are 1, 4, 9, ...
We get them from $1^2$, $2^2$, $3^2$, ...

We can use the $\boxed{x^2}$ key on a calculator to work out square numbers.

*Example*

Work out $6^2$

Key in: $\boxed{6}$ $\boxed{x^2}$

Answer: 36

---

## Exercise 2:1

**1** Use $\boxed{x^2}$ to work out:

| | | | | |
|---|---|---|---|---|
| **a** $4^2$ | **c** $7^2$ | **e** $10^2$ | **g** $21^2$ | **i** $31^2$ | **k** $29^2$ |
| **b** $5^2$ | **d** $9^2$ | **f** $13^2$ | **h** $26^2$ | **j** $43^2$ | **l** $54^2$ |

**2** Use $\boxed{x^2}$ to work out:

**a** $20^2$ **b** $30^2$ **c** $40^2$

Without using your calculator, write down the answers to:

**d** $50^2$ **e** $60^2$ **f** $70^2$

**3** Use  $\boxed{x^2}$ to work out:
   **a** $4.3^2$       **c** $2.6^2$       **e** $100^2$
   **b** $7.5^2$       **d** $31.2^2$     **f** $130^2$

---

*Example*      Find the area of this square.

Area = length × width
      = 4 × 4
      = 16 cm²

4 cm

4 cm

4 × 4 is $4^2$. You can use $\boxed{x^2}$

Key in: $\boxed{4}$ $\boxed{x^2}$

Answer: 16 cm²

---

**4** Use $\boxed{x^2}$ to find the areas of these squares:

**a**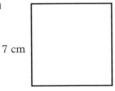
7 cm
7 cm

**b**
12 cm

**c**
2.3 cm

**5** This bowling green is a square.
The length of a side is 25 m.
Tom mows the lawn with a
mower with a cutter which is
50 cm wide.
   **a** What is the area in cm² of each
      square in the mowing pattern?
   **b** What is the area of the lawn in cm²?

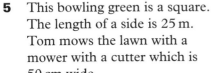

**6**  **a** Find the area of this square
      chessboard.
      The length of a side is 48 cm.
   **b** Find the area of each square on the
      board.

*Example* **1**    The area of this square is 25 cm².
What is the length of a side?

We know that
    5×5 = 25
So the length of a side is 5 cm.

> area
> = 25 cm²

**Square root**    On a calculator there is a  key.
This is called a **square root** key.
This key will find the length of a side of a square for you.

**2**    The length of a side of this square is √25

Key in: **2** **5** ▢

Answer: 5 cm

## Exercise 2:2

**1**   Use ▢ to find the length of a side of these squares.

**a**
> area
> = 36 cm²

**b**
> area = 121 cm²

**c**
> area = 49 cm²

**d**
> area
> = 100 mm²

**2**   Work out:

| | | | |
|---|---|---|---|
| **a** √25 | **d** √169 | **g** √361 | **j** √676 |
| **b** √64 | **e** √196 | **h** √225 | **k** √900 |
| **c** √144 | **f** √324 | **i** √256 | **l** √3136 |

The area of this square is 7 cm².
The length of a side is √7

**7** ▢ on the calculator gives

2.6457513

> area
> = 7 cm²

2.6                    ↑                    2.7

2.64 is nearer to 2.6 than to 2.7

The length of the side is 2.6 cm correct to one decimal place (1 dp).

To round to any number of decimal places look at the first
unwanted digit.
If it is 1, 2, 3 or 4 miss off all the unwanted digits.
If it is 5, 6, 7, 8 or 9 add one to the last digit that you keep.

*Examples*       62.346       correct to 2 decimal places is 62.35

24.34427     correct to 3 decimal places is 24.344

## Exercise 2:3

**1**  Work these out.
Give your answers correct to 1 decimal place.

| | | | | | | | |
|---|---|---|---|---|---|---|---|
| **a** | $\sqrt{29}$ | **d** | $\sqrt{189}$ | **g** | $\sqrt{378}$ | **j** | $\sqrt{670}$ |
| **b** | $\sqrt{60}$ | **e** | $\sqrt{200}$ | **h** | $\sqrt{206}$ | **k** | $\sqrt{809}$ |
| **c** | $\sqrt{42}$ | **f** | $\sqrt{569}$ | **i** | $\sqrt{287}$ | **l** | $\sqrt{5231}$ |

**2**  Copy this table.
Fill it in.

| Area of square | $\sqrt{\phantom{x}}$ from calculator | Length of side | Accuracy needed |
|---|---|---|---|
| 11 cm² | 3.3166248 | | 1 dp |
| 20 m² | | 4.47 m | 2 dp |
| 34 km² | | | 3 dp |
| 19 mm² | | | 1 dp |
| 431 m² | | | 2 dp |
| 243 cm² | | | 1 dp |
| 14 563 km² | | | 3 dp |
| 13.6 mm² | | | 1 dp |
| • 145 m² | | 12.0 m | |
| • ... km² | 15.8113883 | | 3 dp |

**3**  The area of a square floor tile is 800 cm².
Find the length of a side.

## ◄◄REPLAY►

You sometimes have to multiply a number by itself lots of times.

$$2 \times 2 \times 2 \times 2 \times 2$$

A quick way of writing this is $2^5$

The small number 5 is called a **power**.

$$2^5 = 2 \times 2 \times 2 \times 2 \times 2$$

| **Power** | $4^3$. The **power** '3' tells you how many fours are multiplied together. |
|---|---|
| *Examples* **1** | Work out $3^5$ <br> $3^5 = 3 \times 3 \times 3 \times 3 \times 3$ <br> $3^5 = 243$ |
| **2** | We can use the $\boxed{x^y}$ key on a calculator to work out powers. <br><br> To find the value of $3^2$ <br> Key in: $\boxed{3}$ $\boxed{x^y}$ $\boxed{2}$ $\boxed{=}$    Answer: 9 <br><br> To find the value of $5^3$ <br> Key in: $\boxed{5}$ $\boxed{x^y}$ $\boxed{3}$ $\boxed{=}$    Answer: 125 |

## Exercise 2:4

**1** Use $\boxed{x^y}$ to work out:

| | | | |
|---|---|---|---|
| **a** $5^4$ | **d** $6^4$ | **g** $8^3$ | **j** $15^3$ |
| **b** $3^6$ | **e** $4^7$ | **h** $6^5$ | **k** $4.1^3$ |
| **c** $7^3$ | **f** $2^8$ | **i** $21^2$ | **l** $3.7^5$ |

**2** Copy this number pattern.
Fill it in.
The numbers in the last column have a special name.
Guess what they are called.

$$
\begin{array}{lcllcl}
1^3 & = & 1 \times 1 \times 1 & = & 1 \\
2^3 & = & 2 \times 2 \times 2 & = & 8 \\
3^3 & = & 3 \times 3 \times 3 & = & \dots \\
4^3 & = & \dots \times \dots \times \dots & = & \dots \\
5^3 & = & \dots \times \dots \times \dots & = & \dots \\
\dots^3 & = & \dots \times \dots \times \dots & = & \dots \\
\dots^3 & = & \dots \times \dots \times \dots & = & \dots \\
\dots^3 & = & \dots \times \dots \times \dots & = & \dots \\
\dots^3 & = & \dots \times \dots \times \dots & = & \dots \\
\dots^3 & = & \dots \times \dots \times \dots & = & \dots \\
\end{array}
$$

| **Roots** | $25 = 5 \times 5$ <br> 5 is the **square root** of 25. We write $\sqrt{25} = 5$ <br><br> $125 = 5 \times 5 \times 5$ <br> 5 is the **cube root** of 125. We write $\sqrt[3]{125} = 5$ <br><br> $625 = 5 \times 5 \times 5 \times 5$ <br> 5 is the **fourth root** of 625. We write $\sqrt[4]{625} = 5$ |
|---|---|

Calculators usually have $\sqrt{\phantom{x}}$ and $\sqrt[3]{\phantom{x}}$ keys for square roots and cube roots.

For the other roots there is a key like this

$\sqrt[x]{y}$ or $\sqrt[y]{x}$ or $y^{\frac{1}{x}}$ or $x^{\frac{1}{y}}$

We will use the last one.

*Examples*

Work out $\sqrt[3]{216}$

Key in: $\boxed{2}\ \boxed{1}\ \boxed{6}\ \boxed{x^{\frac{1}{y}}}\ \boxed{3}\ \boxed{=}$   Answer: 6

Work out $\sqrt[5]{1024}$

Key in: $\boxed{1}\ \boxed{0}\ \boxed{2}\ \boxed{4}\ \boxed{x^{\frac{1}{y}}}\ \boxed{5}\ \boxed{=}$   Answer: 4

---

**3**  Use $\boxed{x^{\frac{1}{y}}}$ to work out:

a $\sqrt[3]{6859}$    d $\sqrt[4]{6561}$    g $\sqrt[9]{19\,683}$    j $\sqrt[10]{1024}$

b $\sqrt[5]{59\,049}$    e $\sqrt[6]{15\,625}$    h $\sqrt[7]{78\,125}$    k $\sqrt[11]{177\,147}$

c $\sqrt[3]{13\,824}$    f $\sqrt[8]{256}$    i $\sqrt[6]{262\,144}$    l $\sqrt[9]{10\,077\,696}$

**4**  Use $\boxed{x^{\frac{1}{y}}}$ to work these out.
Give your answers correct to 1 dp.

a $\sqrt[3]{76}$    d $\sqrt[4]{5643}$    g $\sqrt[9]{67\,584}$    j $\sqrt[10]{382\,956}$

b $\sqrt[5]{9125}$    e $\sqrt[6]{35\,479}$    h $\sqrt[5]{278\,192}$    k $\sqrt[11]{37\,590}$

c $\sqrt[3]{14\,564}$    f $\sqrt[8]{564}$    i $\sqrt[8]{558\,396}$    l $\sqrt[9]{999\,487}$

**5**  Use your calculator to work these out.
Give your answers correct to 1 dp when you have to round them.

a $6^4$    d $9^4$    g $\sqrt[9]{10\,077\,696}$    j $8.7^6$

b $7^6$    e $\sqrt[4]{456\,976}$    h $3^{11}$    k $\sqrt[8]{679\,036}$

c $\sqrt[8]{65\,536}$    f $2^{12}$    i $24.2^3$    l $5.78^4 + 9.76^4$

**6**  16 has a square root of 4 and a fourth root of 2.
Find three more numbers that have whole number square roots *and* whole number fourth roots.

**7**  $\sqrt{64} = 8$    $\sqrt[3]{64} = 4$
Find three more numbers that have whole number square roots *and* whole number cube roots.

# 2 Mental maths

Ruth, Andrew and Allison have £2 to spend on ice cream. They need to know which ice creams they can buy.

Sometimes we have to work things out in our heads.

## Exercise 2:5 Adding

1   Work these out in your head.
    Write down the answers.
    **a**  30 + 40     **c**  80 + 70     **e**  50 + 16     **g**  27 + 40
    **b**  50 + 20     **d**  900 + 400   **f**  70 + 19     **h**  54 + 30

---

*Example*          Work out    38 + 24

                24 = 4 + 20      Add 4              38 + 4 = 42
                                 Now add 20      42 + 20 = 62

---

2   Do these in your head in the same way as the example.
    Write down the answers.
    **a**  35 + 23     **c**  45 + 34     **e**  57 + 34     **g**  65 + 36
    **b**  28 + 24     **d**  36 + 17     **f**  44 + 36     **h**  73 + 28

3   Do these in your head.
    Write down the answers.
    **a**  123 + 45     **b**  34 + 152     **c**  247 + 28     **d**  263 + 129

4   Ruth, Andrew and Allison have £2 to spend on ice cream.
    Work out all the different combinations of three ice creams that they could buy.

ICE CREAMS
SMALL 60p
MEDIUM 70p
LARGE 80p

## Game   Run from six

This is a game for any number of players.
You need a dice and a piece of paper and a pencil to keep the score.

Throw the dice.
Add up the score as you go along.
You can throw the dice as many times as you like.
If you throw a six you lose the score for that go!

Sally is playing the game.
She throws the dice and keeps a total in her head.
Here are Sally's throws: $4 + 1 + 3 + 5 + 3 = 16$

If Sally throws a six she will score 0.
Sally decides to stop.
She writes down her score of 16.

It is Stewart's turn.
He throws $5 + 2 + 6$. So Stewart scores 0.

The winner is the first person to get to 100.

Play this game with some friends.

## Exercise 2:6 Subtracting

**1** Work these out in your head.
Write down the answers.

| | | |
|---|---|---|
| **a** $20 - 2$ | **b** $16 - 7$ | **c** $27 - 13$ |
| $30 - 9$ | $23 - 6$ | $45 - 34$ |
| $50 - 4$ | $45 - 7$ | $36 - 25$ |
| $20 - 7$ | $34 - 5$ | $58 - 47$ |
| $70 - 6$ | $17 - 8$ | $29 - 17$ |
| $90 - 3$ | $53 - 4$ | $44 - 23$ |
| $40 - 8$ | $68 - 7$ | $56 - 34$ |
| $80 - 5$ | $85 - 6$ | $39 - 18$ |

**2** Work these out in your head.
Write down the answers.

| | | | |
|---|---|---|---|
| **a** $90 - 50$ | **c** $120 - 30$ | **e** $60 - 51$ | **g** $50 - 42$ |
| **b** $700 - 500$ | **d** $200 - 60$ | **f** $56 - 40$ | **h** $64 - 50$ |

---

*Example*  Work out  $53 - 27$

$27 = 7 + 20$  Subtract 7  $53 - 7 = 46$
  Subtract 20  $46 - 20 = 26$

---

**3** Do these in your head in the same way as the example.
Write down the answers.

| | | | |
|---|---|---|---|
| **a** $45 - 17$ | **c** $54 - 27$ | **e** $51 - 28$ | **g** $83 - 64$ |
| **b** $63 - 35$ | **d** $72 - 43$ | **f** $65 - 36$ | **h** $74 - 55$ |

**4** Copy these.
Fill in the missing numbers.

**a** $18 - 9 = ...$      **b** $23 - 6 = ...$      **c** $42 - 28 = ...$
$... + 9 = 18$      $... + 6 = 23$      $... + 28 = 42$

**5** Write down the answers to these subtractions.
For each one, write down an addition sum using the same numbers.

**a** $17 - 8$     **b** $34 - 16$     **c** $47 - 29$     **d** $96 - 78$

## Game    Take away dice

This is a game for any number of players.
You will need a dice. (Try an 8 or 10 sided dice.)
Each player makes a score sheet like this.

One player throws the dice.
All the players write the number somewhere
above the line on their score sheet.
You cannot move a number once you have written it down.

After 8 throws all the boxes will be filled up.

Game 1

| 6 | 2 | 5 | 4 |
| 4 | 3 | 4 | 2 |

Now do 4 subtraction sums.
Take the bottom number away from the top one.
If the top number is smaller than the bottom one,
leave the answer blank.

| 6 | 2 | 5 | 4 |
| 4 | 3 | 4 | 2 |
| 2̶ |   | 1 | 2̶ |

Score: 1

Cross out any answers that are the same.
Add the rest of the answers together to get
your score.

The player with the highest score wins.

Game 2

| 5 | 6 | 4 | 6 |
| 3 | 2 | 1 | 6 |
| 2 | 4 | 3 |   |

Play this game with some friends.

Score: $2 + 4 + 3 = 9$

## Exercise 2:7   Multiplying

**1** Work these out in your head.
Write down the answers.

**a** $6 \times 5$     **d** $7 \times 8$     **g** $6 \times 7$     **j** $8 \times 9$
**b** $7 \times 4$     **e** $9 \times 12$     **h** $9 \times 5$     **k** $7 \times 7$
**c** $8 \times 6$     **f** $6 \times 9$     **i** $12 \times 7$     **l** $5 \times 8$

---

*Example*     Work out   **a** $7 \times 500$     **b** $40 \times 60$

**a** $500 = 5 \times 100$                            **b** $40 = 4 \times 10$      $60 = 6 \times 10$
Multiply by 5        $7 \times 5 = 35$                       $4 \times 6 = 24$
Multiply by 100    $35 \times 100 = 3500$                $40 \times 6 = 240$
                                             $40 \times 60 = 2400$

---

**2**   Work these out in your head.
Write down the answers.

**a**  $6 \times 30$      **d**  $60 \times 70$      **g**  $4 \times 9000$      **j**  $700 \times 80$

**b**  $7 \times 300$     **e**  $8 \times 300$      **h**  $50 \times 40$       **k**  $500 \times 80$

**c**  $40 \times 70$     **f**  $400 \times 8$      **i**  $70 \times 60$       **l**  $90 \times 800$

**3**   Copy these.
Fill in the missing numbers.

**a**  $24 \times 6 = 12 \times 12$         **c**  $14 \times 15 = 7 \times \ldots$
$\qquad = \ldots$                          $\qquad\qquad = \ldots$

**b**  $36 \times 3 = 18 \times \ldots$     **d**  $24 \times 35 = \ldots \times 70$
$\qquad = 9 \times \ldots$                  $\qquad\qquad = \ldots$
$\qquad = \ldots$

**4**   Do these in the same way as question **3**.

**a**  $18 \times 4$      **b**  $28 \times 3$      **c**  $16 \times 45$      **d**  $22 \times 15$

---

*Example*          Work out   **a**  $8 \times 29$       **b**  $7 \times 42$

**a**  $29 = 30 - 1$                 **b**  $42 = 40 + 2$

$\qquad 8 \times 30 = 240$              $\qquad 7 \times 40 = 280$
$\qquad 8 \times 1 = 8$                 $\qquad 7 \times 2 = 14$
$\qquad 240 - 8 = 232$                 $\qquad 280 + 14 = 294$

---

**5**   Work these out in your head.
Write down the answers.

**a**  $6 \times 39$      **c**  $9 \times 58$      **e**  $7 \times 27$      **g**  $8 \times 78$

**b**  $8 \times 73$      **d**  $67 \times 4$      **f**  $82 \times 9$      **h**  $43 \times 7$

**6**   Copy these.
Fill in the missing numbers.

**a**  $67 \times 5 = 67 \times \dfrac{10}{2}$         **b**  $84 \times 25 = 84 \times \dfrac{100}{4}$

$\qquad = \dfrac{?}{2}$                                $\qquad\qquad = \dfrac{?}{4}$

$\qquad = \ldots$                                     $\qquad\qquad = \ldots$

**7**   Do these in the same way as question **6**.

**a**  $86 \times 5$      **b**  $28 \times 25$      **c**  $36 \times 25$      **d**  $64 \times 50$

## Month's choice

**a**

| 7 | 8 |
|---|---|
| 14 | 15 |

What do you notice
about 7 + 15 and 8 + 14?

Try other four-number squares.
Is there a rule?

Try a larger square.
Does this square follow your rule?

**b** What happens if you multiply instead of adding?

**c** Do the same rules work for rectangles?

**AUGUST**

| S | M | T | W | T | F | S |
|---|---|---|---|---|---|---|
| ... | ... | 1 | 2 | 3 | 4 | 5 |
| 6 | 7 | 8 | 9 | 10 | 11 | 12 |
| 13 | 14 | 15 | 16 | 17 | 18 | 19 |
| 20 | 21 | 22 | 23 | 24 | 25 | 26 |
| 27 | 28 | 29 | 30 | 31 | ... | ... |

## Exercise 2:8  Dividing

*Example*   $5 \times 4 = 20$

We can write down two divisions using the same numbers.

$20 \div 5 = 4$     $20 \div 4 = 5$

**1** Work these out in your head.
Write down the answers.
For each one, write down two divisions using the same numbers.
**a** $8 \times 5$    **b** $7 \times 9$    **c** $12 \times 8$    **d** $7 \times 6$

**2** Write down the answers to these.
**a** $35 \div 7$    **c** $36 \div 9$    **e** $56 \div 8$    **g** $72 \div 6$
**b** $48 \div 6$    **d** $42 \div 7$    **f** $64 \div 8$    **h** $72 \div 8$

**3** Write down the answers to these.
**a** $27 \div 3 =$    **c** $32 \div 8 =$    **e** $450 \div 90$
$270 \div 3 =$         $320 \div 8 =$
                       $3200 \div 8 =$       **f** $720 \div 80$

**b** $35 \div 5 =$    **d** $42 \div 6 =$    **g** $1500 \div 30$
$350 \div 5 =$         $420 \div 6 =$
                       $4200 \div 6 =$       **h** $4200 \div 700$

*Example*          Work out    $48 \div 24$

$24 = 4 \times 6$          Divide by 4          $48 \div 4 = 12$
                         Divide by 6          $12 \div 6 = 2$

**4**   Work these out in your head.
     Write down the answers.
     **a**   $56 \div 28$          **b**   $36 \div 18$          **c**   $48 \div 16$          **d**   $72 \div 24$

**5**   Work these out in your head.
     Write down the answers.
     **a**   $240 \div 48$          **b**   $180 \div 36$          **c**   $560 \div 28$          **d**   $720 \div 48$

Here are two rules to help you divide by 5 and by 25.

To divide by 5: multiply by 2 and divide by 10
To divide by 25: multiply by 4 and divide by 100

*Examples* **1**          $65 \div 5 = 65 \times 2 \div 10$
                         $= 130 \div 10$
                         $= 13$

         **2**          $175 \div 25 = 175 \times 4 \div 100$
                         $= 700 \div 100$
                         $= 7$

**6**   Use the rules to work these out in your head.
     Write down the answers.
     **a**   $85 \div 5$          **b**   $350 \div 25$          **c**   $135 \div 5$          **d**   $115 \div 5$

**7**   Work these out in your head.
     Write down the answers.
     **a**   $24 \div 5$          **b**   $220 \div 25$          **c**   $17 \div 5$          **d**   $52 \div 25$

# 3 Estimation

Susan is choosing the wallpaper for her bedroom.
She knows that she needs 7 rolls.

The flowers pattern costs £6.30 a roll.
The teddy bears pattern costs £7.85 a roll.
Susan's mum has £50 to spend.

Susan estimates the cost of each type of paper.
She says that the flowers cost about £6 a roll,
  7 rolls cost about 7 × £6 = £42

She says that the teddy bears cost about £8 a roll,
  7 rolls cost about 7 × £8 = £56

Susan knows that she can only have the flowers.

◄◄REPLAY►
*Rounding*

*Exercise 2:9*

**1** Round these numbers to the nearest whole number.
   **a** 4.6      **c** 5.9      **e** 8.1      **g** 9.9
   **b** 3.8      **d** 6.5      **f** 4.3      **h** 13.6

**2** Round these numbers to the nearest 10.
   **a** 18      **c** 57      **e** 101      **g** 247
   **b** 46      **d** 55      **f** 134      **h** 185

**3** Round these numbers to the nearest 100.
   **a** 127      **c** 757      **e** 1234      **g** 8935
   **b** 426      **d** 650      **f** 4563      **h** 7165

| **Significant figure** | In any number the first **significant figure** is the first digit which isn't a 0. For most numbers this is the first digit. |
|---|---|
| *Examples* | The first significant figure is the red digit:<br>21.4    312    45.78    0.81    0.000 030 042 |
| **Rounding to 1 significant figure (1 sf)** | To **round to 1 significant figure (1 sf)**:<br>**a** look at the first digit after the first significant one<br>**b** use the normal rules of rounding<br>**c** be careful to keep the number about the right size |
| *Examples* | 21.4 to 1 sf is 20. It is *not* 2!<br>312 to 1 sf is 300<br>45.78 is 50 to 1 sf<br>0.81 is 0.8 to 1 sf |

**4** Round these numbers correct to 1 sf.

| | | | | | | | |
|---|---|---|---|---|---|---|---|
| **a** | 22.7 | **d** | 780 | **g** | 6.9 | **j** | 6661 |
| **b** | 346 | **e** | 672 | **h** | 0.78 | **k** | 4012 |
| **c** | 75 | **f** | 6.5 | **i** | 1375 | **l** | 99 |

| **Rounding to any number of significant figures** | To **round to any number of significant figures**:<br>**a** look at the first unwanted digit<br>**b** use the normal rules of rounding<br>**c** be careful to keep the number about the right size |
|---|---|
| *Examples* | 341.4 to 2 sf is 340. It is *not* 34!<br>42 312 to 3 sf is 42 300<br>7845.78 to 1 sf is 8000<br>0.000 031 542 to 2 sf is 0.000 032<br>0.002 034 5 to 3 sf is 0.002 03<br><br>Here the 0 after the 2 is significant because it comes after the first significant figure.<br>A 0 is only significant when it appears to the right of the first significant figure. |

**5** Round these numbers:

| | | | | | |
|---|---|---|---|---|---|
| **a** | 23.47 to 2 sf | **d** | 0.020 344 5 to 4 sf | **g** | 9091 to 2 sf |
| **b** | 456 621 to 3 sf | **e** | 129 835 to 2 sf | **h** | 0.099 125 to 2 sf |
| **c** | 2.365 12 to 3 sf | **f** | 103 523.46 to 3 sf | **i** | 0.030 987 6 to 3 sf |

## Estimating

We often work things out on a calculator.
It is a good idea to check that your answer is about right.
It is very easy to hit the wrong key by accident!

To get an estimate, round each number to one significant figure.

*Examples* **1**    Work out    $4.9 \times 3.2$

Calculation:    [4] [·] [9] [×] [3] [·] [2] [=]
Answer: 15.68
Estimate:    4.9 is 5 to 1 sf
3.2 is 3 to 1 sf
$4.9 \times 3.2$ is about $5 \times 3 = 15$

15 is near to 15.68 So the answer is probably right.

**2**    Work out    $36 \times 82$

Calculation:    [3] [6] [×] [8] [2] [=]
Answer: 2952
Estimate:    36 is 40 to 1 sf
82 is 80 to 1 sf
$36 \times 82$ is about $40 \times 80 = 3200$

3200 is near to 2952. So the answer is probably right.

## Exercise 2:10

Work these out.
Write down the answer and an estimate for each one.

**1**  **a** $4.6 \times 3.1$    **b** $2.4 \times 4.7$    **c** $3.2 \times 7.5$    **d** $4 \times 7.3$

**2**  **a** $54 \times 36$    **b** $26 \times 72$    **c** $58 \times 23$    **d** $80 \times 45$

**3**  **a** $124 \times 356$    **b** $278 \times 312$    **c** $578 \times 123$    **d** $234 \times 652$

**4**  **a** $3.3 \times 21$    **c** $231 \times 34$    **e** $345 \times 85$    **g** $256.1 \times 22$
  **b** $4.9 \times 35$    **d** $1.9 \times 435$    **f** $25.3 \times 768$    **h** $201.3 \times 350$

**5**  **a** $3.2 + 3.6$    **d** $8.9 - 2.7$    **g** $234 + 567$    **j** $3.6 \div 1.2$
  **b** $2.4 + 7.5$    **e** $21.5 \div 4.3$    **h** $315 - 189$    **k** $248 \div 49.6$
  **c** $5.7 - 2.1$    **f** $18 \div 4.8$    **i** $535 - 95$    **l** $499.2 \div 9.6$

When you answer questions you should always make an estimate to check your answer.

## Exercise 2:11

In this exercise:
**a** work out the answers using a calculator
**b** write down an estimate to check that each answer is about right.

**1** The height of the television and the stand is 118 cm.
The height of the stand is 53 cm.
What is the height of the television?

**2** This set of garden furniture costs £137.50.
The table costs £39.50.
What is the cost of one chair?

**3** 126 pupils from Year 8 go ten-pin bowling.
Only six people can play in one lane.
How many lanes do they need?

**4** 54 pupils from Year 8 have a day out at Alton Towers.
It costs £375.30.
How much does each pupil have to pay?

At Alton Towers each pupil buys a can of drink.
If one can costs 58 p, how much does this cost altogether?

● **5** Find the area of this picture.
Give your answer correct to 3 sf.
Explain why it is not sensible to give the answer that you get on the calculator.

25.3 cm

11.8 cm

### Exercise 2:12

**1 a** Copy this list of square numbers.
Fill in the gaps.

| $1^2$ | $2^2$ | $3^2$ | $4^2$ | $5^2$ | $6^2$ | $7^2$ | $8^2$ | $9^2$ | $10^2$ |
|---|---|---|---|---|---|---|---|---|---|
| 1 | 4 | 9 | ... | ... | ... | ... | ... | ... | ... |

**b** (1) Copy this.
Fill in the missing numbers.

Estimate of $\sqrt{13}$

$\sqrt{9} = 3$ $\qquad$ $\sqrt{16} = 4$

$\sqrt{13}$ is between ... and ...

$\sqrt{13}$ is about ... (Guess an estimate here)

(2) Check with a calculator to see how close you are.

**c** Estimate these in the same way.

(1) $\sqrt{46}$ $\qquad$ (2) $\sqrt{51}$ $\qquad$ (3) $\sqrt{90}$ $\qquad$ (4) $\sqrt{20}$

**2** Estimate the value of $\sqrt{478}$

**3** Estimate the value of $3.6^2 + \sqrt{47}$
You need to decide how to round the numbers in question.
Show all of your working.
Use a calculator to find the accurate answer. Write it correct to 3 sf.

### Game 3 guesses

This is a game for two players.
One player has red counters. The other player has blue counters.

You need a game card like this:

| 13 | 19 | 26 | 35 | 46 | 57 | 69 |
|---|---|---|---|---|---|---|

and a table like this:

| | | | |
|---|---|---|---|
| 598 | 741 | 3174 | 665 |
| 3933 | 455 | 247 | 1083 |
| 1196 | 494 | 2622 | 874 |
| 1311 | 897 | 1482 | 338 |

Each number in the table comes from multiplying two of the numbers on the game card.

You can cover a number in the table with one of your counters if you can guess which two numbers it comes from.

Use estimation to guess which two numbers you need.

The winner is the first person to get 3 counters in a row: across, down or diagonally.

Play the game with a friend.

Make up your own table and game card and swap with another pair.

**1**  **a**  Use $x^2$ to work out the area of this square.

**b**  Copy this. Fill in the missing number.
$1 \text{ m}^2 = \dots \text{ cm}^2$

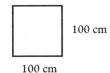

100 cm

100 cm

**c**  A small carpet is a square of side 220 cm.

Use $x^2$ to work out the area of the carpet in $\text{cm}^2$.

**d**  Use your answer to **b** to convert the area to $\text{m}^2$.

220 cm

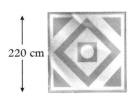

**2**  **a**  Use $x^y$ to work out:

(1) $3^4$      (3) $9^5$      (5) $5.2^3$      (7) $0.4^3$

(2) $5^3$      (4) $8^6$      (6) $1.8^7$      (8) $0.2^4$

**b**  What sort of number gets smaller when you press $x^y$ ?

**c**  Use your answer to **b** to predict which of these numbers will get larger when you press $x^{\frac{1}{y}}$

Give your answers correct to 1 dp when you have to round.

(1) $\sqrt{59}$      (3) $\sqrt[5]{0.0776}$      (5) $\sqrt[7]{6000}$      (7) $\sqrt[7]{5.34}$

(2) $\sqrt[3]{2744}$      (4) $\sqrt[6]{6.5}$      (6) $\sqrt[4]{0.2401}$      (8) $\sqrt{0.1}$

Work out the answers to check your predictions.

**3**  Brian has a square piece of card of side 35 cm.

He is going to use the card to mount a picture.

**a**  Use $x^2$ to work out the area of the card.

**b**  Brian cuts a square hole of side 18 cm in the card.

Use $x^2$ to work out the area of the piece cut out.

**c**  Use your answers to **a** and **b** to find the area of Brian's picture mount.

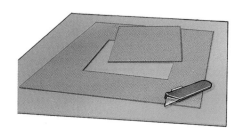

**4**  Work these out in your head.
Write down the answers.

**a**  $139 + 53$      **c**  $76 - 47$      **e**  $7 \times 69$      **g**  $360 \div 24$

**b**  $46 + 237$      **d**  $93 - 68$      **f**  $44 \times 25$      **h**  $95 \div 5$

**5** Copy these.
Fill in the missing numbers.

**a** $34 + 28 = ...$
$... - 28 = 34$

**c** $32 \times 8 = ...$
$... \div 8 = 32$

**b** $56 - 19 = ...$
$... + 19 = 56$

**d** $72 \div 18 = ...$
$... \times 18 = 72$

Do these the same way as **a** to **d**.
Work them out. Then write down a new question using the same numbers.

**e** $56 + 25 =$    **f** $83 - 47 =$    **g** $58 \times 6 =$    **h** $80 \div 5 =$

**6** Round each number to the accuracy given in brackets.

**a** 34.875 (3 sf)
**b** 4037 (3 sf)
**c** 7 506 320 (4 sf)
**d** 5.745 (2 sf)
**e** 5.3498 (4 sf)

**f** 0.6753 (2 sf)
**g** 0.506 742 (3 sf)
**h** 0.003 427 (2 sf)
**i** 0.070 68 (3 sf)
**j** 0.0796 (2 sf)

**7** **a** Estimate the answers to these using numbers rounded to 1 sf.
Write down whether you think your estimate is low, high or 'about right'.

(1) $3.8 \times 6.7$
(2) $4.2 \times 7.3$
(3) $8.9 \times 6.1$

(4) $73 \times 84$
(5) $66 \times 53$
(6) $27 \times 39$

(7) $617 \times 53$
(8) $875 \times 7.9$
(9) $125 \times 218$

**b** Find the accurate answer and compare it with your estimate.

**8** The headteacher says that there are 1265 pupils in Years 7 to 11 in the school, with 253 pupils in each year.

**a** Rewrite the sentence with the numbers rounded to 2 sf.
**b** Rewrite the sentence with the numbers rounded to 1 sf.
**c** Which estimate would the headteacher use? Explain your answer.

**9** **a** (1) Copy this pattern.
Use ▆ to fill in the missing numbers.

$\sqrt{1} = ...$
$\sqrt{10} = ...$
$\sqrt{100} = ...$
$\sqrt{1000} = ...$

(2) Predict $\sqrt{10\,000}$
Use your calculator to check your prediction.

**b** Give estimates for these.

(1) $\sqrt{48}$    (2) $\sqrt{90}$    (3) $\sqrt{18}$    (4) $\sqrt{500}$    (5) $\sqrt{1300}$

**1** **a** Copy this number pattern.
Write down the next two
rows in the pattern.

$$1 = 1$$
$$4 = 1 + 3$$
$$9 = 1 + 3 + 5$$

Some Chinese mathematicians found this method of getting an
approximate square root.
Can you see how it is based on the number pattern?
(1) Subtract as many consecutive odd numbers as you can.
  Start with 1, then 3, 5, etc.
(2) Count the *number* of odd numbers that you have subtracted.
(3) What is the *remainder*?
(4) Add 1 to the *last* number you subtracted.
The approximate square root is $n\frac{r}{l+1}$

*Example*   Work out an estimate for $\sqrt{27}$

| $27 - 1 = 26$ | $23 - 5 = 18$ | $11 - 9 = 2$ |
| $26 - 3 = 23$ | $18 - 7 = 11$ | The remainder is 2 |

So  $n = 5$,  $r = 2$,  $l = 9$

$\sqrt{27} \approx 5\frac{2}{9+1}$   $\sqrt{27} \approx 5\frac{2}{10}$ or 5.2 ($\approx$ means approximately equal to)

**b** Use the method to work out estimates for these.

(1) $\sqrt{31}$          (2) $\sqrt{12}$          (3) $\sqrt{45}$          (4) $\sqrt{73}$

**2** The rectangle and the square are equal in area.
The rectangle is 7 cm long and 4 cm wide.
Calculate the length of a side of the square.
Give your answer correct to 2 dp.

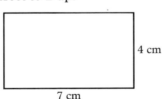

4 cm

7 cm

**3** **a** $3 + 6 + 12 + 24 + \ldots$
(1) Write down the rule for this number pattern.
(2) Use your rule to write down the next two terms.
**b** Add the six terms of your number pattern.

**c** A formula to find the total is $\dfrac{a(r^n - 1)}{r - 1}$   $a$ = first term
$r$ = number used to
multiply in rule
$n$ = number of terms

Use the formula to check your addition in **b**.
**d** Use the formula to add the first 10 terms of the number pattern.

**4**  **a**  Work these out in your head.

Write down the answers.

(1)  $453 + 238$          (4)  $93 - 35$          (7)  $540 \div 18$
(2)  $1046 + 227$        (5)  $8 \times 48$          (8)  $64 \div 25$
(3)  $67 - 48$             (6)  $32 \times 25$

**b**  For each of these, write down a new question using the same numbers but with an inverse operation.
For example, write a subtraction using the numbers from an addition.

**5**  **a**  Estimate the area of a sheet of A4 paper:
(1)  in mm²
(2)  in cm²

**b**  In inches, A4 paper is 11.69 inches by 8.27 inches. Estimate the area of a sheet of A4 in inches².

**c**  Use your answers to **a** and **b** to estimate the number of cm² in 1 inch².

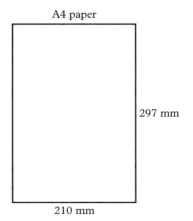

A4 paper

297 mm

210 mm

**6**  Stanthorne High has a total of 1168 pupils in Years 7 to 11.

**a**  (1)  Estimate the number of pupils in each year.
(2)  There are eight forms in each year.
Estimate the number of pupils in a form.

**b**  Do you think that your estimates in **a** are higher or lower than the actual answer?
Explain why.

**c**  (1)  Use a calculator to find the mean number of pupils in a year.
(2)  Find the mean number of pupils in a form.
(3)  Compare the answers with your estimates.

**d**  There are 220 pupils in Year 8.
Suggest how many pupils are in each of the Year 8 forms.

- We can use the $x^2$ key on a calculator to work out square numbers.

  *Example*     Work out $6^2$

  Key in: **6** **$x^2$**     Answer: 36

- **√** is the **square root** key.
  It will work out the sides of squares.

  *Example*     The length of a side of a square of area 25 cm² is $\sqrt{25}$

  Key in: **2** **5** **√**     Answer: 5 cm

- To round to any number of decimal places, look at the first unwanted digit.
  If it is 1, 2, 3 or 4, miss off all the unwanted digits.
  If it is 5, 6, 7, 8 or 9, add 1 to the last digit that you keep.

  *Example*     62.346 correct to 2 dp is 62.35
                24.344 27 correct to 3 dp is 24.344

- $4^3$ means $4 \times 4 \times 4 = 64$

  **$x^y$** will work out powers.           **$x^{\frac{1}{y}}$** will work out roots.

  *Example*     Work out $4^3$           *Example*     Work out $\sqrt[3]{216}$

  Key in: **4** **$x^y$** **3** **=**       Key in: **2** **1** **6** **$x^{\frac{1}{y}}$** **3** **=**

  Answer: 64                              Answer: 6

- To work out questions in your head, do them a bit at a time.

  *Examples*   **1**  $38 + 24$       Add the 4, then add the 20
               **2**  $53 - 27$       Take away 7, then take away 20
               **3**  $7 \times 500$   Multiply by 5, then by 100
               **4**  $48 \div 24$     Divide by 4, then by 6

  To divide by 5: multiply by 2 and divide by 10.
  To divide by 25: multiply by 4 and divide by 100.

- To round to any number of significant figures, look at the first unwanted digit.
  Then use the normal rules of rounding.

  *Examples*   341.4 to 2 sf is **340** not 34   7845.78 to 1 sf is **8000**

- To make an estimate, round each number correct to 1 sf.

  *Examples*   **1**  $2.8 \times 34$           **2**  $589 - 128$
               Estimate: $3 \times 30 = 90$        Estimate: $600 - 100 = 500$
               Answer: 95.2                    Answer: 461

- You can estimate square roots.

  *Example*     $\sqrt{13}$ is between $\sqrt{9}$ and $\sqrt{16}$

                It is nearer to $\sqrt{16}$

                $\sqrt{13}$ is about 3.6

**1** Use $x^2$ to work out:

   **a** $17^2$       **b** $3.6^2$       **c** $0.08^2$

**2** Use $\sqrt{\phantom{x}}$ to work these out.
Give your answer correct to 2 dp when you need to round.

   **a** $\sqrt{625}$    **b** $\sqrt{7.9}$    **c** $\sqrt{12\,345}$    **d** $\sqrt{0.0121}$

**3** Use $x^y$ to work out:

   **a** $7^5$       **b** $13^4$       **c** $8.4^3$       **d** $0.2^6$

**4** Use $x^{\frac{1}{y}}$ to work these out.
Give your answer correct to 3 dp when you need to round.

   **a** $\sqrt[7]{78\,125}$    **b** $\sqrt[8]{256}$    **c** $\sqrt[5]{5.7}$    **d** $\sqrt[4]{0.0081}$

**5** Work these out in your head.
Write down the answers.

   **a** $137 + 56$    **c** $72 - 38$    **e** $8 \times 38$    **g** $56 \div 14$
   **b** $39 + 44$    **d** $38 - 19$    **f** $36 \times 4$    **h** $34 \div 5$

**6** Write these numbers correct to the number of significant figures given.

   **a** $73.467$ (3 sf)       **c** $6.8972$ (3 sf)
   **b** $0.068\,51$ (2 sf)    **d** $0.030\,415$ (3 sf)

**7** **a** Round the numbers correct to 1 sf to make estimates for these.

     (1) $327 + 589$      (3) $5.6 \times 3.2$
     (2) $1270 - 943$     (4) $504 \div 18$

   **b** Work out the answers.
     Compare them with your estimates.

**8** Make estimates for these.

   **a** The number of people on six buses.
     Each bus has 87 passengers.
   **b** The total cost of items costing £5.22, £7.87, £22.19 and £8.63.

**9** Make estimates for these.

   **a** $\sqrt{30}$    **b** $\sqrt{61}$    **c** $\sqrt{800}$    **d** $\sqrt{1750}$

# 3 Statistics: questions and answers

The first opinion poll was done by **George Gallup** in **1935**.

Opinion polls are now often called Gallup polls. Gallup is one of the biggest survey companies in the world.

# 1   Diagrams and charts

### ◄◄ REPLAY ►

All of Year 8 have taken part in a survey.
The questions were about how much TV they watched.
They were also asked about their favourite type of programme and
their favourite channel.

Here are the results of the survey.

**Number of hours watched per day**

| Hours per day | 0 | 1 | 2 | 3 | 4 | 5 | 6 |
|---|---|---|---|---|---|---|---|
| Number of pupils | 20 | 45 | 75 | 60 | 10 | 5 | 5 |

**Favourite type of TV programme**

| Type of programme | children's | soaps | sport | comedy | films | drama | news |
|---|---|---|---|---|---|---|---|
| Number of pupils | 15 | 55 | 40 | 25 | 35 | 25 | 25 |

**Favourite channel**

| Channel | BBC1 | BBC2 | ITV | C4 | Sky | other |
|---|---|---|---|---|---|---|
| Number of pupils | 73 | 22 | 66 | 19 | 24 | 16 |

Year 8 display this data.
Here is some of their work.

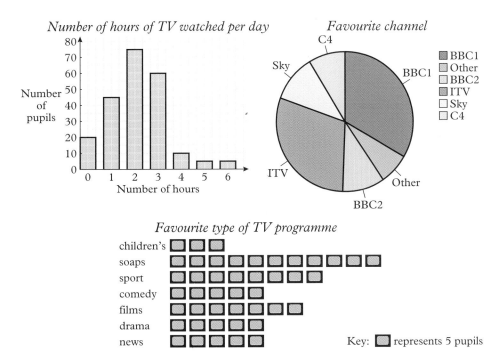

Number of hours of TV watched per day

Favourite channel

Favourite type of TV programme

Key: ▢ represents 5 pupils

## Exercise 3:1

**1** Look at the bar-chart.
   **a** How many pupils are there in Year 8?
   **b** What is the modal number of hours?
   **c** How many people watch TV for *more* than 3 hours a day?
   **d** There are 20 people in the 0 hours bar.
      How do you think the data was rounded before the diagram was drawn?

**2** Look at the pictogram.
   **a** How many people does ▢ stand for?
   **b** How many more people liked soaps than liked news?
   **c** What percentage of people liked soaps the most?
   **d** What is the greatest accuracy the diagram can be read to?

**3** Look at the pie-chart.
   **a** Which are the least and most popular channels?
   **b** Explain how you could work out the number of people in each category.

## Exercise 3:2

1. Draw a bar-chart of the favourite types of programme.
   Don't forget a title and labels.

2. Draw a bar-chart to show the favourite channel.
   Don't forget a title and labels.

3. Draw a pictogram of the number of hours of TV watched.
   Choose your own symbol.
   Make sure that your diagram has a key.

4. Draw a pictogram of the favourite channels.
   Choose a different symbol.
   Don't forget the key.

• 5. Compare each of your diagrams with the ones on page 53.
   Write down which diagram you think is best for each set of data.
   Explain your answer.

Year 8 were also asked how many videos they had hired in the last month.

Here are the answers from 8J and 8K.

**8J**

| 0 | 6 | 9 | 5 | 4 | 6 | 0 | 4 | 5 | 11 |
| 3 | 6 | 5 | 8 | 7 | 4 | 6 | 2 | 2 | 0 |
| 11 | 3 | 1 | 9 | 7 | 5 | 6 | 2 | 3 | 10 |

**8K**

| 2 | 5 | 4 | 9 | 6 | 8 | 2 | 3 | 4 | 0 |
| 1 | 8 | 5 | 3 | 10 | 5 | 9 | 4 | 2 | 6 |
| 4 | 5 | 8 | 9 | 6 | 3 | 5 | 10 | 2 | 0 |

## Exercise 3:3

1. **a** Make a tally-table for the 8J data.
   **b** Draw a pictogram of these results.

2. **a** Make another tally-table for the 8K data.
   **b** Draw a pictogram of these results.

3. Describe the differences between the two diagrams.

It is sometimes useful to collect data into groups.
This means that you have fewer categories.
It often makes diagrams easier to draw.

For the number of videos hired sensible groups might be:
0–2   3–5   6–8   9–11

| Number of videos | |
| --- | --- |
| 0 | |
| 1 | this becomes group 0–2 |
| 2 | |
| 3 | |
| 4 | this becomes group 3–5 |
| 5 | |

## Exercise 3:4

1  **a**  Make a tally-table for 8J using the groups suggested.
   **b**  Draw a bar-chart of your grouped data.

2  **a**  Make a grouped tally-table for 8K.
      Use the same groups.
   **b**  Draw a bar-chart for this data.
      Use the same scale as in question **1**.
      Remember that bar-charts of grouped data have their bars touching.

3  Here is the data for the videos hired by 8L.

| 5 | 1 | 9 | 0 | 0 | 6 | 7 | 10 | 5 | 7 |
| 9 | 8 | 3 | 5 | 6 | 8 | 9 | 0 | 0 | 5 |
| 1 | 4 | 5 | 10 | 1 | 7 | 3 | 6 | 7 | 4 |

   **a**  Make a grouped tally-table for this data.
   **b**  Draw a bar-chart for 8L.

## 2 Pie-charts

| **Pie-chart** | A **pie-chart** shows how something is divided up. The angle of the sector represents the number of items. It is not useful for reading off accurate figures. |
|---|---|

As you saw last year, sometimes the data splits up easily into fractions of the circle.
Often this does not happen and then you have to work out the angles.

Remember there are 360° in a full circle.
This 360° needs dividing up.

*Example*
30 people were asked which national newspaper they read.
The results were:

| | | | |
|---|---|---|---|
| *The Guardian* | 8 | *The Sun* | 6 |
| *Daily Mirror* | 7 | *Daily Express* | 6 |
| *The Times* | 3 | | |

Show these results in a pie-chart.

**1** Divide up the 360°.

There are 30 people in the survey so 360° ÷ 30 = 12°.
This means that each person gets 12° of the circle.

**2** Work out the angle for each newspaper. This is easy to do in a table.

| Newspaper | Number of people | Working | Angle |
|---|---|---|---|
| *The Guardian* | 8 | 8 × 12° = | 96° |
| *Daily Mirror* | 7 | 7 × 12° = | 84° |
| *The Times* | 3 | 3 × 12° = | 36° |
| *The Sun* | 6 | 6 × 12° = | 72° |
| *Daily Express* | 6 | 6 × 12° = | 72° |
| **Total** | 30 | | 360° |

**3** Check that the angles add up to 360°.
$96° + 84° + 36° + 72° + 72° = 360°$

**4 a** Draw a circle. Mark the centre.
Draw a line to the top of the circle.

**b** Draw the first angle (96°).

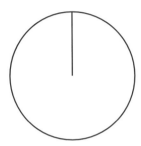

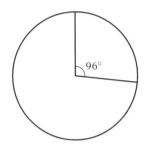

**c** Measure the next angle (84°) from the line that you have just drawn.

**d** Carry on until you have drawn all the angles.

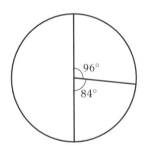

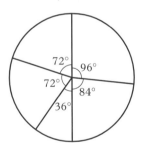

**e** Colour your pie-chart. Add a key.

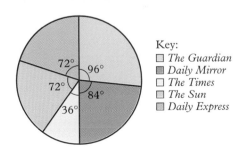

Key:
☐ *The Guardian*
▨ *Daily Mirror*
☐ *The Times*
☐ *The Sun*
☐ *Daily Express*

## Exercise 3:5

1  Class 8J were asked how they travelled to school.
   **a**  Copy this table.

| Method of travel | Number of pupils | Working | Angle |
|---|---|---|---|
| walk | 14 | | |
| bus | 7 | | |
| car | 6 | | |
| bike | 3 | | |
| private jet | 0 | | |
| **Total** | 30 | | 360° |

   **b**  Fill in the rest of the table.
   **c**  Draw a pie-chart to show this information.
       Don't forget the key.

2  Class 8P has 24 pupils.
   Here are their answers to the travel survey.

| Method of travel | Number of pupils |
|---|---|
| walk | 10 |
| bus | 7 |
| car | 6 |
| bike | 1 |

   Draw a pie-chart to show this information.
   Don't forget the key.

3  90 people were asked to say which month they were born in.
   Here are the results.

| Month | People | Month | People |
|---|---|---|---|
| January | 7 | July | 6 |
| February | 4 | August | 8 |
| March | 9 | September | 11 |
| April | 8 | October | 7 |
| May | 7 | November | 10 |
| June | 6 | December | 7 |

   Draw a pie-chart to show this information.
   Don't forget the key.

Sometimes the angle does not come out as a whole number.
You can't draw angles more accurately than to the nearest degree.
So you have to round off each sector to the nearest degree.

After rounding you need to check that the angles still add up to 360°.
If they don't, change the biggest angle so that they do.

This means that the pie-chart is not completely accurate.
Nobody takes accurate readings from pie-charts so this does not matter.

**4** Here is the most watched channel data from the beginning of the chapter.

| Channel | BBC1 | BBC2 | ITV | C4 | Sky | other |
|---|---|---|---|---|---|---|
| Number of pupils | 73 | 22 | 66 | 19 | 24 | 16 |

There are 220 people in the survey.
**a** Calculate the angle for each person.
**b** Calculate the angle for each channel.
**c** Round off the angles and then add them up.
You will be 1° short. Add 1° to the biggest sector (BBC1).
**d** Draw a pie-chart to show this data.
Compare it with the one on page 53.

**5** Here is the favourite type of programme data.

| Type of programme | children's | soaps | sport | comedy | films | drama | news |
|---|---|---|---|---|---|---|---|
| Number of pupils | 15 | 55 | 40 | 25 | 35 | 25 | 25 |

Draw a pie-chart to show this data.

**6** These were the votes in a recent by-election:

| | |
|---|---|
| Liberal Democrat | 16 000 |
| Labour | 14 000 |
| Conservative | 10 000 |
| Others | 2 000 |

Figures are to the nearest 1000.

Draw a pie-chart to show these results.

# 3  Designing a questionnaire

To get information, you need to ask people questions.

You need to think carefully about the questions that you ask.
You must make sure that you get all the information that you need.
Your questions must be easy to answer.

| Questionnaire | A **questionnaire** is a set of questions on a given topic. |
|---|---|
| | There are two types of questionnaire. Sometimes an interviewer asks the questions and fills in the answers. Sometimes you are given a form to fill in yourself. |

There are some rules that you need to know when you write your own
questionnaire.

| *Rule 1* | Questions should not be **biased**. They should not make you think that a particular answer is right. A question that does is called a **leading question**. |
|---|---|
| *Example* | Normal people like to watch football. Do you watch football? |
| | This question is biased. The first sentence should not be there. It makes you think that you aren't normal if you don't watch football. |

## Exercise 3:6

Here is a list of questions.

**a** Most people think that you should be able to learn to drive at 16.
Do you agree?

**b** Do you think you should eat less chocolate and more fruit?

**c** How many weeks of school holiday should children get each year?

**d** Most clever pupils watch the TV news.
Do you watch the news?

**e** Do you read a daily newspaper?

**1** Which of these questions do you think are biased?
Write down their letters.

**2** Write down what makes each of these questions biased.

**3** Write better questions to replace the ones that you thought were biased.

**Rule 2**  Questions should not upset people or embarrass them.

## Exercise 3:7

Here is a list of questions.

**a** How much do you weigh?

**b** How much money have you got in your bank account?

**c** How often do you have a shower?

**d** Do you have any pets at home?

**e** Most people use a deodorant. Do you?

**1** Which of these questions do you think are upsetting or embarrassing?
Write down their letters.

**2** Write down what is wrong with each of the questions that you chose.

**3** Write better questions to replace the ones that you didn't like.

**Rule 3**  Questions can give a choice of possible answers. This could be:

**A** Yes, No or Don't know.

**B** Agree, Disagree or Don't know.

**C** A set of boxes with answers that you tick.

**D** A scale where you circle your choice.
This can be useful when you are asking for an opinion.

## Exercise 3:8

Here is a list of questions.
Choose the style of answer that you would use for each one.
Write down **A**, **B**, **C** or **D**.

**A** ☐ Yes          ☐ No          ☐ Don't know

**B** ☐ Agree          ☐ Disagree          ☐ Don't know

**C** ☐ 0–2          ☐ 3–5          ☐ more than 5

**D** Strongly agree    1    2    3    4    5    Strongly disagree

**1** How many chocolate biscuits do you eat each day?

**2** The National Lottery is a good way of raising money for charity.

**3** Do diesel cars cause less pollution than petrol cars?

**4** Will you vote in the next general election?

**5** How many brothers and sisters do you have?

---

| | |
|---|---|
| **Rule 4** | Questions should be clear.<br>If people do not know what you mean you will not get the information that you need. |
| **Rule 5** | Don't ask questions that allow people to give lots of different answers.<br>This makes it very difficult to draw diagrams to show your results. |
| **Rule 6** | Don't ask questions that have nothing to do with your survey. |
| **Rule 7** | Questions should be in a sensible order.<br>Don't jump from one idea to another and back again. |

## Exercise 3:9

▼  You need the **Fitness questionnaire worksheet** for this exercise.

**1**  Fill in the questionnaire.

**2**  For each question, write down the number of the rule that it has broken.

**3**  Rewrite the questionnaire using the rules that you have learned.

## Exercise 3:10

You are now going to design your own questionnaire.
You can choose any topic that interests you.

You can't 'do' a wide topic like 'sport'. You need to focus on one
particular thing.
For example, you could find out how much sport people in Year 8 play.

When you have decided what you are going to do, you should guess what you
think you will discover.
For example, you might guess that Year 8 pupils spend less than 1 hour per
week doing sport.
This guess is called a hypothesis.
Then you design your questions to test whether your hypothesis is right or wrong.

You should plan your work like this:

**1**  Decide on your topic.
**2**  Decide on your hypothesis.
**3**  Decide who you will ask to fill in the
   questionnaire.

**4**  Write the questions for your questionnaire.
**5**  Try the questionnaire out on a friend.
**6**  Change the questions if you need to.

**7**  Do your survey!

**8**  Tally your results.
**9**  Decide which type of diagrams to use.
**10**  Draw your diagrams.
**11**  Work out some averages.

**12**  Write up your results.
**13**  Explain whether or not your hypothesis was right.

**1**   In a survey of 30 trains: 12 were on time, 10 were early and 8 were late.
Draw a pie-chart to show this information.

**2**   Class 8J were asked how long it took them to get to school.

The results are given correct to the nearest minute.

| Time taken | Number of pupils |
|------------|------------------|
| 1–5        | 6                |
| 6–10       | 3                |
| 11–15      | 5                |
| 16–20      | 4                |
| 21–25      | 8                |
| 26–30      | 4                |

**a**   Draw a bar-chart to show this information.
**b**   How many pupils took 15 minutes or less to get to school?
**c**   How many pupils took more than 20 minutes to get to school?

**3**   A doctor recorded the length of time she spent with each patient.
Here are the times correct to the nearest minute.

| | | | | | | | | |
|---|---|---|---|---|---|---|---|---|
| 10 | 5  | 9  | 20 | 14 | 3  | 8  | 6  | 9  |
| 4  | 25 | 16 | 11 | 15 | 17 | 8  | 6  | 3  |
| 9  | 5  | 6  | 8  | 19 | 21 | 6  | 10 | 11 |
| 5  | 9  | 29 | 3  | 6  | 14 | 18 | 17 | 8  |

**a**   Copy this tally-table.
Add the extra rows that it needs.

| Number of minutes | Tally | Total |
|-------------------|-------|-------|
| 1–5               |       |       |
| 6–10              |       |       |
| 11–15             |       |       |
| 16–20             |       |       |

**b**   Fill in your tally-table.
**c**   Draw a bar-chart to show this information.

**4**   The 250 pupils in Year 8 chose the language that they would like to learn next.
The results are shown in this pie-chart.

50 pupils chose Italian.

**a**   How many pupils chose Spanish?

**b**   How many pupils chose Russian?

**c**   How many pupils chose German?

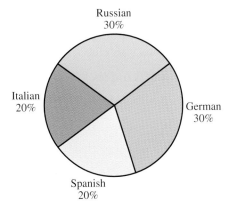

**5**   The charity UNICEF did a survey of the number of children short of food in different areas of the world.
The results were:

| | | | |
|---|---|---|---|
| Africa | 35 000 000 | Asia but not China | 42 000 000 |
| Americas | 10 000 000 | South Asia | 78 000 000 |

Draw a pie-chart to show this information.

**6**   Rajiv is planning a survey on smoking.
He has written some questions.

**a**   Which of Rajiv's questions do you think are biased?
Say what makes them biased.

**b**   Which of his questions should have boxes to tick?
Rewrite these questions showing the boxes.

**c**   Which questions are not clear enough?
Rewrite these questions to make them clearer.

**1** People in different areas of the world spend their money on different things.
A survey was done in three different areas of the world:

OECD, Organisation for Economic Co-operation and Development: This is a 'club' for rich countries.

Latin America: South American countries

South Asia: India, Pakistan and the surrounding countries.

The table shows the percentage of money that they spend on different things.

| Area | food and tobacco | clothing and footwear | housing and energy | furniture and household | transport and communication | health | leisure and other |
|------|------------------|----------------------|--------------------|------------------------|----------------------------|--------|-------------------|
| OECD | 21.2 | 7.1 | 18.2 | 7.1 | 13.6 | 9.4 | 23.5 |
| Latin America | 34.9 | 6.7 | 21 | 7 | 10.1 | 5 | 15.3 |
| South Asia | 52.3 | 9.4 | 8.8 | 4.3 | 7 | 2 | 16.2 |

**a** Draw pie-charts to show the spending in the three different areas of the world.
You will need to divide 360° by 100 to find the angle for 1%.
**b** Write a few sentences describing the differences between them.
**c** Show the data in a different way.
Use another type of diagram.
**d** Which of the two sets of diagrams shows the differences most clearly?

**2** Chantelle did a survey of the 210 pupils in Year 8.
She asked which of the following they considered to be most important in their diet:

fat     sugar     protein     fibre     vitamins

Here is a pie-chart of her results.

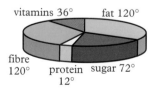

vitamins 36°     fat 120°

fibre 120°     protein 12°     sugar 72°

How many people are there in each category?

- **Pie-chart**
  A **pie-chart** shows how something is divided up.
  The angle of the sector represents the number of items.
  Sometimes the data does not work out into simple fractions.
  When this happens you have to work out angles.
  A pie-chart has 360° in it.
  This 360° needs dividing up.

  *Example*
  30 people were asked which national newspaper they read.

  There are 30 people in the survey so $360° \div 30 = 12°$
  This means that each person gets 12° of the circle.

  Work out the angle for each newspaper. This is easy to do in a table.

| Newspaper | Number of people | Working | Angle |
|-----------|------------------|---------|-------|
| The Guardian | 8 | $8 \times 12° =$ | 96° |
| Daily Mirror | 7 | $7 \times 12° =$ | 84° |
| The Times | 3 | $3 \times 12° =$ | 36° |
| The Sun | 6 | $6 \times 12° =$ | 72° |
| Daily Express | 6 | $6 \times 12° =$ | 72° |
| **Total** | 30 | | 360° |

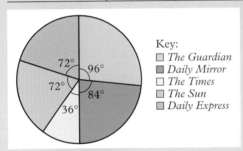

Key:
- ☐ *The Guardian*
- ■ *Daily Mirror*
- ☐ *The Times*
- ☐ *The Sun*
- ■ *Daily Express*

- **Questionnaire**
  A **questionnaire** is a set of questions on a given topic.
  There are two types of questionnaire.
  Sometimes an interviewer asks the questions and fills in the answers.
  Sometimes you are given a form to fill in yourself.

  Remember:
  1 Questions should not be biased.
  2 Questions should not upset people or embarrass them.
  3 Questions can give a choice of possible answers.
  4 Questions should be clear.
  5 Don't ask questions that allow lots of different answers.
  6 Don't ask questions that have nothing to do with your survey.
  7 Questions should be in a sensible order.

**1** Phil is doing a survey into the time taken by Class 8J to get to school.
Here are the times correct to the nearest minute.

| 15 | 10 | 14 | 8  | 3  | 9  | 24 | 23 | 6  | 4  |
|----|----|----|----|----|----|----|----|----|----|
| 7  | 18 | 26 | 7  | 5  | 12 | 17 | 4  | 21 | 19 |
| 5  | 8  | 17 | 24 | 28 | 10 | 3  | 9  | 7  | 25 |

   **a** Think of sensible time ranges to group this data.
   **b** Make a grouped tally-table for this data.
   **c** Draw a bar-chart to show this information.

**2** Pritti asked 8J to choose their favourite radio station.
Their answers were:   Radio 1          10
                       Radio 2          4
                       Radio 5 Live     9
                       Atlantic 252     7
Draw a pie-chart to show this data.

**3** There are 28 pupils in class 8L.
Their favourite radio stations are:   Radio 1          11
                                       Radio 2          3
                                       Radio 5 Live     8
                                       Atlantic 252     6
Draw a pie-chart to show this data.

**4** These questions came from a survey about what adults think of
young people.
   (1) Most people think that there is a lack of discipline in schools.
       Do you agree?
   (2) What do you think of children today?
   (3) Do you think children have too much freedom?
   (4) How much time do you think they should spend at school?

   **a** Write down what you think is wrong with each question.
   **b** Write some better questions which are not biased.

# 4 Algebra

**Muhammed ibn Musa al-Khwarizmi
c780 – c850**

Al-Khwarizmi was a well known mathematician and astronomer who lived in Baghdad in the early 9th century. He wrote a book called *Kitab al-jabr wa al-nuqabalah*, which was about solving equations.

The word algebra comes from the word *al-jabr*.

# 1 Number patterns

Steve is making patterns with counters.
They are in the shapes of capital letters.

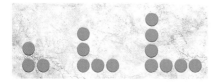
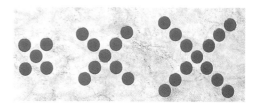

He wants to find the rules for his patterns.

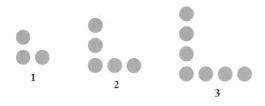

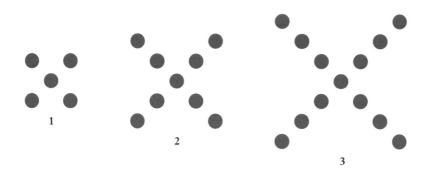

### Exercise 4:1 Alphabet patterns

**1** **a** Copy L shapes 1, 2 and 3 from the picture.
   **b** Draw L shapes 4 and 5.
   **c** Count the number of circles in each shape.
   **d** Copy this table.
      Fill it in.

| L shape number | 1 | 2 | 3 | 4 | 5 |
|---|---|---|---|---|---|
| Number of circles | 3 | 5 | | | |

   **e** Look at your table.
      How many circles are you adding each time?
   **f** Copy and fill in:
         The rule is add ... circles each time.

**2** **a** Copy X shapes 1, 2 and 3 from the picture.
   **b** Draw X shapes 4 and 5.
   **c** Count the number of circles in each shape.
   **d** Copy this table.
      Fill it in.

| X shape number | 1 | 2 | 3 | 4 | 5 |
|---|---|---|---|---|---|
| Number of circles | 5 | 9 | | | |

   **e** Look at your table.
      How many circles are you adding each time?
   **f** Copy and fill in:
         The rule is add ... circles each time.

**3** Can you find some more letters that give patterns?
   Draw your letters.
   Fill in a table and find the rule.

---

*Example*          Lizzy is making triangles out of matchsticks.

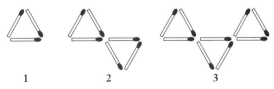

      1              2                3

This table shows how many matchsticks she needs.

| Number of triangles | 1 | 2 | 3 | 4 | 5 |
| --- | --- | --- | --- | --- | --- |
| Number of matchsticks | 3 | 6 | 9 | 12 | 15 |

$+3$　$+3$　$+3$　$+3$

The rule is shown in red. It is $+3$.

Lizzy also finds a formula.
If she knows the number of triangles, she can work out the number of matchsticks.

Her formula is:
  number of *m*atchsticks equals $3 \times$ number of *t*riangles.
  In algebra this is $m = 3 \times t$

## Exercise 4:2

**1** Hitesh is making pentagons out of matchsticks.

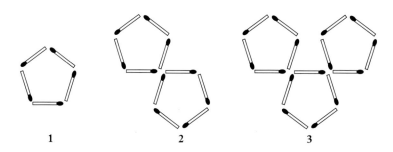

1　　　　　　2　　　　　　3

**a** Copy this table.
Fill it in.

| Number of pentagons | 1 | 2 | 3 | 4 | 5 |
| --- | --- | --- | --- | --- | --- |
| Number of matchsticks | | | 15 | | |

$+?$　$+?$　$+?$　$+?$

**b** Fill in the rule on your table.
**c** Write down the formula.
**d** Write this formula in algebra.

**2** Apples are sold in trays of four.

  **a** Make a table to show the number of apples.
Go up to 5 trays.

  **b** Write down the formula for finding the number of apples.

  **c** Write this formula in algebra.

  **d** Use this formula to find the number of apples in:

    (1) 8 trays    (2) 11 trays    (3) 25 trays

**3** Lucy is making *h*exagons out of *m*atchsticks.

The formula is: $m = 6 \times h$

Use this formula to find the number of matchsticks in:

  **a** 3 hexagons

  **b** 12 hexagons

  **c** 100 hexagons

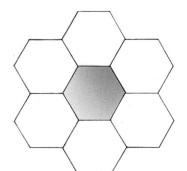
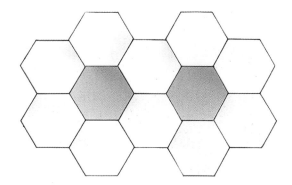

Rod is building a new patio.
He is using red and white slabs.
He wants to work out how many white slabs he needs for each red slab.

The formula is: $w = 4 \times r + 2$

## Exercise 4:3

**1** Use the slabs formula to find the number of white slabs needed for:

  **a** 7 red slabs

  **b** 10 red slabs

  **c** 16 red slabs

**2** Angela is tiling her bathroom.
She uses a formula to work out the number of tiles she needs.
The formula is:
$$t = 10l + 8$$
($t$ = number of tiles, $l$ = length of wall)
The wall is measured in metres.

Work out the number of tiles she needs if the length of the wall is:
**a** 3 m      **b** 5 m      **c** $2\frac{1}{2}$ m      **d** 350 cm

**3** This formula tells you how long to cook a turkey.
$$t = 10w + 30$$

The weight ($w$) is in kilograms and the time ($t$) is in minutes.
How long does it take to cook a turkey which weighs:
**a** 3 kg      **b** 6 kg      **c** 7 kg      **d** 1500 g

Aisha is working on an investigation into squares.

She has to find the formula for the number of matchsticks.

She has made a table.

| Number of squares | 1 | 2 | 3 | 4 | 5 |
|---|---|---|---|---|---|
| Number of matchsticks | 4 | 7 | 10 | 13 | 16 |

Aisha notices that the pattern goes up in 3s.
She knows that this means that the formula will have ×3 in it.

She calculates that she needs to add 1 to get the number of matchsticks.

She writes the full formula:
number of *m*atchsticks = 3 × number of *s*quares + 1
$$m = 3s + 1$$

Aisha checks her formula with $s = 6$
number of matchsticks = 3 × 6 + 1
$$= 19$$

She makes 6 squares with matchsticks to check that her answer is right.

## Exercise 4:4

**1** These patterns are made from square tiles.

 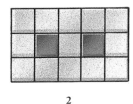 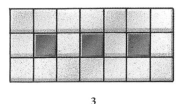

1          2          3

  **a** Look at the patterns
     Draw the next two.
  **b** Copy this table.
     Fill it in.

| Number of blue tiles | 1 | 2 | 3 | 4 | 5 |
|---|---|---|---|---|---|
| Number of yellow tiles | 8 | 13 | | | |

  **c** How many yellow tiles do you add each time?
  **d** What must your formula have in it?
  **e** What do you have to add to get the numbers in your table?
  **f** Write out the full formula.

**2** Here are some diagrams of C shapes made out of squares.

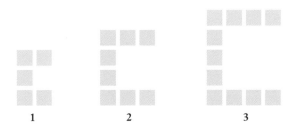

1          2          3

  **a** Draw the next two diagrams.
  **b** Make a table to show the number of squares in each diagram.
  **c** How many squares do you add each time?
  **d** What must your formula have in it?
  **e** What do you have to add to get the numbers in your table?
  **f** Write down the full formula.
  **g** Use your formula to find the number of squares in the 10th diagram.

**3**

**a** Draw the next two diagrams.
Count the dots in them.
**b** Work out the formula for these dots.
**c** Use your formula to work out the number of dots in the 20th diagram.

| Number sequence | A **number sequence** is a pattern of numbers. |
| --- | --- |

| Term | Each number in the sequence is called a **term**. There is always a rule to work out the next term in the sequence. |
| --- | --- |

*Example*

| Term number | 1 | 2 | 3 | 4 | 5 | 6 |
| --- | --- | --- | --- | --- | --- | --- |
| Term | 4 | 7 | 10 | 13 | 16 | 19 |

The rule to get the next term is $+3$.

Each term can also be worked out from a formula.
If you use the formula to work out the 20th term then you do not have to work out all the previous 19 terms!

In this example the formula is: $t = 3 \times n + 1$
$n$ is the term number and $t$ is the term.

The 20th term is $t = 3 \times 20 + 1$
$$= 60 + 1$$
$$= 61$$

## *Exercise 4:5*

**1** For each of these sequences find:
   **a** the next three terms
   **b** the rule to get from one term to the next
   **c** the formula to work out each term from the term number

| | | | | | | | |
| --- | --- | --- | --- | --- | --- | --- | --- |
| (1) | 7 | 9 | 11 | 13 | ... | ... | ... |
| (2) | 5 | 8 | 11 | 14 | ... | ... | ... |
| (3) | 6 | 10 | 14 | 18 | ... | ... | ... |
| (4) | 20 | 30 | 40 | 50 | ... | ... | ... |
| (5) | 18 | 36 | 54 | 72 | ... | ... | ... |
| (6) | 18 | 16 | 14 | 12 | ... | ... | ... |

**2** For each of these sequences:
  **a** fill in the gaps
  **b** find the formula to work out each term from the term number
    (1)  5     8     ...     14
    (2)  7     ...     13     16
    (3)  4     9     ...     ...
    (4)  12     ...     ...     33

---

If you know the formula you can work out the sequence.

*Example*        The formula for a sequence is:   $t = 4n + 3$
        Work the first 3 terms of the sequence.
        1st term:     $t = 4 \times 1 + 3 = 7$
        2nd term:     $t = 4 \times 2 + 3 = 11$
        3rd term:     $t = 4 \times 3 + 3 = 15$

---

**3** From each of these formulas, work out the first 4 terms of the sequence.
  **a** $t = 2n + 3$        **b** $t = 5n + 2$        **c** $t = 3n + 1$

**4** The formula for a sequence is $t = 6n - 3$
  **a** Work out the 20th term.
  **b** Which term is equal to 417?
  **c** Which is the first term to go over 1000?
    What is this term?

**5** The formula for a sequence is $t = n^2 + 3$
  **a** Work out the first five terms of this sequence.
  **b** Work out the differences between each term and the next.
    Why do you think they are not all the same?

## 2 Reversing rules

Rod has ordered 26 white slabs for his patio.
He has forgotten how many red slabs he needs.

Rod needs the inverse of his formula.
The formula is: $w = 4r + 2$

First he writes his formula on robot screens.

$r \longrightarrow \boxed{\times 4} \longrightarrow \boxed{+ 2} \longrightarrow 26$

The inverse machine is:

$6 \longleftarrow \boxed{\div 4} \xleftarrow{24} \boxed{- 2} \longleftarrow 26$

He needs 6 red slabs.

### Exercise 4:6

**1** How many red slabs does Rod need for:
  **a** 34 white slabs    **b** 22 white slabs    **c** 42 white slabs

**2** Zeta needs a new cycle helmet. The helmet costs £23.

Zeta earns money delivering leaflets.
Her wages are £2 for every packet of leaflets she delivers.
She also gets £5 for lunch and bus fares.

The formula is: $w = 2p + 5$

  **a** Draw the inverse machine for this formula.
  **b** How many packets does Zeta need to deliver to buy her cycle helmet?

**3** George takes part in a sponsored silence.
His parents give him £5.
His friends sponsor him £2 per hour.

The formula is:  $m = 2h + 5$

**a** Draw the inverse machine.
**b** How long does George need to stay silent to raise:
   (1)  £11            (2)  £23            (3)  £53

You can also solve problems using equations.
To solve an equation you look to see what has been done to $x$.
You then find the inverse of this.

*Example*      **1**   Solve $x + 9 = 17$
The inverse of $+9$ is $-9$ so subtract 9 from both sides.

$$x + 9 - 9 = 17 - 9$$
$$x = 8$$

**2**   Solve $4r + 2 = 30$
$4r$ means $4 \times r$

This is the formula for the red and white slabs.
Solving this will answer the question
'How many red slabs does Rod need for 30 white slabs?'

The inverse of $+2$ is $-2$ so subtract 2 from both sides.

$$4r + 2 - 2 = 30 - 2$$
$$4r = 28$$

The inverse of $\times 4$ is $\div 4$ so divide both sides by 4.

$$\frac{4r}{4} = \frac{28}{4}$$
$$r = 7$$

◄◄ **REPLAY** ►

### Exercise 4:7

Solve these equations.

**1**   $x + 4 = 10$          **4**   $3x = 12$          **7**   $2x + 1 = 9$

**2**   $x - 7 = 12$          **5**   $4x = 24$          **8**   $7x - 3 = 46$

**3**   $x + 15 = 23$          **6**   $\frac{1}{2}x = 5$          **9**   $2x - 5 = 15$

**10**  $3x - 2 = 8$

**12**  $\dfrac{x}{2} = 14$

**14**  $\dfrac{x}{5} + 1 = 6$

**11**  $6x + 7 = 19$

**13**  $\dfrac{x}{3} = 5$

**15**  $8 + 2x = 20$

Some equations have letters on both sides.
The rules for solving them are the same.
You must still try to find inverses.

*Examples*

**1**  Solve the equation $6x = 4x + 8$

Your aim is to change the equation so that $x$ only appears on one side.
Look to see which side has least $x$.
In this example the RHS has only $4x$.
Subtract $4x$ from each side

$$6x - 4x = 4x - 4x + 8$$
$$2x = 8$$

Divide by 2
$$x = 4$$

**2**  Solve the equation $5x + 3 = 2x + 18$

This time we need to subtract $2x$ from each side
$$5x - 2x + 3 = 2x - 2x + 18$$
$$3x + 3 = 18$$

Now subtract 3
$$3x + 3 - 3 = 18 - 3$$
$$3x = 15$$

Divide by 3
$$x = 5$$

## Exercise 4:8

Solve these equations.

**1**  $5x = 3x + 8$

**2**  $9x = 6x + 21$

**3**  $2x = x + 9$

**4**  $7x = x + 36$

**5**  $5x + 2 = 3x + 10$

**6**  $7x + 1 = 4x + 19$

**7**  $6x - 4 = 3x + 8$

**8**  $9x - 3 = 7x + 23$

**9**  $8x - 11 = 2x + 25$

**10**  $5x + 1 = x + 13$

# 3 Substitution

Lots of equations used in maths and science have powers in them.

◄◄ **REPLAY** ►

### Exercise 4:9

The letters represent the numbers shown:

$$a = 2 \quad b = 5 \quad c = 3 \quad d = 4 \quad e = 10$$

Work these out.
(*Remember:* $3 \times a$ is written $3a$ in algebra and $a \times b$ is written $ab$.)

**1** $b + 8$      **3** $d + e$      **5** $d + b - c$      **7** $ab$

**2** $3a$      **4** $2c - a$      **6** $5d - 4b$      **8** $2cd - e$

**9** A formula used in science is $F = ma$ where $F$ is a force.
Find $F$ if $m = 6$ and $a = 9$.

**10** $P = 2l + 2w$ gives the perimeter of a rectangle.
Find $P$ when $l = 8$ and $w = 2$.

---

| **Power** | $a^2$ | The **power** '2' tells you how many $a$'s are multiplied together. |
|---|---|---|
| | | $a \times a = a^2$ |
| | | $a \times a \times a = a^3$ |

---

**11** Write these as a power.

    **a** $d \times d \times d$                      **c** $y \times y$

    **b** $a \times a \times a \times a \times a$         **d** $c \times c \times c \times c$

**12** Find the value of:

    **a** $4^2$          **b** $2^4$          **c** $5^3$

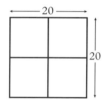

Kerry and Sapna are helping on a farm during their holiday. The farmer asks them to find the area of these fields.

Kerry and Sapna work out the area in different ways.

**Kerry's method**

Area of 1 field $= 10 \times 10$

             $= 100$

Area of 4 fields $= 4 \times 100$

              $= 400$

**Sapna's method**

Area of big square $= 20 \times 20$

                  $= 400$

They both get the same answer.

They write a formula that gives the area of any size field.

**Kerry's method**

Area of 1 field $= y \times y$

             $= y^2$

Area of 4 fields $= 4 \times y^2$

              $= 4y^2$

**Sapna's method**

Area of big square $= 2y \times 2y$

                  $= 2 \times y \times 2 \times y$

                  $= 4 \times y \times y$

                  $= 4y^2$

They both get the same answer again.

$y \times y$ is written $y^2$    so $2y \times 2y$ is written $(2y)^2$

       $(2y)^2$ is the same as $4y^2$

In algebra their formulas are:

    $A = 4y^2$     $A = (2y)^2$

*Example*

Use Kerry and Sapna's formulas to find the area of the fields when $y = 30$.

$$A = 4y^2$$
$$= 4 \times 30^2$$
$$= 4 \times 900$$
$$= 3600$$

$$A = (2y)^2$$
$$= (2 \times 30)^2$$
$$= (60)^2$$
$$= 60 \times 60$$
$$= 3600$$

## Exercise 4:10

**1** Use Kerry and Sapna's formulas to find the area of the fields when the value of $y$ is:

   **a** 20    **b** 35    **c** 40    **d** 25    **e** 33

**2** John is using the formula $D = 3t^2$ in science.
Find the value of $D$ when the value of $t$ is:

   **a** 2    **b** 5    **c** 9    **d** 10

**3** The area of a shape is given by the formula $a = (4d)^2$
Find the value of $a$ when the value of $d$ is:

   **a** 3    **b** 4    **c** 5    **d** 6

*Example*

$c = 2$     $d = 3$     $e = 5$     $f = 10$

Work out   **a** $3f^2$      **b** $4c^3$

**a** $3f^2 = 3 \times f^2$
       $= 3 \times 10^2$
       $= 3 \times 100$
       $= 300$

**b** $4c^3 = 4 \times c^3$
       $= 4 \times 2^3$
       $= 4 \times 8$
       $= 32$

Work these out.

**4** $d^3$       **6** $e^3$       **8** $4e^2$       **10** $7f^4$

**5** $c^4$       **7** $2d^2$       **9** $5c^3$       **11** $3e^2$

| Example | Work out | **a** $(4d)^2$ | **b** $(2e)^3$ |

**a** $(4d)^2 = (4 \times d)^2$
$= (4 \times 3)^2$
$= 12^2$
$= 144$

**b** $(2e)^3 = (2 \times e)^3$
$= (2 \times 5)^3$
$= 10^3$
$= 1000$

## Exercise 4:11

$$c = 2 \qquad d = 3 \qquad e = 5 \qquad f = 10$$

Work these out.

**1** $(2f)^2$      **6** $4f^3$

**2** $(3d)^3$      **7** $(4f)^3$

**3** $(4c)^2$      **8** $3c^4$

**4** $5d^2$      **9** $(3c)^4$

**5** $(5d)^2$

**10** Fill in the missing numbers.
  **a** $(y^2)^3 = y^?$      **b** $(m^4)^2 = m^?$      **c** $(s^3)^4 = s^?$

**11** In science we use the formula Energy $= 8x^2$
Find the energy when:
  **a** $x = 12$      **b** $x = 20$

**12** In science we use the formula Kinetic energy $= \frac{1}{2}mv^2$
Find the energy when:
  **a** $m = 5$ and $v = 3$
  **b** $m = 8$ and $v = 12$

**13** The formula for distance is:
$$\text{distance} = ut + \frac{1}{2}at^2$$
Find the distance when:
  **a** $u = 4$, $t = 3$ and $a = 8$
  **b** $u = 6$, $t = 5$ and $a = 6$

**14** In science we use the formula
$$\text{Potential Energy} = mgh$$
The value of $g$ is 9.8
Find the energy when:
**a** $m = 40$ and $h = 7$
**b** $m = 9$ and $h = 10$

**15** The formula $\quad \text{Tension} = \dfrac{\lambda x}{l}\, '$ is used for elastic strings.

($\lambda$, a Greek letter, is said 'lambda'.)
Find the tension when:
**a** $\lambda = 20, \ x = 5, \ l = 40$
**b** $\lambda = 100, \ x = 6, \ l = 15$

---

### Exercise 4:12 Traffic light squares

Look at these patterns of coloured squares.

1

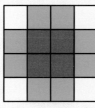

2

How many yellow and green squares would there be in the 50th traffic light square?
How many red squares would there be in the 50th traffic light square?

Design some square patterns of your own.
You could use more colours.
For each pattern, work out how many of each colour there would be in the 50th square.

How about three-dimensional problems?

**1**  The cost of having a car repaired is £10 plus £15 for each hour that the job takes.
   **a**  Copy and fill in:
       The formula is:
           cost = ... × number of *h*ours + **10**
   **b**  Write the formula in algebra.
   **c**  Find the cost of a repair that takes 3 hours.

**2**  Roundabouts are put at crossroads like this:

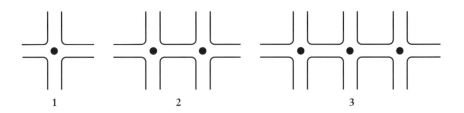

1          2                    3

   **a**  Draw the next two diagrams in this pattern.
   **b**  Copy this table.
       Fill it in.

| Number of roundabouts | 1 | 2 | 3 | 4 | 5 |
|---|---|---|---|---|---|
| Number of roads | 4 | 7 | | | |

   **c**  Look at the table.
       How many roads are you adding each time?
   **d**  Copy and fill in:
       The formula is:
           number of *r*oads = ... × ..................... + ...
   **e**  Write your formula in algebra.
           *r* = ... × ... + ...

**3**  Jane is having a party.
   The cost of the food is £15 plus £3 for each person.
   **a**  Write down the formula for the cost of the food.
   **b**  Work out the cost of food for 40 people.
   **c**  Write down the inverse formula.
   **d**  The food costs £78.
       How many people are coming to the party?

**4** For each of these sequences find:
  **a** the next three terms
  **b** the rule to get from one term to the next
  **c** the formula to work out each term from the term number

|      |   |    |    |    |     |     |     |
|------|---|----|----|----|-----|-----|-----|
| (1)  | 1 | 3  | 5  | 7  | ... | ... | ... |
| (2)  | 7 | 11 | 15 | 19 | ... | ... | ... |
| (3)  | 1 | 6  | 11 | 16 | ... | ... | ... |
| (4)  | 9 | 12 | 15 | 18 | ... | ... | ... |
| (5)  | 4 | 14 | 24 | 34 | ... | ... | ... |

**5** The formula for a sequence is $t = 8n - 7$
  **a** Find the 26th term.
  **b** Which term is equal to 65?

**6** Solve these equations.
  **a** $x + 6 = 11$          **f** $8d + 11 = 35$

  **b** $y - 9 = 15$          **g** $\dfrac{x}{2} = 4$

  **c** $7x = 21$          **h** $\dfrac{y}{3} = 12$

  **d** $2x + 3 = 15$          **i** $\dfrac{t}{2} + 6 = 20$

  **e** $5y - 8 = 12$          **j** $\dfrac{y}{2} - 7 = 11$

**7** Write these as a power.
  **a** $t \times t$          **b** $s \times s \times s \times s$          **c** $y \times y \times y$

**8** Find the value of:
  **a** $5^2$          **b** $4^3$          **c** $2^5$          **d** $3^4$

**9** $a = 5 \quad b = 3 \quad c = 2 \quad d = 10$
  Work out:
  **a** $4 + b$          **e** $2a + 3c$          **i** $b^2$
  **b** $c + d$          **f** $4d - 3a$          **j** $a^2 + c^2$
  **c** $3d$          **g** $d^2$          **k** $5c^2$
  **d** $5 + 3c$          **h** $c^4$          **l** $(5c)^2$

**1**  The formula for a sequence is $5n^2 - 3$
   **a**  Work out the first 3 terms of this sequence.
   **b**  What is the 10th term?
   **c**  Which term is equal to 177?

**2**  Solve these equations.
   **a**  $2y - 3 = y + 2$        **b**  $7x - 8 = 4x + 4$

**3**  Fill in the gaps in these sequences.
   **a**  $\frac{2}{11}$    …    $\frac{4}{11}$    …    …    $\frac{7}{11}$
   **b**  $\frac{7}{12}$    $\frac{1}{2}$    …    $\frac{1}{3}$    …    …
   **c**  $2\frac{1}{3}$    3    …    …    5    …
   **d**  $\frac{3}{4}$    …    …    …    …    …    $\frac{1}{2}$

**4**  Find the formula for the sequence:
        15        13        11        9        7        5

**5**  Look at these sequences:

| Term number | 1 | 2 | 3 | 4 | 5 |
|---|---|---|---|---|---|
| sequence A | 2 | 4 | 6 | 8 | 10 |
| sequence B | 2 | 5 | 8 | 11 | 14 |
| sequence C | 2 | 6 | 10 | 14 | 18 |

   **a**  Find the formula for each
       sequence.
   **b**  On graph paper, draw a set of
       axes as shown.
   **c**  Draw graphs of sequences A,
       B and C all on the same
       diagram.
   **d**  Write about what you notice.
       What sort of graph would the
       sequence in question **1**
       produce?

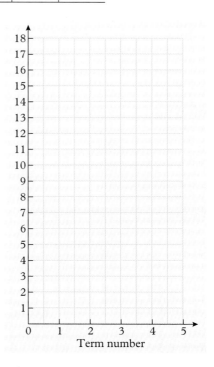

- **Number sequence** A **number sequence** is a pattern of numbers
  **Term** Each number in the sequence is called a **term**.

*Example*

| Term number | 1 | 2 | 3 | 4 | 5 | 6 |
|---|---|---|---|---|---|---|
| Term | 4 | 7 | 10 | 13 | 16 | 19 |

The rule to get to the next term is $+3$.

Each term can also be worked out from a formula.
In this example the formula is $t = 3n + 1$
$n$ is the term number and $t$ is the term.

The 20th term is: $t = 3 \times 20 + 1$
$$= 61$$

- You can work out the sequence from the formula.

*Example*
The formula for a sequence is $t = 4n + 3$
The first 3 terms of the sequence are:

| 1st term | 2nd term | 3rd term |
|---|---|---|
| $t = 4 \times 1 + 3$ | $t = 4 \times 2 + 3$ | $t = 4 \times 3 + 3$ |
| $= 7$ | $= 11$ | $= 15$ |

- ***Solving equations***
  Some equations have letters on both sides.
  Change the equation so that $x$ only appears on one side.

*Example*

| | |
|---|---|
| Solve the equation | $5x + 3 = 2x + 18$ |
| Subtract $2x$ from each side | $5x - 2x + 3 = 2x - 2x + 18$ |
| | $3x + 3 = 18$ |
| Now subtract 3 from each side | $3x + 3 - 3 = 18 - 3$ |
| | $3x = 15$ |
| Divide by 3 | $x = 5$ |

- **Power** $a^2$ The **power** '2' tells you how many $a$'s are multiplied together.
  $$a \times a = a^2 \qquad a \times a \times a = a^3$$

Be careful when substituting into powers.
Look at these when $d = 3$.
They give different answers.

| | |
|---|---|
| $4d^2 = 4 \times 3^2$ | $(4d)^2 = (4 \times 3)^2$ |
| $= 4 \times 9$ | $= 12^2$ |
| $= 36$ | $= 144$ |

**1**  Wesley is tiling his bathroom in a pattern like this:

  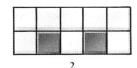  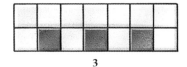

1                    2                              3

**a**  Copy the table.
Fill it in.

| Number of blue tiles | 1 | 2 | 3 | 4 | 5 |
|---|---|---|---|---|---|
| Number of white tiles | 5 | 8 | | | |

**b**  How many white tiles do you add each time?
**c**  Write down the first part of the formula.
**d**  What do you have to add to get the numbers in your table?
**e**  Copy and fill in the full formula:
number of *white* tiles = … × number of *blue* tiles + …
**f**  Wesley uses 17 blue tiles.
How many white tiles does he use?
**g**  Write your formula on robot screens.
**h**  Draw the inverse machine.
**i**  Wesley used 62 white tiles.
How many blue tiles did he use?

**2**  The formula for a sequence is   $t = 4n + 3$
Work out the first 3 terms of the sequence.

**3**  $a = 2$   $b = 5$   $c = 7$
Work out:
**a**  $2a + 10$          **c**  $c^2$          **e**  $2b^2$
**b**  $2b + c$          **d**  $b^3$          **f**  $(2b)^2$

**4**  Solve these equations.
**a**  $4x + 5 = 3x + 12$
**b**  $7x - 10 = 3x + 2$

# 5 Transformations

QUESTIONS

EXTENSION

SUMMARY

TEST YOURSELF

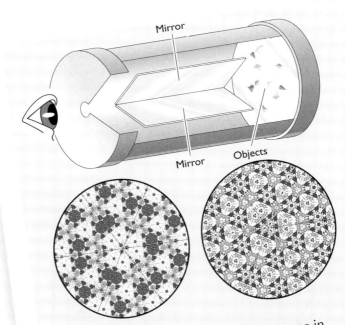

David Brewster invented the kaleidoscope in 1816. It is made with two mirrors in a tube. The angle between the mirrors can be 45° or 60°. When the end of the tube is rotated, coloured pieces of plastic between the two mirrors are reflected to make symmetrical patterns.

Which other angles would work? Why?

# 1   Reflections

The lake acts like a mirror.
The trees are reflected in it.
The mirror line is a line of symmetry.

◄◄ REPLAY ►

### Exercise 5:1

Copy these diagrams on to squared paper.
Draw their reflections in the mirror lines.

**1**
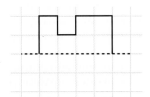

**2**
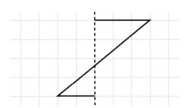

The object does not have to touch the mirror line.
The reflection is the same distance from the mirror line as the object.

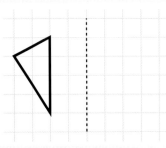

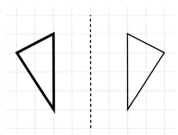

Put an object 2 squares
in front of a mirror line.

Its reflection is 2 squares
behind the mirror line.

Copy these diagrams on to squared paper.
Draw their reflections in the mirror lines.

**3**

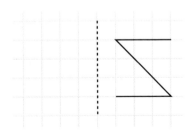

**5**

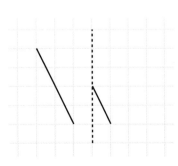

**4**

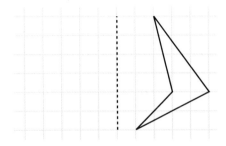

**6**

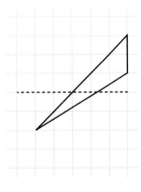

The mirror line is not always a line of the grid.

The reflection or image is still the same distance from the mirror line as the object.
Here the distance is diagonally across two squares.

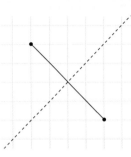

**Image**

The **image** is how the object appears after reflection or rotation.

Copy these diagrams on to squared paper.
Draw their reflections in the mirror lines.

**7** 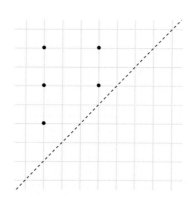 **8**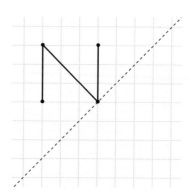

**9** Trace these diagrams on to tracing paper.
Fold the tracing paper along the mirror line.
Trace the object again.

Open out the tracing paper and hold it up to the light.
You will see the object and its reflection.

**a**  **b**  **c**

## Exercise 5:2

**1** Draw axes like these on squared paper.
  **a** Plot these points:
    A (1, 2)   B (2, 4)   C (5, 1)
    Label each point with its letter.
    Join the points to get triangle ABC.
  **b** Reflect triangle ABC in the $y$ axis to
    get a new triangle $A_1B_1C_1$.
    The reflection of A is $A_1$, etc.

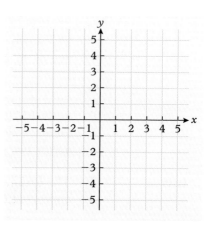

**c** Copy this table for the reflection.
Fill it in.

| Co-ordinates of ABC | A(1, 2) | B(2, 4) | C(5, 1) |
|---|---|---|---|
| Co-ordinates of $A_1B_1C_1$ | $A_1(-1, 2)$ | $B_1$ | $C_1$ |

**d** The reflection changes the co-ordinates.
Write down the rule for this change.

**e** Reflect the original triangle ABC in the $x$ axis to get triangle $A_2B_2C_2$

**f** Make a table for the reflection like the one in part **c**.

**g** The reflection changes the co-ordinates.
Write down the rule for this change.

**h** To complete the pattern triangle $A_3B_3C_3$ could be drawn in the
third quadrant.
Use your rules from part **d** and part **g** to predict the co-ordinates of
triangle $A_3B_3C_3$.
Draw $A_3B_3C_3$ to see if you are right.

**2** Copy the axes from question **1** again.

**a** This co-ordinate table is for the line $y = x$.
The $y$ co-ordinate equals the $x$ co-ordinate.
Copy the table.
Fill it in.

| $x$ | −5 | −4 | −3 | −2 | −1 | 0 | 1 | 2 | 3 | 4 | 5 |
|---|---|---|---|---|---|---|---|---|---|---|---|
| $y$ | −5 | | | | | | | | | | |

**b** Plot the points. Join them with a ruler.
Label your line $y = x$

**c** Plot these points: A(−2, 1)   B(−2, 5)   C(3, 5)   D(2, 3)
Label each point with its letter.
Join the points to get quadrilateral ABCD.

**d** Reflect ABCD in the line $y = x$.
Label the reflected shape $A_1B_1C_1D_1$.

**e** Copy this table for the reflection.
Fill it in.

| Co-ordinates of ABCD | A(−2, 1) | B(−2, 5) | C(3, 5) | D(2, 3) |
|---|---|---|---|---|
| Co-ordinates of $A_1B_1C_1D_1$ | $A_1$ | $B_1$ | $C_1$ | $D_1$ |

**f** The reflection changes the co-ordinates.
Write down the rule for this change.

This shape made from cubes
is reflected in a mirror.

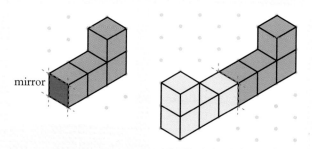

mirror

## Exercise 5:3

You will need some cubes and some dotty isometric paper for
this exercise.

**1** Make these shapes from cubes.
Make their reflections.
Draw your shapes on isometric paper.

a 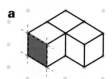    b 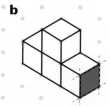    c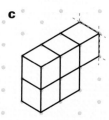

These pairs of arrangements of four cubes are reflections of each other.

a      b

In pair **b** the arrangements can be rotated to be identical with each other.

● **2** Make a pair of arrangements of five cubes which are reflections of each other:
  **a** so that the pair can be rotated to be identical
  **b** so that the pair cannot be rotated to be identical
  Draw your pairs on isometric paper.

## 2  Movement – translations

There are different rides at the fair.
You can go straight down the field on the train.
You can go round and round on a roundabout.

| | |
|---|---|
| **Translation** | A **translation** is a movement in a straight line. |
| **Rotation** | A **rotation** is a movement round in a circle. |

### Exercise 5:4

**1**  Write down whether these movements are translations or rotations.
   **a**  opening an ordinary door
   **b**  running 100 metres
   **c**  going up in a lift
   **d**  opening a book
   **e**  swimming a length
   **f**  unscrewing the top of a bottle

**2**  Give two examples of your own of translations.

**3**  Give two examples of your own of rotations.

**5**

## Translations

*Example*

Translate the L shape 4 squares to the right.

Choose one point.
Move the point 4 squares to the right.
Move the other points in the same way.

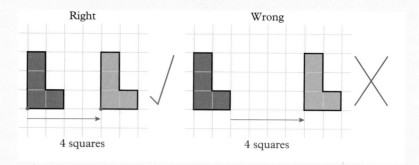

## Exercise 5:5

You will need squared paper for this exercise.

**1** Copy this L shape on to squared paper.
You will need a new copy for each part of the question.
Label each copy with the question number.

Translate your L:
**a** 5 squares to the right
**b** 4 squares down
**c** 3 squares to the left
**d** 5 squares up

**2** Draw a pair of axes from 0 to 10.
  **a** Plot these points: A (1, 1)  B (4, 1)  C (3, 3)
    Join the points to make a triangle.
  **b** Translate triangle ABC 5 units to the right and 2 units up.
    Label the image triangle $A_1B_1C_1$.
  **c** Translate triangle ABC 2 units to the right and 6 units up.
    Label the image triangle $A_2B_2C_2$.
  **d** Write down the translation that takes $A_1B_1C_1$ to $A_2B_2C_2$.
  **e** Write down the translation that takes $A_2B_2C_2$ to $A_1B_1C_1$.

## Exercise 5:6

**1** Draw a pair of axes from $-5$ to 5.
  **a** Plot these points but do not join them:
  A(1, 1)  B(0, 0)  C(2, 2)  D(-2, 4)
  **b** Translate each point 3 units to the right.
  Label the new positions $A_1$, $B_1$, $C_1$ and $D_1$.
  **c** Make a table for the points A, B, C, D.
  **d** The translation changes the co-ordinates.
  Write down the rule for a translation
  3 units to the right.
  **e** What is the rule for a translation 3 units
  to the left?

| Point | Image after translation of 3 units to right |
|---|---|
| A(1, 1) | $A_1$ ... |
| B(0, 0) | |

**2** Use the same diagram as question **1**.
  **a** Plot E(4, 4)  F(0, 3)  G(-4, -1)  H(-2, 0)
  **b** Translate each point 2 units down.
  Label the new positions $E_1$, $F_1$, $G_1$ and $H_1$.
  **c** Make a new table for the points E, F, G, H.
  **d** Write down the rule for the change of co-ordinates.
  **e** What is the rule for a translation 2 units up?

**3** Write down the co-ordinates of the images of these points.
  Do not draw a diagram.
  **a** (2, 3) is translated 4 units to the right
  **b** (1, 6) is translated 5 units down
  **c** (-4, 4) is translated 3 units to the right
  **d** (2, -3) is translated 6 units up
  **e** (0, -2) is translated 4 units up
  **f** (-1, 2) is translated 2 units to the left
  **g** (4, 1) is translated 4 units to the right and 3 units up
  **h** (5, -3) is translated 6 units to the left and 2 units down
  **i** (a, b) is translated p units to the right and q units up

· · · · · · · · · · · · · · · · · · · · · · · · · · · · · · · · · · · · · · · · · · · · · · · · · · · · · · · · · · · · · · · · · · · · · · ·

## Game  Translate a cube

This is a game for two players.
You need a board like this,
a red dice and a blue dice, and
a small cube.
Put the cube on 'start'.

The first player rolls both dice.

The red dice gives the number of squares to move the cube across.
You can move left or right.
The blue dice gives the number of squares to move the cube
up or down.
The first player moves the cube.

The second player now rolls both dice and moves the cube.

You score points if you land on a coloured square.

= 1 point          = 3 points

The first person to score 5 points or more wins.

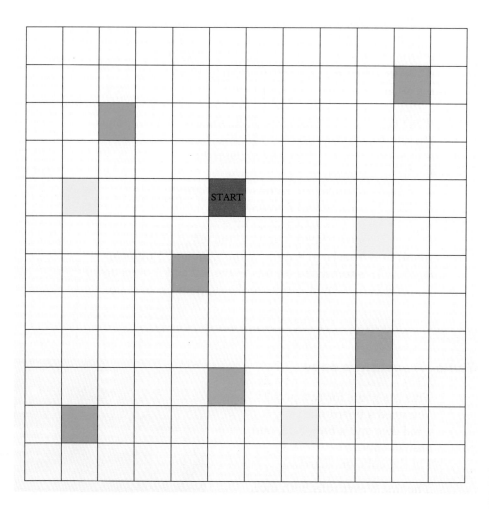

## 3 Rotation

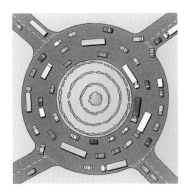

When the traffic is on the roundabout it goes in circles. The centre of the circles is the middle of the roundabout.

A rotation or turning can be clockwise or anti-clockwise.
The amount of turning can vary.

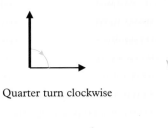

Quarter turn clockwise

Half turn anti-clockwise

### Exercise 5:7

**1** Are these rotations clockwise or anti-clockwise?
How much have they turned?

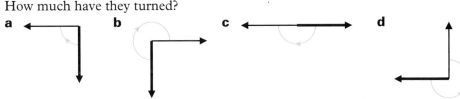

a    b    c    d

| **Centre of rotation** | When an object rotates it turns about a **centre of rotation**. Here centres of rotation are shown in red. |

The centre of rotation can be in different places.

The centre of rotation does not have to be on the arrow.

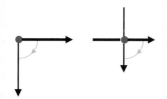

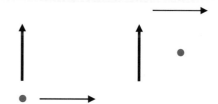

The arrow has moved a quarter turn clockwise about different centres. The arc showing the turn need not be drawn.

In this exercise centres of rotation are shown in red.

Start by copying an arrow into your book.
Use tracing paper to trace the arrow.
Put your pencil point on the centre. Rotate the tracing paper. The tracing paper shows you the new position of the arrow.
Draw the new position of the arrow in your book.

*Rotate the tracing paper*

**2** Give the arrow a quarter turn anti-clockwise about the centre. The centre each time is marked with ●

   **a** ●⟶     **b** ⟶●     **c** ⟶●⟶

**3** Give the arrow a half turn clockwise about the centre.

   **a** ⟵ ●     **b** ●

   ⟵

◄◄**REPLAY**►

| **Rotational symmetry** | A shape has **rotational symmetry** if it fits on top of itself more than once as it makes a complete turn. |
|---|---|
| **Order of rotational symmetry** | The **order of rotational symmetry** is the number of times that the shape fits on top of itself. This must be 2 or more. |

This shape has rotational symmetry of order 3.

## Exercise 5:8

C marks the centre of rotation.

**1** **a** Copy the diagram on to squared paper.
   **b** Give the flag a half turn about C.
      Draw the new position.
   **c** Write down the order of rotational symmetry of your diagram.

**2** **a** Copy the diagram on to squared paper.
   **b** Give the flag a quarter turn clockwise about C.
      Draw the new position.
   **c** Give the flag two more quarter turns clockwise about C.
      Draw each new position.
   **d** Write down the order of rotational symmetry of the finished diagram.

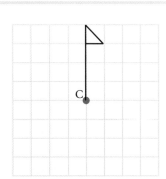

## Exercise 5:9

**1** Draw a pair of axes from −6 to 6.
   **a** Plot these points:
      A(2, 1)   B(6, 1)   C(6, 3)   D(4, 3)
      Join the points to make a trapezium.
   **b** Rotate ABCD 180° (a half turn) about the origin.
      Label the image $A_1B_1C_1D_1$.
   **c** Copy this table for the rotation.
      Fill it in.

| Co-ordinates of ABCD | A(2, 1) | B(6, 1) | C(6, 3) | D(4, 3) |
|---|---|---|---|---|
| Co-ordinates of $A_1B_1C_1D_1$ | $A_1$ (..., ...) | $B_1$ | $C_1$ | $D_1$ |

   **d** Write down the rule for the change in co-ordinates after the rotation.

●  **2**  Use the diagram from question **1**.
  **a** Rotate ABCD 90° clockwise about the origin.
      Label the image $A_2B_2C_2D_2$.
  **b** Make a table for the co-ordinates of ABCD and $A_2B_2C_2D_2$.
  **c** Write down the rule for the change in co-ordinates.
  **d** Rotate ABCD 90° anti-clockwise about the origin.
      Label the image $A_3B_3C_3D_3$.
      Make a table.
      Write down the rule.
  **e** Compare the rules for the clockwise and anti-clockwise rotations.
      Write down what you notice.

### *Patterns with reflections, translations and rotations*

You need some large squared paper.
Cut out a $4 \times 4$ grid of squares.

Draw a pattern in the top left-hand corner.

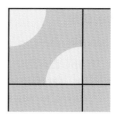

Translate the pattern to
each square to get this.

Reflect the pattern in each
line of the grid to get this.

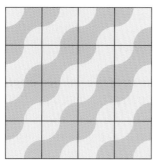

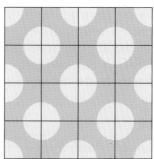

This pattern has
been rotated through
a quarter turn clockwise
each time.

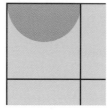

Try some patterns of your own.

# 4  Enlargement

The photographs of the school play at Stanthorne High are ready.

There is a standard size or an enlargement.
The enlargement is twice as wide and twice as long as the
standard size.

---

| **Enlargement** | An **enlargement** changes the size of an object. The change is the same in all directions |

| **Scale factor** | The **scale factor** tells us how many times bigger the enlargement is. |

*Example*  Enlarge the rectangle by a scale factor of 2.

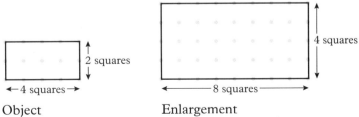

|  |  |
|---|---|
| 2 squares | 4 squares |
| ←4 squares→ | ←————— 8 squares —————→ |
| Object | Enlargement |

The enlargement is 2 times as long and 2 times as wide as
the object.

---

## Exercise 5:10

**1** Copy these shapes on to squared paper.
Enlarge each shape by a scale factor of 2.

**a**

**c**

**b**

**d**

**2** Enlarge the shapes in question **1** by a scale factor of 3.

## Exercise 5:11

**1** Draw an $x$ axis from 0 to 9 and a $y$ axis from 0 to 12.
  **a** Plot these points in order.
     Join them as you go.
     (2, 2) (2, 4) (1, 6) (3, 6) (3, 2) (2, 2)
  **b** Copy this table.
     Fill it in.

| Co-ordinates of object | (2, 2) | (2, 4) | (1, 6) | (3, 6) | (3, 2) | (2, 2) |
|---|---|---|---|---|---|---|
| Co-ordinates $\times$ 2 | | (4, 8) | | | | |

  **c** Plot the new co-ordinates in order.
     Join them as you go.
  **d** Write down the scale factor of the enlargement.

**2** Draw an $x$ axis from 0 to 9 and a $y$ axis from 0 to 12.
  **a** Plot these points in order.
     Join them as you go.
     (1, 1) (1, 4) (2, 4) (3, 2) (3, 1) (1, 1)
  **b** Make a table like the one in question 1.
     On the second line put 'Co-ordinates $\times$ 3'
  **c** Plot the new co-ordinates in order.
     Join them as you go.
  **d** Write down the scale factor of the enlargement.

**Centre of enlargement**

An enlargement can be done from a **centre**.

Measure the distances of points on the object from the centre.
Multiply these distances by the scale factor.
This gives the distances of points on the image from the centre.

*Example*

Enlarge the triangle by a scale factor of 2.
Use C as the centre of enlargement.

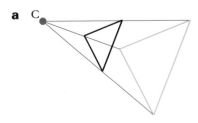

## Exercise 5:12

**1** Copy these diagrams.
Use C as the centre of enlargement.
Enlarge the triangle by a scale factor of 2.

**2** Copy these diagrams.
Use C as the centre of enlargement.
Enlarge the quadrilateral by a scale factor of 3.

**a** C

**c**

C

**b**

C

**3** Draw a pair of axes from −6 to 6.
  **a** Plot these points:
    A(−2, 4)  B(0, 2)  C(1, 4)
    Join them to make triangle ABC.
  **b** Plot these points:
    $A_1(-6, 6)$  $B_1(0, 0)$  $C_1(3, 6)$
    Join them to make triangle $A_1B_1C_1$.
  **c** Write down the scale factor for the enlargement.
  **d** Draw lines on the diagram to find the centre of enlargement.
    Write down its co-ordinates.

**4** Use the same diagram as for question 3.
  **a** Plot these points:
    D(−2, −1)  E(−3, −3)  F(0, −3)  G(0, −1)
    Join them to make trapezium DEFG.
  **b** Plot these points:
    $D_1(1, -1)$  $E_1(-1, -5)$  $F_1(5, -5)$  $G_1(5, -1)$
    Join them to make trapezium $D_1E_1F_1G_1$.
  **c** Write down the scale factor for the enlargement.
  **d** Draw lines on the diagram to find the centre of enlargement.
    Write down its co-ordinates.

**5** Write down the centre for the two enlargements in Exercise 5:11.

**1** Copy these diagrams on to squared paper.
Draw their reflections in the mirror lines.

**a**

**b**

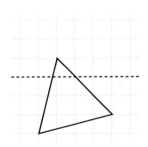

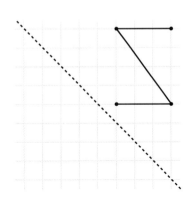

**2** Copy the diagram.
Draw the reflection in the
mirror line.

**3** Draw an *x* axis from 0 to 10 and a *y* axis from 0 to 16.
  **a** Plot these points:
  $(4, 1)$ $(9, 1)$ $(9, 3)$ $(4, 3)$
  Join the points to make a rectangle.
  Translate the rectangle 5 units up.
  **b** Plot these points:
  $(2, 13)$ $(4, 13)$ $(4, 16)$
  Join the points to make a triangle.
  Translate the triangle 5 units down.
  **c** Plot these points: $(0, 8)$ $(1, 10)$
  Join the points to make a line.
  Translate the line 9 units to the right.
  **d** Plot these points: $(0, 5)$ $(0, 6)$ $(1, 6)$
  Join the points to make a triangle.
  Translate the triangle 4 squares to the right.
  Translate the triangle another 4 squares to the right.
  **e** Plot the point $(1, 4)$.
  Translate the point 2 units to the right and 5 units up.

**4 a** Make these arrangements of cubes.
Imagine a mirror to the right of each shape.
Make a reflection of each shape in the mirror.
The first one has been done for you.

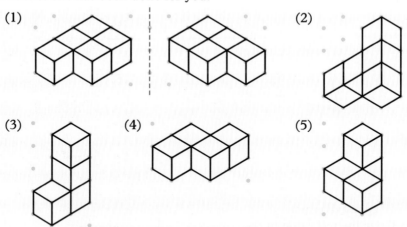

**b** Draw the reflections of these on dotty isometric paper.

**5** Copy each diagram on to squared paper.
Rotate about C each time.

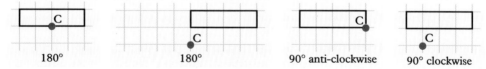

**6** Copy the diagram on to squared paper.
  **a** Give the arrow a quarter turn anti-clockwise
    about C.
    Draw the new position.
  **b** Give the arrow two more quarter turns
    anti-clockwise.
    Draw each one.
  **c** Write down the order of rotational symmetry
    of the finished diagram.

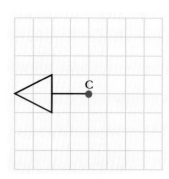

**7** Copy these shapes on to squared paper.
Enlarge them by a scale factor of 3.

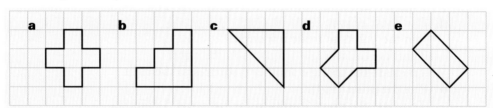

**1**   Traditional Islamic patterns are made like this.

Make a pattern   Reflect the pattern across   Colour the pattern.
in a square.    and down.

   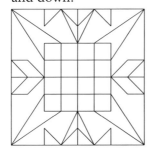   

Make your own pattern like this.

**2**   Start with a simple shape that tessellates.
You can make a more interesting shape with rotations and translations.

Cut a semicircle from the shape.
Give the semicircle a half turn.

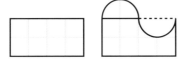   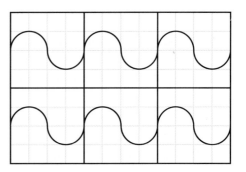

Cut a triangle from the shape.
Translate the triangle to the opposite side.

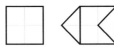

Try some patterns of your own.

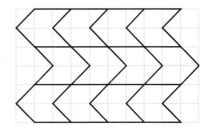

**3** This triangle has been given a
half turn about the midpoint
of one of its sides.

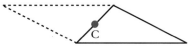

The triangle and its rotation make a parallelogram.
  **a** What shape triangle would you start with to get these quadrilaterals?
    (1) rhombus          (2) rectangle          (3) square
  **b** It is impossible to make a kite or a trapezium this way.
    Explain why.

**4** On squared paper, draw a pair of axes from −5 to 5.
  **a** Plot these points.
    Join them in order as you go.
    (1, 1) (1, 4) (3, 4) (3, 2) (1, 2)
    Label your shape P.
  **b** Reflect P in the *x* axis.
    Label the reflection Q.
  **c** Reflect Q in the *y* axis.
    Label the reflection R.
  **d** Describe the single transformation that takes P to R.
  **e** Rotate P 90° anti-clockwise about the origin.
    Label the image S.
  **f** Describe the single transformation that takes S to Q.

**5** The enlargement that takes shape P to
shape Q has a scale factor of 2.
To go from Q to P we need an
enlargement by scale factor $\frac{1}{2}$.
Copy these diagrams on to
squared paper.
Enlarge the shapes by scale factor $\frac{1}{2}$.

Use C as the centre of enlargement.

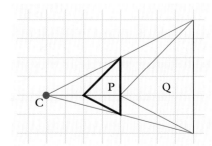

**a**

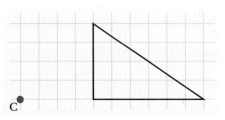

**b**

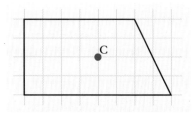

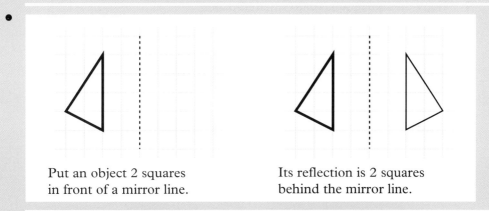

Put an object 2 squares
in front of a mirror line.

Its reflection is 2 squares
behind the mirror line.

**Translation**    A **translation** is a movement in a straight line.
**Rotation**    A **rotation** is a movement round in a circle.

*Example*    Translate the L shape 4 squares
to the right.

Choose one point.
Move the point 4 squares to
the right.
Move the other points in the
same way.

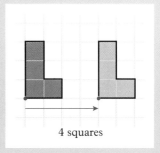

4 squares

The centre of rotation can be in
different places.

The arrow has been moved a
quarter turn clockwise about
different centres.

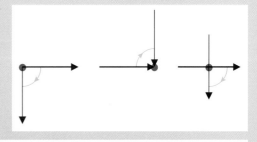

**Enlargement**    An **enlargement** changes the size of an object.
**Scale factor**    The **scale factor** tells us how many times bigger the
enlargement is.

*Example*
Enlarge the rectangle by a
scale factor of 2.

The enlargement is 2 times
as long and 2 times as wide
as the object.

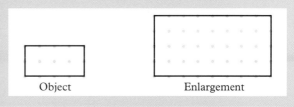

Object           Enlargement

**1** Copy these diagrams on to squared paper.
Draw their reflections in the mirror lines.

**a**

**b**

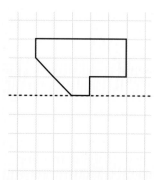
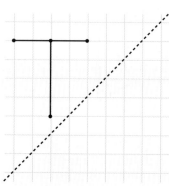

**2** For each part start with a new copy of
this L shape drawn on squared paper.
Label each copy with the question number.

Translate your L:
**a** 3 squares to the right
**b** 5 squares down
**c** 2 squares to the left and 4 squares up

**3 a** Copy the diagram.
Give the flag a
quarter turn anti-clockwise
about C.

**b** Copy the diagram
Give the flag a
half turn clockwise
about C.

**4** Copy the diagram on to squared paper.
Rotate this shape about C a quarter turn at
a time.
Make a new shape with rotational symmetry
of order 4.

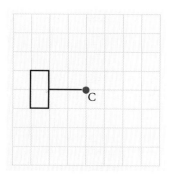

**5 a** Copy this shape on to
squared paper.
Enlarge it by a scale factor of 2.

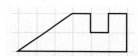

**b** Copy this shape on to squared paper.
Enlarge it by a scale factor of 3.
Use C as the centre of enlargement.

# 6 Don't be negative!

The coldest place in the world is the Pole of Inaccessibility in Antarctica. Its annual mean temperature is −58°C.

Braemar, in Scotland, is the coldest weather station in the UK. Its annual mean temperature is 6.3°C. On cold nights, Braemar has had temperatures down to −27°C.

The lowest temperature possible is absolute zero, 0 K on the Kelvin scale or −273.15°C. The lowest temperature reached on Earth is 0.000 000 000 28 K. This was at the Low Temperature Laboratory of Helsinki University, Finland, in February 1993.

## 1 ◄◄REPLAY►

You have already met negative numbers.

| **Negative** numbers | Numbers with minus signs in front are called **negative** numbers. |
|---|---|
| **Positive** numbers | Other numbers except nought are **positive**. Positive numbers are sometimes written with a plus sign in front. Nought is not positive or negative. |
| **Number line** | We can show positive and negative numbers on a **number line**. |

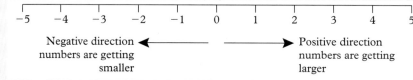

Negative direction numbers are getting smaller

Positive direction numbers are getting larger

| *Examples* | 1 is smaller than 4 | $-2$ is smaller than 1 | $-4$ is smaller than $-1$ |
|---|---|---|---|
| | 3 is larger than 2 | 1 is larger than $-2$ | $-1$ is larger than $-3$ |

### Exercise 6:1

**1** Put these numbers in order, smallest first.

    **a** $-4, 5, -2, 3, -7$     **b** $5, -3, 0, -2, 7$     **c** $-6, 1, -1, -3, 0, 4$

**2** Put these numbers in order, largest first.

    **a** $-5, 2, -1, 0, -3$     **b** $-2, 5, 1, -1, 2$     **c** $-11, 8, -5, -9, 2, -1$

**3** Write down the next two terms in these number patterns.
  **a** 4, 2, 0, −2, −4, ..., ...
  **b** 8, 5, 2, −1, −4, ..., ...
  **c** 13, 8, 3, −2, −7, ..., ...
  **d** −28, −25, −22, −19, ..., ...
  **e** 7, 1, −5, ..., ...
  **f** 6, 5, 3, 0, −4, −9, ..., ...

**4** Copy these number patterns.
  Fill in the missing numbers.
  **a** 5, 3, 1, ..., −3, ..., −7
  **b** 9, 6, 3, ..., −3, ..., −9
  **c** 100, 50, ..., −50, ..., −150

---

| **Less than <** **Greater than >** | We often use the signs < and > with numbers. |
|---|---|
| | < means **'less than'**     > means **'greater than'** |

*Examples*      −5 < −2 means −5 is less than −2
                2 > −4 means 2 is greater than −4

---

**5** Copy the pairs of numbers.
  Write in < or >
  **a** 4   2
  **b** 0   −3
  **c** −5   −1
  **d** 6   −6
  **e** −2   1
  **f** −3   −8

**6** The normal height of a river is
  marked as zero on the scale.
  At the beginning of the month the
  level was at 4 metres.
  **a** What is the level of the river
     now?
  **b** How much has the water level
     fallen?

**7** How many degrees difference is there between these night and day
  temperatures?
  **a** 6 °C and 11 °C
  **b** −2 °C and 14 °C
  **c** −5 °C and 0 °C
  **d** −1 °C and 10 °C
  **e** −5 °C and −1 °C
  **f** −10 °C and 20 °C

**8** The temperature in a freezer is −18 °C.
  A frozen pizza is thawed to room temperature.
  Room temperature is 21 °C.
  How many degrees does the temperature of the pizza rise?

We can use calculators for questions with negative numbers.
We use the **+/−** key.

---

*Example*    One night the temperature is −4 °C. The following day the
temperature rises to 9 °C.
How many degrees difference is there between the day and
night temperatures?

Key in:    **9**    **−**    **4**    **+/−**    **=**

Answer: 13 °C

---

**9** Here are some night and day temperatures.
Use your calculator to find the difference between each pair.
**a** −3 °C and 7 °C          **d** 2 °C and 17 °C
**b** −1 °C and 13 °C         **e** −9 °C and −1 °C
**c** −5 °C and 10 °C         **f** −9 °C and 0 °C

**10** Jane is standing on a cliff.
This picture shows what is above
and below sea level.
**a** What is at about +60 m?
**b** How far below the fish is the
top of the wreck?
**c** How far above the fish is the
seagull?
**d** Estimate the distance of the
seabed below sea level.

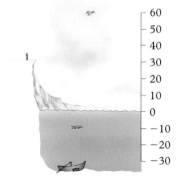

**11** On a quiz show contestants score 2 points for a correct answer.
They lose a point for a wrong answer.
What is the final score for:
**a** 9 correct and 2 wrong answers?
**b** 4 correct and 8 wrong answers?
**c** 2 correct and 11 wrong answers?
In the same quiz these contestants all scored 11 points.
**d** Mark gave 5 wrong answers.
How many questions did he answer correctly?
**e** Jamila gave 7 correct answers.
How many questions did she get wrong?
**f** Luke got the same number of correct and wrong answers.
How many questions did he answer?

**12** Leanne drew a bar-chart to
show her bank balance at
the end of each month from
September to February
last year.

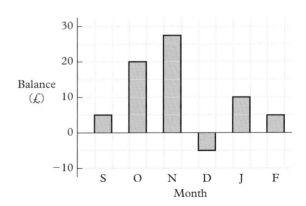

  **a** How much did Leanne:
  (1) pay in to the bank in
      October?
  (2) withdraw from the
      bank in December?
  **b** By how much did her
  bank balance change in
  January?

**13** The table shows the average monthly temperatures for St Petersburg.
  **a** Draw a bar-chart to show the temperatures.
  Use squared paper or graph paper.

| Month | J | F | M | A | M | J | J | A | S | O | N | D |
|---|---|---|---|---|---|---|---|---|---|---|---|---|
| Temperature °C | −7 | −8 | −4 | 3 | 10 | 15 | 18 | 17 | 11 | 5 | 0 | −4 |

  **b** What is the difference between the average temperatures for the
  hottest month and the coldest month?

## 2 The rules for directed numbers

Sally and Peter enjoy scuba diving.
They are talking about their dives.
They call sea level 0.
Sally says she dived to $-5$ m.
Peter says he dived 4 m further down.
Sally knows how to work this out:
$-5 - 4 = -9$
Peter dived to $-9$ m.

| **Directed numbers** | **Directed numbers** are numbers with signs in front of them, for example $-3$, $+5$, $-7$ |
| --- | --- |

### *Adding and subtracting directed numbers*

*Example*

Use the number ladder to answer these:

**a** $7 - 4$     **b** $3 - 6$     **c** $-5 - 2$

*Always start at 0.*
*Count up for positive numbers.*
*Count down for negative numbers.*

**a** $7 - 4$
Start at 0 on the line.
Count 7 spaces up.
Count 4 spaces down.
Answer: 3

**b** $3 - 6$
Start at 0 on the line.
Count 3 spaces up.
Count 6 spaces down.
Answer: $-3$

**c** $-5 - 2$
Start at 0 on the line.
Count 5 spaces down.
Count 2 spaces down.
Answer: $-7$

## Exercise 6:2

**1** Copy the number ladder from the Example into your book.
Put it down the side of the page.
Use the number ladder to answer these:

| | | | | | |
|---|---|---|---|---|---|
| **a** | $6 - 4$ | **g** | $-6 + 7$ | **m** | $9 - 10$ |
| **b** | $3 - 5$ | **h** | $-5 + 8$ | **n** | $-1 + 3 - 4$ |
| **c** | $5 - 7$ | **i** | $-3 - 4$ | **o** | $5 - 6 + 3$ |
| **d** | $2 - 8$ | **j** | $-5 + 5$ | **p** | $-2 - 3 - 1$ |
| **e** | $6 - 10$ | **k** | $-3 - 3$ | **q** | $-2 + 6 - 8$ |
| **f** | $-3 + 4$ | **l** | $-6 - 2$ | **r** | $-1 - 5 - 3$ |

**2** **a** Copy this addition table on to squared paper.
**b** Fill it in.
Start in the area shaded blue.
Look at the pattern in each line.
Use the pattern to complete the table.

second number

| + | -3 | -2 | -1 | 0 | 1 | 2 | 3 |
|---|---|---|---|---|---|---|---|
| 3 | | | | | | 5 | 6 |
| 2 | | | | | | | 5 |
| 1 | | | | | | | |
| 0 | | | | | | | |
| -1 | | | | | | | |
| -2 | | | | | | | |
| -3 | | | | | | | |

first number

**3** Copy these and fill them in.

**a** Use your addition table to help you.
(1) $3 + -2 = \ldots$
(2) $2 + -1 = \ldots$
(3) $1 + -3 = \ldots$
(4) $3 + -1 = \ldots$
(5) $2 + -3 = \ldots$
(6) $1 + -2 = \ldots$

**b** Use your number ladder to help you.
(1) $3 - 2 = \ldots$
(2) $2 - 1 = \ldots$
(3) $1 - 3 = \ldots$
(4) $3 - 1 = \ldots$
(5) $2 - 3 = \ldots$
(6) $1 - 2 = \ldots$

**c** Compare the two sets of answers.
Write down what you notice.
**d** Copy this rule in to your book:
$+ -$ **is the same as just** $-$

**4** Use your rule and the number ladder to answer these:

| | | | | | |
|---|---|---|---|---|---|
| **a** | $4 + -2 = 4 - 2 = \ldots$ | **d** | $-5 + -2$ | **g** | $9 + -7$ |
| **b** | $5 + -4 = 5 \ldots 4 = \ldots$ | **e** | $-6 + 3$ | **h** | $-8 + 1$ |
| **c** | $2 + -7 = 2 \ldots 7 = \ldots$ | **f** | $-3 + -4$ | **i** | $-5 + -5$ |

**5** **a** Copy this subtraction table on to squared paper.

**b** Fill it in.
Start in the area shaded blue.
Use number patterns to help you complete the table.

second number

| − | −3 | −2 | −1 | 0 | 1 | 2 | 3 |
|---|----|----|----|---|---|---|---|
| **3** | | | | | 2 | 1 | 0 |
| **2** | | | | | | | −1 |
| **1** | | | | | | | −2 |
| **0** | | | | | | | −3 |
| **−1** | | | | | | | |
| **−2** | | | | | | | |
| **−3** | | | | | | | |

first number

**6** Copy these and fill them in.

**a** Use your subtraction table to help you.
(1) $1 - -2 = \ldots$
(2) $3 - -1 = \ldots$
(3) $2 - -3 = \ldots$
(4) $3 - -3 = \ldots$

**b**
(1) $1 + 2 = \ldots$
(2) $3 + 1 = \ldots$
(3) $2 + 3 = \ldots$
(4) $3 + 3 = \ldots$

**c** Compare the two sets of answers.
Write down what you notice.

**d** Copy this rule in to your book.

$- -$ **is the same as just** $+$

**7** Use your rule and the number ladder to answer these:

**a** $6 - -4 = \quad 6 + 4 = \ldots$    **d** $-5 - -7$    **g** $-7 - -2$

**b** $3 - -7 = \quad 3 \ldots 7 = \ldots$    **e** $1 - -6$    **h** $-6 - -3$

**c** $-9 - -8 = \quad -9 \ldots 8 = \ldots$    **f** $8 - -2$    **i** $-1 - -5$

**8** Use your two rules and your number ladder to answer these:

**a** $5 - -4$    **c** $3 + -5$    **e** $-5 + 4$    **g** $-3 + 7$

**b** $4 + -2$    **d** $7 - -1$    **f** $-3 - -6$    **h** $-3 - 4$

*Multiplying and dividing directed numbers*

*Exercise 6:3*

**1** Copy these number patterns.
Fill in the missing numbers.

**a** $-3, \ldots, -1, 0, \ldots, 2, 3$

**b** $-6, -4, \ldots, 0, 2, \ldots, 6$

**c** $\ldots, -6, -3, 0, 3, 6, \ldots$

**2 a** Copy this multiplication table on to squared paper.
**b** Fill it in.
Start in the area shaded blue.
Use the number patterns from question **1** to help you.

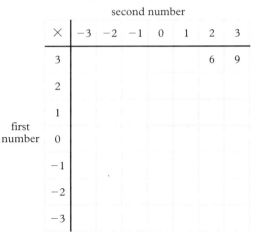

second number

| × | −3 | −2 | −1 | 0 | 1 | 2 | 3 |
|---|---|---|---|---|---|---|---|
| 3 | | | | | | 6 | 9 |
| 2 | | | | | | | |
| 1 | | | | | | | |
| 0 | | | | | | | |
| −1 | | | | | | | |
| −2 | | | | | | | |
| −3 | | | | | | | |

first number

**3** Copy these and fill them in.
Use your multiplication square to help you.

**a** (1) $3 \times 2 = \ldots$
(2) $-2 \times 2 = \ldots$
(3) $-1 \times 2 = \ldots$
(4) $2 \times -3 = \ldots$
(5) $3 \times -1 = \ldots$

**b** (1) $-3 \times -2 = \ldots$
(2) $-2 \times -1 = \ldots$
(3) $-2 \times -2 = \ldots$
(4) $-1 \times -3 = \ldots$
(5) $-3 \times -1 = \ldots$

**c** Copy these rules and fill them in.
Use your answers to part **a** to help you.
**+ × − and − × + are the same as ...**
(**+** represents a positive number and **−** represents a negative number.)

**d** Copy this rule and fill it in.
Use your answers to part **b** to help you:
**− × −** is the same as ...

**4** Use your rules to answer these:

**a** $-2 \times 5$
**b** $-3 \times -6$
**c** $4 \times -7$
**d** $-5 \times -5$

**e** $6 \times -4$
**f** $-10 \times -9$
**g** $-5 \times 8$
**h** $9 \times 9$

**i** $-7 \times -6$
**j** $-6 \times -9$
**k** $-7 \times 5$
**l** $-12 \times -12$

---

Look at the multiplication: $-3 \times 4 = -12$
We can write two divisions using the same numbers: $-12 \div -3 = 4$
$-12 \div 4 = -3$

---

**5** Write two divisions for each of these.

**a** $-5 \times 3 = -15$
**b** $4 \times -5 = -20$

**c** $-3 \times -6 = 18$
**d** $3 \times 11 = 33$

**e** $-5 \times -10 = 50$
**f** $5 \times -6 = -30$

**6** Copy these rules and fill them in.
Use your answers to question 5 to help you.

$+ \div +$ **is the same as ...**      $- \div -$ **is the same as ...**

$+ \div -$ **is the same as ...**      $- \div +$ **is the same as ...**

**7** Use your rules to answer these:

| | | | | | |
|---|---|---|---|---|---|
| **a** | $-16 \div 2$ | **e** | $-30 \div 6$ | **i** | $45 \div -5$ |
| **b** | $-20 \div -5$ | **f** | $-18 \div -6$ | **j** | $70 \div -7$ |
| **c** | $-24 \div -3$ | **g** | $14 \div -7$ | **k** | $-24 \div -12$ |
| **d** | $44 \div -11$ | **h** | $28 \div 4$ | **l** | $-81 \div 9$ |

You can use a calculator to work with directed numbers.

## Adding and subtracting

*Step 1:* Use your rules for directed numbers to simplify the question.

*Step 2:* Use $\boxed{+/-}$ to enter any negative numbers into the calculator.

*Examples*

**a** $15 + -19$      **b** $-13 - -9$

**a** Simplify:

$15 + -19 = 15 - 19$

Key in: $\boxed{1}\ \boxed{5}\ \boxed{-}\ \boxed{1}\ \boxed{9}\ \boxed{=}$

Answer: $-4$

**b** Simplify:

$-13 - -9 = -13 + 9$

Key in: $\boxed{1}\ \boxed{3}\ \boxed{+/-}\ \boxed{+}\ \boxed{9}\ \boxed{=}$

Answer: $-4$

## Multiplying and dividing

*Step 1:* Use your rules for directed numbers to simplify the question.
The rules will give you the sign of the answer without using $\boxed{+/-}$.

*Examples*

**a** $15 \times -14$      **b** $-276 \div -12$

**a** Simplify:

$15 \times -14 = -210$

Sign of the answer is $-$ $(+ \times - \text{ is } -)$     $15 \times 14$ worked out on a calculator

**b** Simplify:

$-276 \div -12 = 23$

Answer is positive so no sign is needed $(- \div - \text{ is } +)$     $276 \div 12$ worked out on a calculator

### Exercise 6:4

**1**   Use a calculator to answer these.

**a**   $17 + -14$      **g**   $-37 - -14$

**b**   $35 - -16$      **h**   $-54 + -28$

**c**   $24 - 38$      **i**   $-36 + -43$

**d**   $27 + -42$      **j**   $-57 - 44$

**e**   $-21 - 28$      **k**   $56 - 97$

**f**   $-19 - -26$      **l**   $-45 - -174$

**2**   Use a calculator to answer these.

**a**   $17 \times -12$      **g**   $-43 \times -12$

**b**   $-13 \times 23$      **h**   $-279 \div 9$

**c**   $27 \times -28$      **i**   $17 \times -26$

**d**   $-165 \div -15$      **j**   $-322 \div -23$

**e**   $-24 \times -6$      **k**   $43 \times -13$

**f**   $1700 \div 25$      **l**   $-306 \div 18$

**3**   Work out the answers to these.

**a**   $-2 \times -6 \times -5$      **g**   $-5 \times 6 \times -7$

**b**   $-56 \div -7 \div 4$      **h**   $-3 \times -3 \times -3$

**c**   $32 \div -4 \div -4$      **i**   $100 \div -5 \div -5$

**d**   $24 \div -3 \div -4$      **j**   $(-2)^3$

**e**   $-40 \div -4 \div -5$      **k**   $(-3)^4$

**f**   $-6 \times -3 \times 2$      **l**   $(-5)^3$

## 3 Using negative numbers

8M are having a science lesson. They are learning about the Kelvin scale for measuring temperature.
The coldest temperature possible is 0 K.
This is about $-273\,°C$.
The formula for converting K to °C is:
$$C = K - 273$$

### Exercise 6:5

**1** Use the formula $C = K - 273$ to convert these temperatures to °C.
   **a** 273 K   **b** 373 K   **c** 1000 K   **d** 0 K   **e** 100 K

The formula for converting °C to K is $K = C + 273$

---

*Example*        Use the formula $K = C + 273$ to convert $-50\,°C$ to K.

Substitute for C      $K = -50 + 273$

Key in:     

Answer: 223 K

---

**2** Use the formula $K = C + 273$ to convert these temperatures.
   **a** $-20\,°C$   **b** $-100\,°C$   **c** $200\,°C$   **d** $-15\,°C$   **e** $-200\,°C$

**3** Use the formula $p = q + 10$ to find $p$ for these values of $q$.
   **a** $-5$   **b** $-10$   **c** $-30$   **d** 18   **e** $-2$

**4** Use the formula $r = s - 25$ to find $r$ for these values of $s$.
   **a** $-15$   **b** 25   **c** 0   **d** $-6$   **e** $-10$

**5** Use the formula $w = 50 + v$ to find $w$ for these values of $v$.
   **a** 25   **b** $-30$   **c** $-85$   **d** $-5$   **e** $-100$

**6** Use the formula $b = 75 - c$ to find $b$ for these values of $c$.
   **a** 50   **b** $-40$   **c** $-10$   **d** $-25$   **e** $-100$

*Example 1*     Use the formula $g = 3h$ to find $g$ when $h = -5$

Substitute for $h$        $g = 3 \times -5$
                         Answer: $-15$

*Example 2*     Use the formula $n = \frac{m}{2}$ to find $n$ when $m = -8$

Substitute for $m$        $n = -8 \div 2$
                         Answer: $-4$

## Exercise 6:6

**1** Use the formula $g = 3h$ to find $g$ for these values of $h$.
   **a** $-7$     **b** $-2$     **c** $0$     **d** $5$     **e** $-20$

**2** Use the formula $n = \frac{m}{2}$ to find $n$ for these values of $m$.
   **a** $-6$     **b** $-3$     **c** $16$     **d** $0$     **e** $-50$

**3** Use the formula $y = 4x$ to find $y$ for these values of $x$.
   **a** $-1$     **b** $0$     **c** $5$     **d** $-0.5$     **e** $-6$

**4** Use the formula $d = \frac{c}{10}$ to find $d$ for these values of $c$.
   **a** $-20$     **b** $-15$     **c** $-35$     **d** $5$     **e** $-150$

**5** Use the formula $y = \frac{12}{x}$ to find $y$ for these values of $x$.
   **a** $-6$     **b** $-2$     **c** $-3$     **d** $10$     **e** $-4$

It is a very cold day. Gary hears on the radio that the temperature is $-6\,°\text{C}$.
Gary's grandmother is old-fashioned. She likes to use the Fahrenheit scale for temperature. Gary knows a formula for converting Celsius to Fahrenheit:
   $F = 1.8 \times C + 32$

Gary works out the temperature on his calculator like this:
Substitute for C     $F = 1.8 \times -6 + 32$
Key in:

| 1 | . | 8 | × | 6 | +/− | + | 3 | 2 | = |

Answer: $21.2\,°\text{F}$

## Exercise 6:7

**1** Use Gary's formula $F = 1.8C + 32$ to convert these temperatures to Fahrenheit.

   **a** $-10\,°C$    **b** $-5\,°C$    **c** $15\,°C$    **d** $-8\,°C$    **e** $-20\,°C$

**2** Use the formula $v = 5t + 20$ to find $v$ for these values of $t$.

   **a** 7    **b** $-4$    **c** $-10$    **d** $-6$    **e** $-2.5$

**3** Use the formula $p = 3q - 15$ to find $p$ for these values of $q$.

   **a** $-4$    **b** $-12$    **c** 0    **d** 5    **e** $-1$

**4** Use the formula $s = 4t - 6$ to find $s$ for these values of $t$.

   **a** $-2$    **b** $-6$    **c** $-20$    **d** 0    **e** 1.5

**• 5**  **a** Write the formula $F = 1.8C + 32$ on robot screens.

     **b** Draw the inverse machine for $F = 1.8C + 32$.

     **c** Use your inverse machine to convert these temperatures to Celsius. Round your answers correct to one decimal place if necessary.

       (1) $50\,°F$    (2) $-4\,°F$    (3) $-40\,°F$    (4) $0\,°F$    (5) $212\,°F$

---

*Example 1*

Find the value of $3t^2$ when $t = -4$

Substitute for $t$       $3 \times (-4)^2$

Without a calculator:    $3 \times -4 \times -4 = 48$

With a calculator:
Key in:

| **3** | **×** | **4** | **+/−** | **$x^2$** | **=** |

Answer: 48

*Example 2*

Find the value of $4p^3$ when $p = -2$

Substitute for $p$       $4 \times (-2)^3$

Without a calculator:    $4 \times -2 \times -2 \times -2 = -32$

With a calculator:
Key in:

| **4** | **×** | **2** | **+/−** | **$x^y$** | **3** | **=** |

Answer: $-32$

## Exercise 6:8

**1** Find the value of these when $t = -4$
   **a** $t^2$      **b** $2t^5$      **c** $5t^4$      **d** $10t^2$      **e** $6t^3$

**2** Find the value of these when $s = -3$
   **a** $s^2$      **b** $4s^4$      **c** $5s^3$      **d** $2s^5$      **e** $9s^2$

**3 a** Copy this table.
     Fill it in.

     $y = 3x^2$

| $x$ | $-3$ | $-2$ | $-1$ | $-0.5$ | 0 | 0.5 | 1 | 2 | 3 |
|-----|------|------|------|--------|---|-----|---|---|---|
| $3x^2$ | 27 | ... | ... | ... | ... | ... | ... | 12 | ... |

   **b** Copy the axes on to
     squared paper.
   **c** Plot the points in your table.
     Join the points with a smooth
     curve.
   **d** Label your graph $y = 3x^2$.
   **e** What line is the line of
     symmetry of the curve?
   **f** Write down the co-ordinates
     of the minimum point.

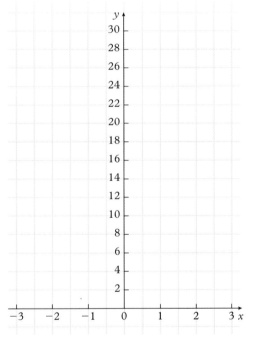

**1** Use your rules to answer these.
  **a** $6 - -2$       **c** $-6 + -2$       **e** $-4 - -4$       **g** $-5 - 4$
  **b** $4 + -5$       **d** $-2 - 4$       **f** $-2 + -3$       **h** $0 - -5$

**2** Use your rules to answer these.
  **a** $-6 \times -4$       **c** $-7 \times 7$       **e** $-9 \times -2$       **g** $-4 \times -4$
  **b** $-3 \times 5$       **d** $4 \times -8$       **f** $-10 \times -8$       **h** $-11 \times -6$

**3** Use your rules to answer these.
  **a** $-20 \div 4$       **c** $-55 \div 11$       **e** $-56 \div 7$       **g** $27 \div -9$
  **b** $-32 \div -4$       **d** $-36 \div -9$       **f** $-42 \div 6$       **h** $-35 \div -7$

**4** Use a calculator to answer these.
  **a** $14 \times -17$       **d** $-45 \times -13$       **g** $-570 \div -19$
  **b** $-37 + -16$       **e** $-55 - 34$       **h** $23 \times -16$
  **c** $-1288 \div -56$       **f** $67 - 86$       **i** $-25 - -30$

**5** **a** Use the formula $e = 25 + f$ to find $e$ for these values of $f$.
      (1) $f = 15$       (2) $f = -16$       (3) $f = -25$       (4) $f = -40$
  **b** Use the formula $g = 80 - h$ to find $g$ for these values of $h$.
      (1) $h = 55$       (2) $h = 85$       (3) $h = -20$       (4) $h = -35$

**6** **a** Use the formula $r = 6s$ to find $r$ for these values of $s$.
      (1) $s = 5$       (2) $s = -4$       (3) $s = -10$       (4) $s = -50$
  **b** Use the formula $m = \dfrac{n}{5}$ to find $m$ for these values of $n$.
      (1) $n = 5$       (2) $n = -10$       (3) $n = -30$       (4) $n = -50$

**7** **a** Use the formula $p = 15 - 3q$ to find $p$ for these values of $q$.
      (1) $q = 4$       (2) $q = -2$       (3) $q = -5$       (4) $q = -7$
  **b** Use the formula $a = 3b + 12$ to find $a$ for these values of $b$.
      (1) $b = -4$       (2) $b = -3$       (3) $b = 0$       (4) $b = -7$

**8** Find the value of $10t^2$ for these values of $t$.
  **a** $t = 1$       **b** $t = 0$       **c** $t = -2$       **d** $t = -6$

**9** Find the value of these when $y = -5$.
  **a** $y^2$       **b** $2y^2$       **c** $5y^3$       **d** $3y^4$

## Game Make it to zero

This game is for two or more players.
You need a dice and a coin.

Megan and Andrew are playing
'Make it to zero'.
Megan tosses the coin and rolls the dice.
The coin decides the sign of the number:
heads is positive, tails is negative.
Megan gets a tail and a 3. Both players
write down the number $-3$.

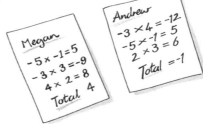

Megan tosses the coin and rolls the dice five more times.
She gets these numbers: $-3, 2, -5, -1, 4, 3$

Megan and Andrew each put the numbers into pairs.
Then they multiply each pair.
Megan adds her answers and Andrew adds his answers.
The winner is the one who gets a total cl

Here are Megan's and Andrew's results:

Megan
$-5 \times -1 = 5$
$-3 \times 3 = -9$
$4 \times 2 = 8$
Total 4

Andrew
$-3 \times 4 = -12$
$-5 \times -1 = 5$
$-5 \times 3 = 6$
$2 \times 3 = 6$
Total $= -1$

Andrew is closest to zero, so he wins.

Play this game with some friends.

**1** Malcolm has a remote controlled car.
He moves the car backwards and forwards and makes it accelerate at a
constant rate.

Here are two equations which describe the way the car moves:
$v = u + at$ $\quad$ $u =$ the speed at the start of a journey in m/s
$s = ut + \frac{1}{2}at^2$ $\quad$ $v =$ the speed at the finish of a journey in m/s
$\quad\quad\quad\quad$ $a =$ the acceleration in m/s$^2$
$\quad\quad\quad\quad$ $s =$ the distance travelled in metres
$\quad\quad\quad\quad$ $t =$ the time taken in seconds
**a** The car makes a journey where $u = 0$, $t = 4$ s, $a = 0.5$ m/s$^2$.
Find:
(1) the speed at the end of the journey
(2) the distance travelled
**b** The car makes a second journey where $u = 1$ m/s, $t = 2.5$ s,
$a = -0.4$ m/s$^2$.
Find:
(1) the speed at the end of the journey
(2) the distance travelled

131

**2** A sequence has the formula $50 - 2n^2$.
  **a** Work out the first three terms of the sequence.
  **b** Which term is 0?
  **c** What is:
   (1) the 6th term
   (2) the 10th term

**3** Copy these sequences.
  Fill in the missing terms.
  **a** $-12, -7, ..., ..., 8, 13$       **c** $17, 8, ..., -10, ..., -28$
  **b** $9, 5, 1, ..., ..., -11$          **d** $..., ..., -25, -19, -13, -7$

**4** Solve these equations.
  **a** $4x + 9 = 1$              **c** $5p - 2 = -12$
  **b** $\frac{y}{2} + 7 = 5$           **d** $2 - x = -5$

**5** $2 \times -6 = -12$
  2 and $-6$ are factors of $-12$.
  Write down all the factors of $-12$.

**6** Work out the answers to these.
  **a** $(-4)^4$        **b** $(-2)^7$        **c** $(-5)^4$        **d** $(-3)^5$

**7** Copy and fill in:
  $10^3 = 1000$
  $10^2 = ...$
  $10^1 = ...$
  $10^? = 1$
  $10^{-1} = \frac{1}{10}$
  $10^{-2} = ...$

**8** **a** Work out the answers to these.
   (1) $(-2)^2$      (2) $(-5)^2$      (3) $(-8)^2$      (4) $(-10)^2$
  **b** Copy and fill in:
   (1) $(-?)^2 = 9$                 (3) $(-?)^2 = 100$
   (2) $(-?)^2 = 36$                (4) $(-?)^2 = 49$
  **c** Explain why it is impossible to find a number so that $(?)^2 = -16$

**9** **a** Write the formula $v = 50 + 10a$ on robot screens.
  **b** Draw the inverse machine for $v = 50 + 10a$
  **c** Use your inverse machine to find $a$ when $v$ takes these values.
   (1) $v = 0$        (2) $v = -10$        (3) $v = 25$        (4) $v = 50$

- **Negative** numbers      Numbers with minus signs in front are called **negative** numbers.

  **Positive** numbers      Other numbers except nought are **positive**. Positive numbers are sometimes written with a plus sign in front.

  Nought is not positive or negative.

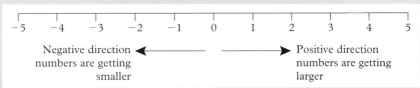

- **Less than <**
  **Greater than >**

  We often use the signs < and > with numbers.
  $-5 < -2$ means $-5$ is less than $-2$
  $2 > -4$ means $2$ is greater than $-4$

- **Directed numbers**      **Directed numbers** are numbers with signs in front of them, for example $-3, +5, -7$.

- **Adding and subtracting directed numbers**

  *Example*      Use the number ladder to answer $3 - 5$

  *Always start at 0.*
  *Count up for positive numbers.*
  *Count down for negative numbers.*

  $3 - 5$
  Start at 0 on the line.
  Count 3 spaces up.
  Count 5 spaces down.
  Answer: $-2$

  ```
   4
   3
   2
   1
   0
  -1
  -2
  -3
  ```

- **Rules for directed numbers**

  $+ \times -$ and $- \times +$ are the same as $-$      $+ -$ is the same as $-$
  $+ \div -$ and $- \div +$ are the same as $-$      $- -$ is the same as $+$

- **Multiplying and dividing directed numbers**

  *Examples*      $5 \times -4 = -20$      $-10 \div 2 = -5$
       $-3 \times -2 = 6$      $-6 \div -2 = 3$

- *Examples*

  **1**    Use the formula $g = 3h$ to find $g$ when $h = -5$

       Substitute for $h$      $g = 3 \times -5$
       Answer: $-15$

  **2**    Use the formula $n = \dfrac{m}{2}$ to find $n$ when $m = -8$

       Substitute for $m$      $n = -8 \div 2$
       Answer: $-4$

**1** Put these temperatures in order, lowest first.

$6\,°C,\quad -5\,°C,\quad -3\,°C,\quad 2\,°C,\quad 1\,°C,\quad -1\,°C,\quad 0\,°C$

**2** Copy the pairs of temperatures.
Write in < or >
**a** $5\,°C$    $3\,°C$      **b** $-6\,°C$    $-8\,°C$    **c** $-4\,°C$    $0\,°C$

**3** The temperature in the desert at night is $-9\,°C$.
During the day it reaches $43\,°C$.
How many degrees does the temperature rise?

**4** Use a number ladder to answer these.
**a** $8-2$      **b** $3-9$      **c** $-4-5$      **d** $3-5+4-1$

**5** Work these out.
**a** $4--6$      **c** $-7--3$      **e** $-3\times5$      **g** $6\times-10$
**b** $-5+-2$      **d** $-5-3$      **f** $-4\times-2$      **h** $-10\div-2$

**6** Use a calculator to answer these.
**a** $31\times-56$      **c** $19+-36$      **e** $-280\div-14$
**b** $175\div-25$      **d** $-25--48$      **f** $-45\times-23$

**7** Use the formula $r=s-25$ to find $r$ for these values of $s$.
**a** $68$      **b** $12$      **c** $-35$

**8** Use the formula $v=5t-12$ to find $v$ for these values of $t$.
**a** $6$      **b** $2$      **c** $-4$

**9** Find the value of these when $t=-2$.
**a** $t^2$      **b** $5t^2$      **c** $8t^3$

**10** Use the formula $E=5v^2$ to find $E$ for these values of $v$.
**a** $3$      **b** $1$      **c** $-5$

# 7 Angles

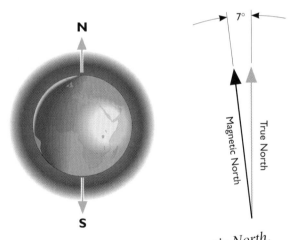

Compass needles point to *magnetic North*. This is slightly different from true North. Maps often have two arrows for North. One arrow is for true North and one is for magnetic North. Magnetic North should have a date by it because it varies from year to year! The angle between true North and magnetic North is around 7°.

# 1 ◀◀ REPLAY ▶

40°

The cable car takes tourists up and down the mountain.
The cable is at an angle of 40° with the horizontal. It is dangerous for
this angle to be too large.

---

**Degree**

We use degrees (written °) to measure angles.

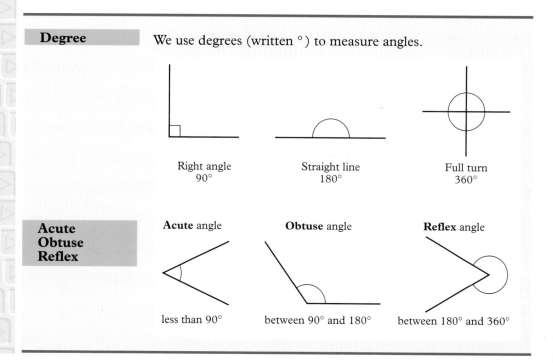

| Right angle | Straight line | Full turn |
|---|---|---|
| 90° | 180° | 360° |

**Acute**
**Obtuse**
**Reflex**

**Acute** angle          **Obtuse** angle          **Reflex** angle

less than 90°      between 90° and 180°      between 180° and 360°

## Exercise 7:1

**1** Write down the angle that is:

        **c** reflex        **d** a right angle

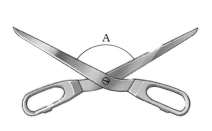

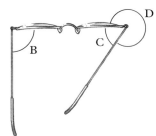

A pair of glasses

**2** Write down the name of each of these angles.
Choose from:
straight line, acute angle, reflex angle, right angle, obtuse angle.

  **a** 30°     **c** 270°     **e** 45°     **g** 320°     **i** 116°
  **b** 125°   **d** 180°   **f** 90°     **h** 170°     **j** 6°

## Exercise 7:2

**1** Take a piece of rough paper.
  **a** Fold it to make a straight line.
  **b** Fold it again to make a right angle.
Keep your right angle to use in the next question.

*Example*

Estimate the sizes of these angles.

Fold 90° in half to get 45°

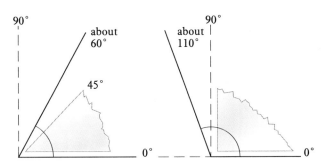

137

**2** Estimate the size in degrees of
each of these angles.
Use your folded right angle to
help you.
Copy this table and fill in your
estimates.
You will need the 'Actual' column
for question **3**.

| | Estimate | Actual |
|---|---|---|
| a | | |
| b | | |
| c | | |
| ... | | |

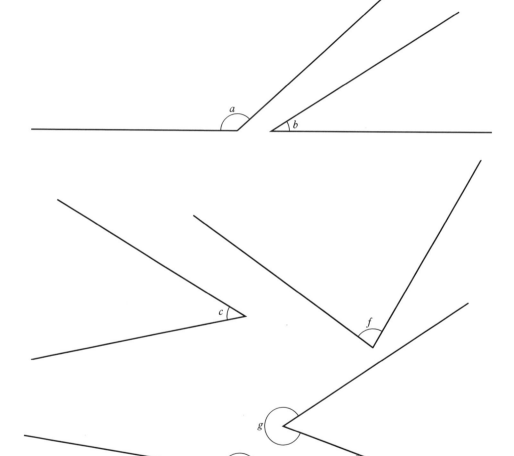

**3** Measure the angles in question **2**.
If you have a 180° protractor, measure the smaller angle for reflex angles.
Then take the answer away from 360°
Write your answers in the 'Actual' column in your table.

**4** Draw and label these angles:

| | | | | |
|---|---|---|---|---|
| **a** 67° | **c** 113° | **e** 165° | **g** 96° | **i** 198° |
| **b** 42° | **d** 270° | **f** 18° | **h** 154° | **j** 315° |

---

*Examples*    Calculate the angles marked with letters.

**1 Angles on a straight line**
add up to 180°
$a = 180° - 55° - 30°$
$a = 95°$

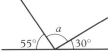

**2 Angles at a point** add up
to 360°
$b = 360° - 140° - 135°$
$b = 85°$

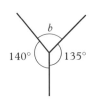

**3 Opposite angles** are equal.
$p$ is opposite 120° and
$q$ is opposite 60°.
$p = 120°$     $q = 60°$
($p$ and $q$ add up to 180°)

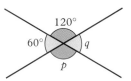

---

## Exercise 7:3

Calculate the angles marked with letters.
Write down a reason for each one.

**1**

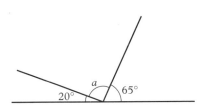

**2**

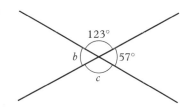

**3**

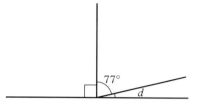

**7**

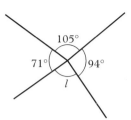

**4**

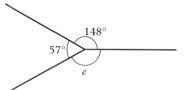

**8**

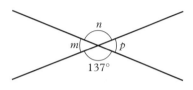

**5**

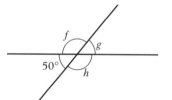

**9**

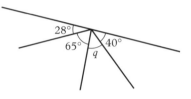

**6**

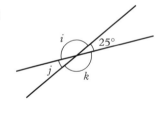

**● 10**

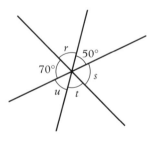

---

*Example*

Calculate angle *c*.

The angles of a triangle
add up to 180°.
*c* = 180° − 30° − 40°
*c* = 110°

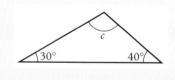

---

## Exercise 7:4

Calculate the angles marked with letters.

**1**

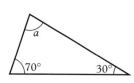

**2**

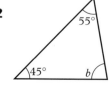

**3**

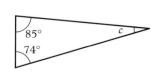

A **scalene triangle** has no equal angles and no equal sides.

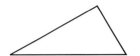

An **isosceles triangle** has two equal angles and two equal sides.

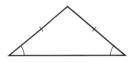

An **equilateral triangle** has three equal angles and three equal sides.

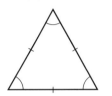

Calculate the angles marked with letters.

**4**

**5**

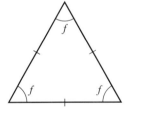

**6**

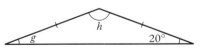

**7**

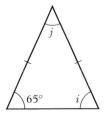

**8** Copy and fill in:
$2k = 180° - 30°$
$2k = ...$
$k = ...$

**9**

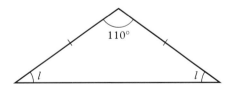

● **10**

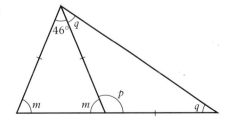

# 2   Parallel lines

Pairs of railway lines are parallel. The two tracks on a railway line never meet. They always stay the same distance apart.

Different pairs of railway lines can cross.
Sometimes a train can change from one pair of lines to another. A system of moveable parts of lines is used. These are called points.

### Exercise 7:5

**1**   **a**   Draw a pair of parallel lines.
Mark them with arrows.
    **b**   Draw a line intersecting both of your parallel lines.
    **c**   Measure and label all eight angles.

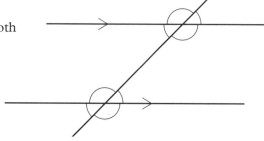

**2**   **a**   Draw another pair of parallel lines.
Mark them with arrows.
    **b**   Draw a line intersecting both of your parallel lines at a different angle.
    **c**   Measure and label all eight angles.

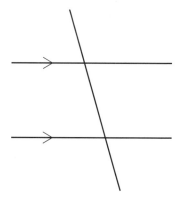

**3  a** Look at the angles you measured
   in questions **1** and **2**.
   What do you notice?
 **b** Copy this diagram.
   Colour the four equal obtuse angles red.
   Colour the four equal acute angles blue.

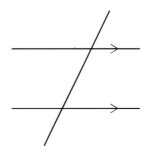

---

*Example*          Find the angles marked with
          letters.

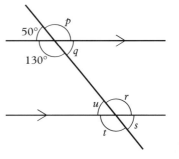

*p* is opposite 130°
*q* is opposite 50°
*p* = 130°        *q* = 50°

The 'bottom' set of four angles
is the same as the 'top' set.
*r* = 130° and *t* = 130°
*s* = 50° and *u* = 50°

---

## Exercise 7:6

Find the angles marked with letters.

**1**

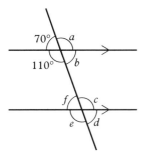

**3**

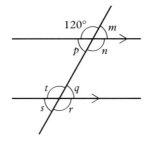

**2**

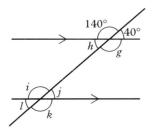

**4**

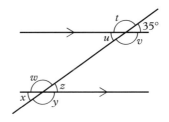

143

**5**

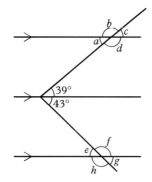

**6**

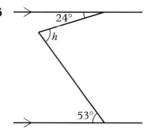

| **Alternate angles** | Angles on opposite sides of the intersecting line are called **alternate angles**. They are found in **Z** shapes. **Alternate angles are equal**. | 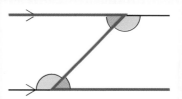 |
| --- | --- | --- |
| **Corresponding angles** | Angles in the same place in 'top' and 'bottom' sets of angles are called **corresponding angles**. They are found in **F** shapes. **Corresponding angles are equal.** | 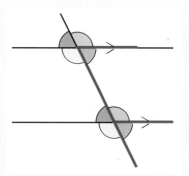 |
| **Interior angles** | Angles between parallel lines are called **interior angles**. **Interior angles add up to 180°** | 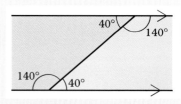 |

## Exercise 7:7

**1 a** Copy the diagram.
**b** Colour one pair of alternate angles red.
  Colour the other pair blue.
**c** Label your diagram 'Alternate angles'.

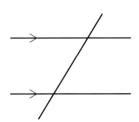

**2 a** Make another copy of the diagram.
**b** Choose four colours.
  Colour each pair of corresponding angles in a different colour.
**c** Label your diagram 'Corresponding angles'.

**3 a** Copy the diagram.
**b** Calculate the missing angles.
**c** Label your diagram 'Interior angles'.

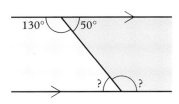

**4** Find the angles marked with letters.
  Write down whether each pair of angles is alternate, corresponding or
  interior.

**a**

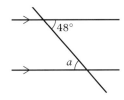

**d**

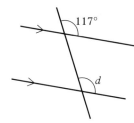

**b**

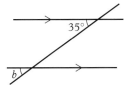

**e**

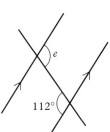

**c**

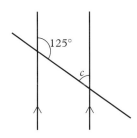

**f**

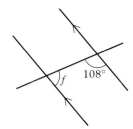

145

*Example*  Find the angles marked with letters.

$p$ and 130° are interior angles
(using the parallel lines with
one arrow)
$p = 180° - 130°$      $p = 50°$

$r$ and 130° are interior angles
(using the parallel lines with
two arrows)
$r = 180° - 130°$      $r = 50°$

$p$ and $q$ are interior angles
(using the parallel lines with two arrows)
$q = 180° - 50°$      $q = 130°$

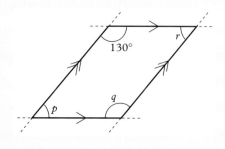

## Exercise 7:8

Find the angles marked with letters.

**1**

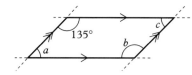

**2**

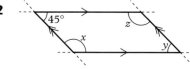

**3**

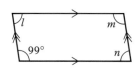

**4**

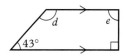

**5**

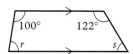

**6**

**7**

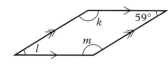

**8**

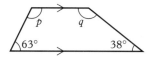

**9**

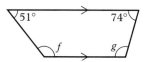

**10**

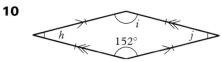

146

# 3  Polygons

Most buildings are rectangular.
Sometimes buildings use a
different polygon in their shape.
Can you see why this building is
called the Octagon?

◀◀ REPLAY ▶

**Polygon**

A **polygon** is a shape with straight sides.

| Number of sides | Name of polygon |
|---|---|
| 3 | triangle |
| 4 | quadrilateral |
| 5 | pentagon |
| 6 | hexagon |
| 7 | heptagon |
| 8 | octagon |

6 sides: hexagon

## Exercise 7:9

**1**  Write down the sum of the angles of a triangle.

**2  a**  Draw any quadrilateral.
  **b**  Divide the quadrilateral into two triangles with a diagonal.
  **c**  A quadrilateral can be divided into two triangles.
     What do its angles add up to?

**3  a**  Draw a pentagon.
  **b**  Draw diagonals from one vertex
     to each of the other vertices.
  **c**  A pentagon can be divided
     into three triangles.
     What do its angles add up to?

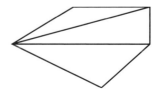

**4**  Repeat question **3** for a hexagon.

**5**  **a**  Copy this table.

| Number of sides | Name of polygon | Number of triangles | Sum of angles of polygon |
|---|---|---|---|
| 3 | triangle | 1 | 180° |
| 4 | quadrilateral | ... | ... |
| ... | | | |

  **b**  Use your answers to questions **1–4** to fill in the table up to hexagons.
  **c**  (1) Look at the patterns of the numbers in your table.
      Use the patterns to fill in the table up to octagons.
    (2) Draw a heptagon and an octagon.
      Divide them into triangles.
      Check that you have filled in your table correctly.

**6**  **a**  (1) How many triangles can a 20-sided polygon be divided into?
    (2) What is the angle sum of a 20-sided polygon?
  **b**  Repeat part **a** for a 100-sided polygon.
  **c**  (1) Copy and fill in:
      The number of triangles a polygon can be divided into is the
      same as the number of ........... of the polygon take away ...
      The angles of the polygon add up to the number of .............
      multiplied by ...°
    (2) Write your rule for finding the angles of a polygon in algebra.
      Use $n$ for the *n*umber of sides of the polygon.
  **d**  The angles of a polygon add up to 2700°.
      Use the inverse of your rule to find the number of sides of the polygon.

---

| **Regular polygon** | **Regular polygons** have all their sides the same length. Also all their angles are equal. |
|---|---|
| | Equilateral triangles and squares are regular polygons. |
| *Example* | Calculate an angle of a regular pentagon. |

A regular pentagon can be divided
into three triangles.
Sum of angles of pentagon
$3 \times 180° = 540°$
One angle of pentagon
$540° \div 5 = 108°$
Answer: 108°

---

## Exercise 7:10

**1** Calculate the angles of regular polygons with these numbers of sides.
   **a** 6     **b** 7     **c** 8     **d** 10     **e** 12     **f** 20

**2** **a** (1) Draw a triangle with extended sides like this.
   (2) Measure each of the marked angles.
   (3) Add your three angles together.

   **b** Draw a quadrilateral with its sides extended in the same way. Repeat part **a** (2) and (3).

   **c** Draw a pentagon with extended sides. Repeat part **a** (2) and (3).

   **d** The angles you have measured are called **exterior angles**. The exterior angles of any polygon always add up to the same number. What do they add up to?

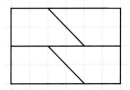

● **3** The exterior angle of a regular polygon is 15°. How many sides does the polygon have?

---

◄◄**REPLAY**►

 **Tessellation**     A **tessellation** is a pattern made by repeating the same shape over and over again. There are no gaps in a tessellation.

A tessellation of trapeziums

---

## An investigation into tessellating shapes

You need a set of tiles in the shapes of regular polygons.
Use the tiles to see which regular polygons tessellate.
What is special about the angles of the regular polygons that tessellate?
Can you find any irregular polygons that tessellate?
Are their angles special in any way?

# 4   Bearings

Simon is orienteering. He has an orienteering map with checkpoints marked on it.
Simon is using a compass to find the direction or bearing of the next checkpoint.

| **Bearing** | A compass gives the **bearing** of an object. This is the direction you travel in to go straight to the object. |

Bearings are measured clockwise from north in degrees.
Bearings always have three figures.

*Examples*

Find the bearing of B from A in each case.

**1**

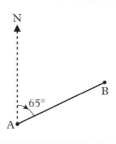

Bearing of B from A
is 065°

**2**

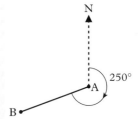

Bearing of B from A
is 250°

## Exercise 7:11

Find the bearing of B from A in each case.

**1**

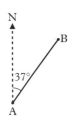

**2**

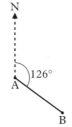

**3**

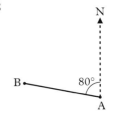

**4**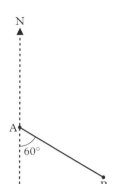

**5**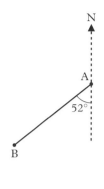

**6**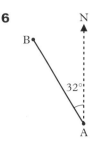

Simon stands on the path. He needs to find an orienteering control point.

Simon uses his compass to find the control point.
It is on a bearing of 070°

Simon then wants to return to the path from the control point.
He makes a half turn to face the way he came.
Simon needs to know the bearing for his return.

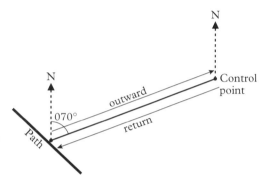

## Exercise 7:12

**1** Here is a diagram for Simon's run.
   **a** Write down the colour of the outward bearing of 070°
   **b** Write down the colour of Simon's return bearing.
   **c** Copy and fill in:
       Return bearing is  070° + 180° = ...°

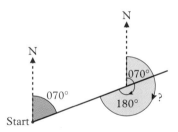

**2** The diagram shows Simon's run to another control point on a bearing of 120°
   **a** Sketch the diagram.
   **b** Colour the outward bearing red. Colour the return bearing blue.
   **c** Copy and fill in:
       Return bearing is  120° + ...° = ...°

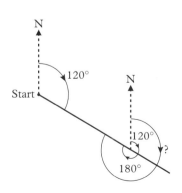

**3** Neena leaves the path on a bearing of 240°

**a** Sketch this diagram of Neena's run.

**b** Colour the outward bearing of 240° red.
Colour the return bearing blue.

**c** Copy and fill in:
Return bearing is 240° − 180° = ...°

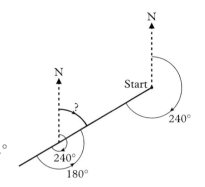

Find the return bearings for these.

**4**
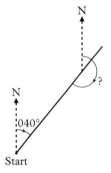

**5**
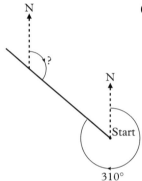

**6**
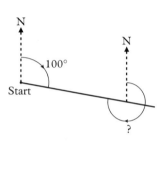

---

There is always a difference of 180° between outward bearings and return bearings.

| Size of outward bearing | Rule for finding return bearing |
| --- | --- |
| less than 180° | outward bearing + 180° |
| more than 180° | outward bearing − 180° |

---

The diagrams give the bearings of point B from point A.
Find the bearing of A from B (the return bearing).

**7**
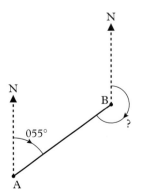

**8**
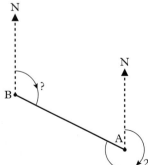

**9**
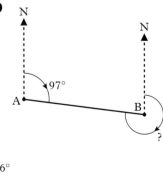

10 The diagram is a scale drawing of a piece of coastline.

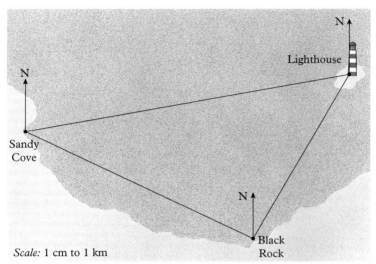

Scale: 1 cm to 1 km

Find these answers by accurate measurement.
a A boat sails from Sandy Cove to Black Rock.
Find the bearing and the distance the boat sails.
b The boat then sails from Black Rock to the lighthouse.
Find the bearing and the distance the boat sails.
c The boat then sails directly from the lighthouse to Sandy Cove.
Find the bearing for this journey and the distance the boat sails.
d The boat makes a second trip to the lighthouse. This time it goes
straight there.
Explain how you can calculate the bearing of the lighthouse from
Sandy Cove using the bearing you found in part c.

● 11 A ship sails 120 miles on a bearing of 245°
Then it sails 80 miles on a bearing of 328°
a Make a sketch of the ship's voyage.
b Make a scale drawing using a scale of 1 cm to 20 miles.
c On the return journey, the ship sails straight back to its
starting point.
Use your scale drawing to find the bearing for the return journey.
Find the distance the ship travels on its return journey.

**1** Find the angles marked with letters.

**a**

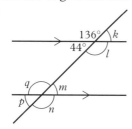

**b**

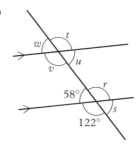

**2** Find the angles marked with letters.
Write down whether the angles are alternate, corresponding or interior.

**a**

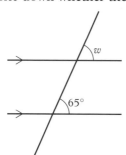

**b**

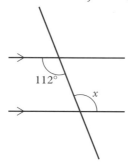

**c**

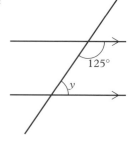

**3** Find the angles marked with letters.

**a**

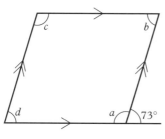

**b**

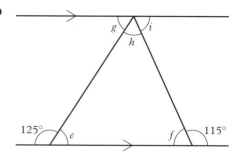

**4** We use the points of the compass
to describe direction.
This method is not very accurate.
We use it to describe the direction
of winds, for example.

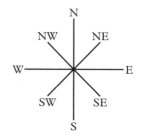

Write these points of the compass as bearings in degrees.
  **a** E       **c** S       **e** NW       **g** SW
  **b** W      **d** SE     **f** NE      **h** N

**5** Find the bearing of A from B in each case.

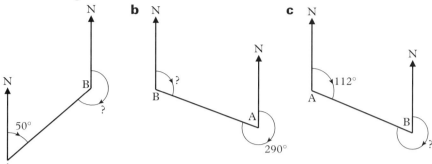

**a**     **b**    **c**

**6 a** Write down the angle sum of the **exterior** angles of any polygon.
  **b** A regular polygon has an exterior angle of 36°
    (1) How many times does 36° divide into 360°?
    (2) How many sides must the polygon have?
  **c** Use 180° − 36° to calculate an interior angle of this polygon.
  **d** Repeat parts **b** and **c** for these exterior angles.
    (1) 30°      (2) 24°      (3) 20°      (4) 18°

**7 a** A boat sails from Red Pier to Whitesands Bay.
    Find the bearing and the distance the boat sails.
  **b** The boat then sails from Whitesands Bay to Cave Point.
    Find the bearing and the distance the boat sails.
  **c** On the return journey the boat sails directly from Cave Point to Red Pier.
    Find the bearing for the return journey, and the distance the boat sails.

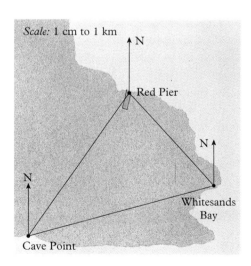

*Scale:* 1 cm to 1 km

Red Pier

Whitesands Bay

Cave Point

**1** Find the angles marked with letters.

**a**

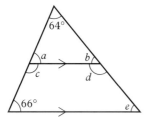

**c**

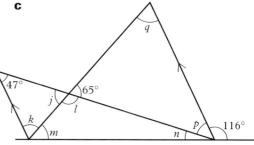

**b**

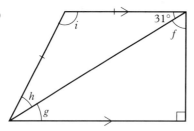

**d**

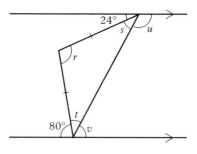

**2** **a** Write down the formula for finding the angle sum of the interior angles of a polygon with *n* sides.
 **b** Work out the angle sum of the interior angles for a polygon with 14 sides.
 **c** A polygon has an interior angle sum of 2520°
 How many sides does it have?

**3** The diagram shows a ship at C, near a straight piece of coast.
 The captain takes the bearings of two lighthouses on the coast.
 The bearing of lighthouse A is 220°. The bearing of lighthouse B is 150°
 The lighthouses are 8 km apart.
 **a** Calculate: (1) the bearing of C from A
  (2) the bearing of C from B
 **b** Make an accurate drawing of triangle ABC.
 Use a scale of 1 cm to 1 km.
 **c** By measuring, find the distance of the ship from the shore.

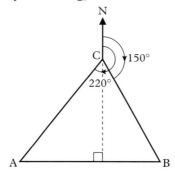

- *Example*

Find the angles marked with letters.

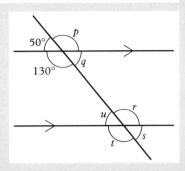

$p$ is opposite 130°
$q$ is opposite 50°
$p = 130°$        $q = 50°$

The 'bottom' set of four angles is equal to the 'top' set.
$r = 130°$ and $t = 130°$
$s = 50°$ and $u = 50°$

**Alternate angles**

Angles on opposite sides of the intersecting line, like $q$ and $u$, are called **alternate angles**.
Alternate angles are equal.

**Corresponding angles**

Angles in the same place in 'top' and 'bottom' sets of angles, like $p$ and $r$, are called **corresponding angles**.
Corresponding angles are equal.

**Interior angles**

Angles between the parallel lines, like $q$ and $r$, are called **interior angles**. Interior angles add up to 180°

- *Example*

Calculate an interior angle of a regular pentagon.

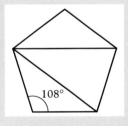

A regular pentagon can be divided into three triangles.
Sum of angles of pentagon   $3 \times 180° = 540°$
One angle of pentagon        $540° \div 5 = 108°$
Answer: 108°

- **Exterior angles**

The **exterior angles** of an polygon add up to 360°

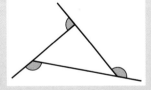

- 

Regular polygons which tessellate are equilateral triangles, squares and regular hexagons.

- **Bearing**

A compass gives the **bearing** of an object. This is the direction you travel in to go straight to the object.
Bearings are measured clockwise from north in degrees.
Bearings always have three figures.

**1** Find the angles marked with letters.

**a**
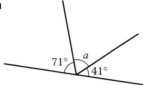

**c**
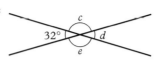

**b**
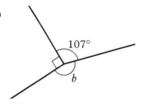

**d**
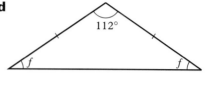

**2** Find the angles marked with letters.

**a**
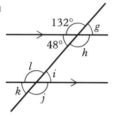

**b**
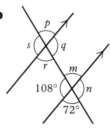

**3** Find the angles marked with letters.
Write down whether the angles are alternate, corresponding or interior.

**a**
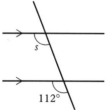

**b**
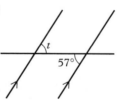

**c**
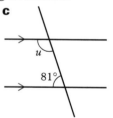

**4** **a** Calculate the angle sum of the interior angles of an octagon.
**b** Calculate an interior angle of a regular octagon.

**5** Find the bearing of A from B in each case.

**a**
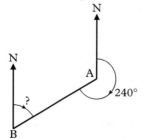

**b**
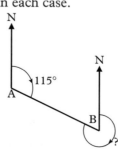

**c**
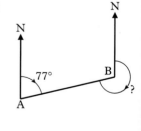

# 8 Probability

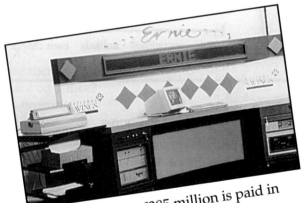

Every year about £385 million is paid in prizes by ERNIE.

ERNIE stands for Electronic Random Number Indicating Equipment.

ERNIE picks the numbers of the winning Premium Bonds each month.

Each Premium Bond costs £1 and every Bond has a 1 in 19 000 chance of winning a prize. Most prizes are £50 or £100 but there is a monthly prize of £1 million.

The chance of any Bond winning the £1 million prize in any month is about 1 in 8 billion!

## 1 ◄◄ REPLAY ►

Last year you used probability to help you decide what to say in the card game Higher or Lower.

**Probability** **Probability** tells us how likely something is to happen.

We can show it on a probability scale:

impossible  very unlikely  unlikely  even chance  likely  very likely  certain

### Exercise 8:1

**1** Draw a probability scale.
Mark on it points **a**, **b** and **c** to show how likely you think each one is.
**a** The next person you see will be over 2 metres tall.
**b** There will be at least one sunny day in June in London.
**c** You will pass your driving test before you are 18 years old.

Probability is written as a number.
We write 0 for impossible and 1 for certain.

We can draw our probability scale like this:

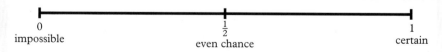

0
impossible

$\frac{1}{2}$
even chance

1
certain

All probabilities must be between 0 and 1.

**2** Draw a probability scale like this one:

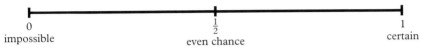

|       |       |       |
|-------|-------|-------|
| 0 | $\frac{1}{2}$ | 1 |
| impossible | even chance | certain |

Mark on it points **a**, **b** and **c** to show how likely you think each one is.

**a** The next person you meet will be older than you.

**b** The next person you meet will have a twin.

**c** The next person you meet will be right-handed.

**3** For each letter that you marked in question **2**, give an estimate of the probability.
Write your answer as a decimal or a fraction.

Probability is usually written as a fraction.

Sally bought 3 raffle tickets.
100 tickets were sold.

The probability that Sally wins the raffle is $\frac{3}{100}$.

## Exercise 8:2

**1** A bag contains 6 yellow counters and 5 green counters.
One counter is taken out at random.
Write down the probability that the counter is

**a** yellow        **b** green        **c** blue

**2** Pat's piggy bank contains four £1 coins, three 50 p coins and five 20 p coins.
She shakes out a coin at random.
Write down the probability that the coin will be

**a** 50 p        **b** £1        **c** worth less than £1

**3** The table shows the membership of a youth club.

|       | Under 13 years old | 13 years old and over |
|-------|--------------------|-----------------------|
| boys | 20 | 15 |
| girls | 18 | 22 |

**a** How many members are there in the club?
A person is chosen at random from the club.
Write down the probability that the person chosen is

**b** a boy

**c** a teenager (13 or older)

**d** a girl who is under 13 years old

**4** A card is picked at random from an ordinary pack of 52 playing cards.
What is the probability that it will be

    **a** red      **b** a spade      **c** a 9      **d** a picture card?

Remember: the picture cards are jack, queen, king and ace.

A box contains 12 counters.
There are 8 red and 4 blue.

Rolf picks a counter from the box
without looking.
He writes down the colour and
puts it back in the box.

He does this 12 times.

Rolf *expects* to get 8 reds and 4 blues.

## Exercise 8:3

**1** Rolf picks a counter 24 times.
    **a** How many reds does he expect to get?
    **b** How many blues does he expect to get?

**2** A bag contains 5 blue balls, 4 yellow balls and 1 black ball.
Malcolm takes a ball at random and writes down the colour.
He then puts the ball back in the bag.
    **a** He does this 10 times.
       Write down how many balls he would expect to be
       (1) blue         (2) black         (3) yellow
    **b** He does this 50 times.
       Write down how many balls he would expect to be
       (1) blue         (2) black         (3) yellow

**3** A fair dice is thrown 300 times.
Write down the number of times you would expect to get
    **a** a 6         **b** a 2 or a 3         **c** an odd number

**4** In a survey of pupils at Stanthorne High, Sunita discovered that
1 in every 10 pupils is left-handed.
Write down the number of left-handed pupils you would expect in
    **a** a group of 10 pupils        **b** a form of 30 pupils

**5** A factory making calculators expects 1 in every 100 calculators to be faulty.

  **a** How many faulty calculators would you expect to find in a batch of 1000?

  **b** In a batch of 3420 calculators, 41 are found to be faulty. Is this more or less than the number of faulty calculators you would expect?

**6** A bag contains 12 balls. Some are red and some are blue.
A ball is chosen at random from the bag and its colour is noted.
The ball is then replaced in the bag.
This is done 360 times and a red ball appears 150 times.

How many of each colour ball do you think are in the bag?
Explain your answer.

## Game   Holder of the box

You will need a box and
3 different colours of counters.
This is a game for 3–5 players.

One player is the 'Holder of the box'.
This player chooses 12 counters of
three different colours and puts them
in the box.
There must be at least one counter of each colour.
The other players must not see the counters.

The other players take turns to choose a counter at random from the box, note the colour and return it to the box.
When a player returns a counter to the box he or she can guess how many counters of each colour there are in the box.

You can only guess when you have just had your turn.
You will probably not want to guess until everyone has had a couple of turns.

The first person to guess correctly wins.
The winner becomes the 'Holder of the box' for the next game.

Once you have played this game a few times you might like to make up a new game of your own.
Write down the rules and explain how to play your game.

# 2   It always adds up to 1

Peter and Jane are going to the fair. The weather forecast says that the probability of rain is 60%.

Peter does not want to get wet. Jane is more cheerful. She says that the probability of it not raining is 40%.

We usually write probabilities as fractions.

60% is $\frac{60}{100}$ and 40% is $\frac{40}{100}$.

$\frac{60}{100} + \frac{40}{100} = \frac{100}{100} = 1$

Probabilities always add up to 1.
We can show this on a probability scale.

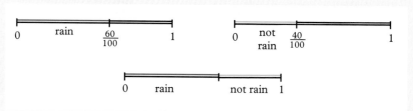

## Exercise 8:4

**1** The scale shows the probability that Siobahn will take her dog for a walk after school.

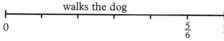

Draw a scale to show the probability that Siobahn will not take her dog for a walk.

**2** The scale shows the probability that Manzoor will be on time for school.

Draw a scale to show the probability that Manzoor will be late for school.

**3** The probability that Liam cooks the tea is $\frac{5}{8}$.
What is the probability that he doesn't cook the tea?
Draw a probability scale to help you.

**4** Gemma likes to talk to her friend Sadie on the phone.
Gemma can only use the phone if her Dad is in a good mood.
The probability that he is in a good mood is $\frac{4}{11}$.

What is the probability that Gemma will not be able to ring Sadie tonight?

---

*Example*

A box contains red, blue and green counters.
One counter is picked at random.
The probability that it is red is $\frac{5}{10}$ and
the probability that it is blue is $\frac{3}{10}$.
What is the probability that it is green?

This time we split the probability scale into tenths.
We have to colour 3 different sections to show
the probabilities of the 3 colours.

The part left over shows the probability of green.
The probability of green is $\frac{2}{10}$.

---

**5** Emma gets the bus to school each morning.
The probability that the bus is early is $\frac{3}{10}$.
The probability that the bus is exactly on time is $\frac{1}{10}$.
  **a** Draw a scale to show the probabilities of the bus being early and on time.
  **b** What is the probability that the bus is late?
Show this probability on your scale.

**6** A box contains yellow, green and red counters.
One counter is picked at random.
The probability that it is yellow is $\frac{7}{20}$ and
the probability that it is green is $\frac{11}{20}$.
What is the probability that the counter is red?

# 3 Probability: how to make it look difficult

We often talk about an important event happening in sport.
We use the word event in probability too.

---

**Event**

An **event** is something that can happen in a probability question.

When you roll a dice, there are lots of events.
One event is 'getting a 6'.
Another event is 'getting an odd number'.

We sometimes call an event by a letter.
The event 'getting a 6' might be called event A.
We write $P(A)$ for the probability of A happening.

**Probability**

The **probability** of an event A is the number of ways that the event A can happen divided by the total number of things that can happen.

*Example*

One card is chosen from an ordinary pack of playing cards.
Let A be the event 'getting a heart'.

There are 13 ways that event A can happen because there are 13 hearts in a pack.
There are 52 things that can happen altogether because there are 52 cards in a pack.

So $P(A) = \frac{13}{52}$

---

## Exercise 8:5

**1**  Find $P(A)$ if the event A is getting
   **a**  a 1 on a fair dice
   **b**  a red card from an ordinary pack of cards
   **c**  a king from an ordinary pack of cards
   **d**  a blue sock from a drawer containing 6 blue socks and 4 grey socks
   **e**  an even number on a 20-sided dice numbered 1–20

**◄◄ REPLAY ►**

| **Cancelling fractions** | When we write probabilities as fractions, we should **cancel the fractions** to their simplest form. We can do this using the $a\frac{b}{c}$ button on the calculator. |
| --- | --- |
| *Example* | To cancel the fraction $\frac{13}{52}$ we press: |

$$\boxed{1}\ \boxed{3}\ \boxed{a\frac{b}{c}}\ \boxed{5}\ \boxed{2}\ \boxed{=}$$

The display shows ⌐⌐⌐⌐ . This means $\frac{1}{4}$.

In the rest of this exercise give all probabilities as fractions in their simplest form.

**2**  Scott has a bag containing 15 sweets. 8 of them are toffees, 4 are fruit drops and 3 are chocolates.
   He takes a sweet out at random.
   Find the probability that the sweet he gets is
   **a**  a toffee
   **b**  a fruit drop
   **c**  a chocolate

Scott actually takes out a fruit drop, which he eats.
He then offers the bag to Natalie and she takes a sweet at random.
Find the probability that Natalie gets
   **d**  a toffee
   **e**  a fruit drop
   **f**  a chocolate

**3** Sinead is not a tidy girl. She has all of her exercise books in a heap in her room.
When she does her homework she picks them up at random until she gets the right one.
In her pile of books are 3 Maths, 4 English, 4 Science, 3 French, 2 History, 2 Geography and 2 Music.

What is the probability that the book she chooses first will be

   **a** Maths             **b** English          **c** Music?

---

| **Probability of something not happening** | The **probability of something not happening** is 1 minus the probability that it does happen.<br>For an event A, the event 'not A' is written A' and<br>    $P(A') = 1 - P(A)$ |
|---|---|
| *Example* | The probability of getting a 6 on a dice is $\frac{1}{6}$.<br>The probability of not getting a 6 is $\frac{5}{6}$.<br>We know this because there are 5 ways of not getting a 6.<br><br>If A is the event 'getting a 6', A' is the event 'not getting a 6' and<br>$P(A') = 1 - P(A) = 1 - \frac{1}{6} = \frac{5}{6}$ |

---

**4** Find $P(A')$ for the events given in question **1**.

**5** The probability that Janice will go round to see her friend tonight is $\frac{7}{12}$.
Find the probability that Janice won't see her friend tonight.

**6** A bag contains a full set of 22 snooker balls.
There are 15 reds, and 1 each of white, yellow, green, brown, blue, pink and black.
One ball is chosen at random.
Write down the probability that it is

   **a** black
   **b** red
   **c** grey
   **d** not black
   **e** not red
   **f** not grey

## 4 Sample space diagrams

Sarah and Gavin are choosing their meal.

Sarah wants to know how many different meals she can choose. She can have soup and fish fingers, soup and sausages, soup and veggie burger, juice and fish fingers, juice and sausages or juice and veggie burger.

There are 6 possibilities.
These can be shown in a table like this:

| Starter | Main course |
|---------|-------------|
| soup | fish fingers |
| soup | sausages |
| soup | veggie burger |
| juice | fish fingers |
| juice | sausages |
| juice | veggie burger |

## Exercise 8:6

**1** Philippa is on an adventure holiday.
In the morning she can choose from Sailing, Windsurfing and Canoeing.
In the afternoon she can choose from Climbing, Horse-riding and Archery.

Draw a table to show all the ways that Philippa can spend her day.

**2** Write down the different breakfasts that you can choose from this menu.

Bill, Rudi and Keith decide to
toss a coin to see who does the
washing up.
As there are 3 of them they need
3 possible outcomes.
They decide to use 2 coins.

If the outcome is 2 heads Bill will wash up.

If the outcome is 2 tails Keith will wash up.

If the outcome is 1 head and 1 tail Rudi will wash up.

Is this fair?

Here are the possible outcomes. There are four.

We can use a table to show these.

|  |  | 20 p coin | |
|---|---|---|---|
|  |  | H | T |
| 2 p coin | H | H, H | H, T |
|  | T | T, H | T, T |

1 outcome gives 2 heads.
1 outcome gives 2 tails.
2 outcomes give 1 head and 1 tail.

Probability of 2 heads = $\frac{1}{4}$

Probability of 2 tails = $\frac{1}{4}$

Probability of 1 head and 1 tail = $\frac{2}{4} = \frac{1}{2}$

So this is not fair. 1 head and 1 tail will happen the most.

## Exercise 8:7

**1** David tosses the coin at the same time as Kelly spins the spinner.

**a** Copy the table to show the possible outcomes.
Fill it in.

|      |   | Spinner |   |   |
|------|---|---------|---|---|
|      |   | 1       | 2 | 3 |
| Coin | H | H, 1    |   |   |
|      | T |         |   | T, 3 |

**b** Write down the number of possible outcomes.
**c** How many ways can you get a tail on the coin and a 3 on the spinner?
**d** What is the probability of getting a tail on the coin and a 3 on the spinner?
**e** What is the probability of getting an odd number and a head?

---

| **Sample space** | A **sample space** is a list of all the possible outcomes. |
|---|---|
| **Sample space diagram** | A table which shows all of the possible outcomes is called a **sample space diagram**. |

**2** Saleem throws a coin and rolls a dice.
**a** Copy this sample space diagram.
Fill it in.

|      |   | Dice |   |   |   |   |   |
|------|---|------|---|---|---|---|---|
|      |   | 1 | 2 | 3 | 4 | 5 | 6 |
| Coin | H |   |   |   |   |   |   |
|      | T |   |   |   |   |   |   |

**b** What is the total number of possible outcomes?
**c** What is the probability of getting a head and a 6?
**d** What is the probability of getting a tail and a number less than 3?
**e** What is the probability of getting a tail and a multiple of 3?
**f** What is the probability of getting a head and a prime number?

**3** The picture shows two tetrahedral dice.
They both have four faces.
The faces are numbered 1, 2, 3 and 4.
The score is the face that the dice
lands on.

Copy this sample space diagram.
Fill it in.

|  |  | Second dice |  |  |  |
|---|---|---|---|---|---|
|  |  | 1 | 2 | 3 | 4 |
| First dice | 1 |  |  | 1, 3 |  |
|  | 2 |  |  |  |  |
|  | 3 |  | 3, 2 |  |  |
|  | 4 |  |  |  |  |

**a** What is the total number of possible outcomes?
**b** What is the probability of getting a 1 on both dice?
**c** What is the probability of getting the same number on both dice?

Surrinder decides to add the two numbers that the dice land on.
He calls this the score.
In the picture above the score is $4 + 1 = 5$
**d** Draw a new sample space diagram to show the score.
**e** What is the probability of scoring 2?
**f** What is the probability of scoring 5?

**4** Each form in Stanthorne High
has a quiz team.
The best teams in Year 8 are 8S
and 8H.
8S has a team of 3 boys and 1 girl.
8H has a team of 2 boys and 2 girls.
One person is chosen from each
team to represent the year.

Copy the sample space diagram to show the possible pairs of pupils.
Fill it in.

|  |  | 8S Team |  |  |  |
|---|---|---|---|---|---|
|  |  | B | B | B | G |
| 8H Team | B |  |  |  |  |
|  | B |  |  |  |  |
|  | G |  |  |  |  |
|  | G |  |  |  |  |

Write down the probability that the pair chosen is
**a** a boy and a girl        **b** two pupils of the same sex

**5** A bag contains 3 blue balls, 1 red ball and 1 white ball.
A second bag contains 1 blue ball and 4 red balls.
A ball is chosen at random from each bag.
**a** Draw a sample space diagram to show the possible outcomes.
**b** What is the probability that the 2 balls are white?
**c** What is the probability that the 2 balls are the same colour?
**d** What is the probability that at least one ball is blue?

## Game – It's not fair

This is a game for two players A and B.
Take turns to roll the dice. Multiply the two numbers scored.
In this picture the score is $4 \times 3 = 12$

For each roll:
player A gets a point if the product is even
player B gets a point if the product is odd

The first player to 10 points wins.

Play the game with a partner.
Who should win? Explain your answer using a sample space diagram.
Can you change the rules of the game to make it fair?

## Chinese dice

For this investigation, you need 3 dice.

| | | | | | | |
|---|---|---|---|---|---|---|
| Dice A has faces labelled | 2 | 2 | 2 | 2 | 6 | 6 |
| Dice B has faces labelled | 1 | 1 | 5 | 5 | 5 | 5 |
| Dice C has faces labelled | 3 | 3 | 3 | 4 | 4 | 4 |

Two players play like this.

The first player chooses a dice.
The second player chooses a dice from the remaining two.

Each player rolls their dice and the player with the higher number scores
1 point.

This is done 12 times. The player with the most points wins.

Using these rules it is possible for one player to win nearly all the time.
How?

**1** Jenny takes one card at random from the 13 hearts from a pack of cards.
What is the probability that she gets
   **a** a 4        **b** a picture card      **c** a heart      **d** a spade?

**2** A 12-sided dice has the numbers 1 to 12 on its faces.
Hiten rolls the dice once.
Write down the probability that he gets
   **a** a 6                        **c** a prime number
   **b** an even number         **d** a number which is greater than 7

**3** A farmer supplies a shop with baking potatoes.
6 out of every 10 potatoes are large.
   **a** How many large potatoes would you expect in a bag of 30 potatoes?
   **b** In a bag of 25 potatoes, 12 are large.
       Is this more or less than you would expect?

**4** 200 tickets are sold for a raffle.
The probability that John wins first prize is $\frac{7}{100}$.
How many raffle tickets has John bought?

**5** Jean has 2 dice. One is fair and the other is biased.
She has thrown both dice 60 times.
Here are her results.

Dice A

| Score | 1 | 2 | 3 | 4 | 5 | 6 |
|---|---|---|---|---|---|---|
| Frequency | 9 | 7 | 18 | 8 | 9 | 9 |

Dice B

| Score | 1 | 2 | 3 | 4 | 5 | 6 |
|---|---|---|---|---|---|---|
| Frequency | 9 | 11 | 12 | 10 | 9 | 9 |

Which do you think is the fair dice?
Explain your answer.

**6** A box contains 20 counters. Some are blue and some are white.
A counter is taken at random from the box and the colour is noted.
The counter is then replaced.
This is repeated 240 times.

A white counter is chosen 84 times.
How many counters of each colour do you think are in the box?

**7** A game uses 2 spinners.
The two numbers that they land
on are added together to give
the score.

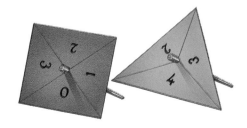

**a** Copy this table to show the score.
Fill it in.

|  |  | Blue spinner | | | |
|---|---|---|---|---|---|
|  |  | 0 | 1 | 2 | 3 |
| Green | 2 | | | | |
| spinner | 3 | | | | |
|  | 4 | | | | |

Find the probability that the score is
**b** 4        **c** less than 6        **d** 6 or more

**8** Copy and complete this sample space diagram to show the possible
outcomes when three coins are thrown.

| First coin | Second coin | Third coin |
|---|---|---|
| H | H | H |
| H | H | T |

What is the probability of getting
**a** 3 heads
**b** head head tail in this order
**c** two heads and one tail?

**9** The probability that Janine will be late for school is $\frac{3}{5}$.
The probability that she will be on time is $\frac{1}{10}$.
What is the probability that she will be early?

**10** Find $P(A)$ if the event A is
**a** rolling an even number on an ordinary fair dice
**b** rolling a multiple of 4 on a 20-sided fair dice numbered 1 to 20
**c** getting an even number and a head when throwing an
ordinary fair dice and tossing a fair coin.

**11** Find $P(A')$ for the events given in question **10**.

**1**   A bag contains 16 balls. The balls are red, blue or yellow.
A ball is chosen at random and the colour is noted.
The ball is then replaced.
When this is done 160 times, a yellow ball appears 20 times.
When this is done 320 times, a blue ball appears 120 times.

How many red balls do you think are in the bag?

**2**   Jamie has four pairs of socks scattered in his drawer. Each pair of socks
is a different colour.
He takes one sock from the drawer and keeps it.
What is the probability that the next sock out of the drawer will make
a pair with the first?

**3**   A box contains 30 balls. The balls are white, blue or pink.
The probability of choosing a pink ball at random is $\frac{1}{3}$.
There are 5 more blue balls than there are pink.

Find the probability of choosing at random
**a**   a white ball
**b**   a white or a blue ball

**4**   Mary and Sian play a game with
this spinner.

If the spinner stops on red,
Mary scores 4 points.
If the spinner stops on green,
Sian scores 2 points.

They add up their score and the first person to 40 points wins.
**a**   Who is more likely to win?
**b**   Explain how you would change the rules to make the game fair.

**5**   There are 2 bags of counters.
The first bag contains 2 blue, 1 red and 1 black.
The second bag contains 1 blue, 3 red and 2 black.
You take a counter at random from each bag.

Draw a sample space diagram to show the possible outcomes.
Find the probability that you get
**a**   2 reds
**b**   a blue and a black
**c**   2 counters of the same colour

- Probability tells us how likely something is to happen.
  We write it as a number.
  We write 0 for impossible and 1 for certain.

  We can show it on a probability scale:

  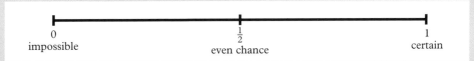

  All probabilities must be between 0 and 1.

- Probability is usually written as a fraction.

  *Example*  Sally bought 3 raffle tickets.
  100 tickets were sold.
  The probability that Sally wins the raffle is $\frac{3}{100}$.

- Probabilities always add up to 1.
  We can show this on a probability scale.

  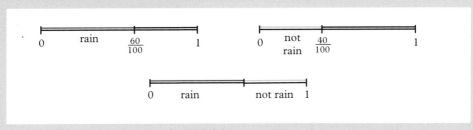

- An **event** is something that can happen in a probability question.
  We sometimes call an event by a letter.
  The event 'getting a 6' might be called event A.
  We write $P(A)$ for the probability of A happening.

- The **probability of something not happening** is 1 minus the probability that it does happen.
  For an event A, the event 'not A' is written A' and $P(A') = 1 - P(A)$

  *Example*  If A is the event 'getting a six on a dice'
  A' is the event 'not getting a six'
  $P(A') = 1 - P(A) = 1 - \frac{1}{6} = \frac{5}{6}$

- A **sample space** is a list of all the possible outcomes.
  A table which shows all of the possible outcomes is called
  a **sample space diagram**.

1   A bag of sweets contains 4 toffees and 10 fruit drops.
    Francis takes 1 sweet at random from the bag.
    Write down the probability that the sweet is
    **a** a toffee              **b** a fruit drop

2   Penny has 3 red, 5 green and 7 black pencils in her pencil case.
    She takes 1 pencil out at random.
    She writes down the colour and puts the pencil back in the case.
    **a** She does this 30 times.
       Write down how many pencils she expects to be
       (1) red                (2) green                (3) black
    **b** She does this 90 times.
       Write down how many pencils she expects to be
       (1) red                (2) green                (3) black

3   The probability that Kirk gets all his homework right is $\frac{2}{5}$.
    What is the probability that he gets something wrong?

4   Lucy rings her friend Vicky.
    The probability that the phone call will last for less than 10 minutes is $\frac{1}{6}$.
    The probability that it will last between 10 and 20 minutes is $\frac{7}{12}$.
    What is the probability that the call will last for more than 20 minutes?

5   The event A is 'getting an odd number' on an ordinary dice.
    Write down
    **a** $P(A)$              **b** $P(A')$

6   A bag contains 3 red balls, 1 blue ball and 1 yellow ball.
    Another bag contains 2 red balls, 3 blue balls and 2 yellow balls.
    Ingrid takes one ball from each bag.
    **a** Draw a sample space diagram to show all the possible outcomes.
    **b** Write down the probability that Ingrid will get
       (1) 2 yellow balls
       (2) 2 balls of the same colour
       (3) at least one blue ball

# 9 Percentages and fractions

Emily owns shares worth £200.
The share value rises by 10%.
Then the value falls by 10%.

*True or False?*
Emily's shares are now worth £200.

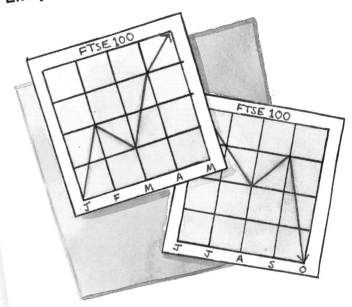

# 1   Simple percentages

82 out of these 100 children have blue eyes.

This is the same as saying that 82% have blue eyes.

8 out of these 50 children are left-handed. This is the same as 16 out of every 100.

This means that 16% of them are left-handed.

### Exercise 9:1

1   Pupils who are right-handed are shaded blue.
What percentage are right-handed?

2   Pupils who take a packed lunch to school are shaded red.
What percentage take a packed lunch?

**3** Pupils who did not do their homework are shaded green.

   **a** What percentage did not do their homework?

   **b** What percentage *did* do their homework?

**4** Pupils who play in a school sports team are shaded pink.

   **a** What percentage of the pupils play for a school team?

   **b** What percentage do *not* play for a school team?

**5** Pupils who own a computer system are shaded yellow. What percentage of the pupils do *not* own a computer?

**6** Pupils who go swimming regularly are shaded blue.

   **a** What percentage go swimming?

   **b** What percentage do *not* go swimming?

**7** Pupils who support Liverpool Football Club are shaded orange.

   **a** What percentage support Liverpool?

   **b** What percentage do *not* support Liverpool?

Shops often have special sale days.
They mark some items with a blue cross.
This means that there is 10% off the price.

They do not change the price on the ticket because the sale only lasts a few days.

You have to work out the sale price for yourself.

It is easy to find 10% of an amount of money.
You divide the amount by 10.

To divide by 10, move all the numbers one place to the right.

*Example*    A T-shirt costing £6.50 is in the blue cross sale.
Work out how much you would save.

$$10\% \text{ of } £6.50 = £6 \,.\, 5 \quad 0 \div 10$$

$$= £0 \,.\, 6 \quad 5$$
$$= 65\,p$$

You would save 65 p

Once you have worked out 10% it is quite easy to work out other percentages.

To work out 20% of an amount:
    First work out 10% of the amount.
    Then multiply by 2.
        $10\% \times 2 = 20\%$

## Exercise 9:2

**1** These items are in the blue cross sale. For each one work out how much you would save.
  **a** A T-shirt costing £7.50
  **b** Shorts costing £9.50
  **c** Socks costing £3.50
  **d** A sweatshirt costing £8.50

**BLUE CROSS SALE**

**10% OFF** ALL MARKED ITEMS

**2** Work out how much these would *cost* in the blue cross sale.
  **a** A T-shirt costing £5.20
  **b** A board game costing £7.40
  **c** A pen costing £1.20
  **d** A diary costing £4.90

**3** A personal stereo costs £24.90
  **a** How much would you save with 10% off?
  **b** How much would the stereo cost?

---

*Example*  A pair of jeans costs £35.90
Work out the cost of the jeans with 20% off.

10% of £35.90 = £3.59
20% of £35.90 = £3.59 × 2 = £7.18

The jeans would cost £35.90 − £7.18 = £28.72

---

**4** A pair of jeans costs £27.90
  **a** How much would you save with 20% off?
  **b** Find the cost of the jeans with 20% off.

**5** A box of computer disks costs £8.50
  **a** How much would you save with 20% off?
  **b** How much does the box of disks cost in the sale?

**6** A ski jacket costs £120
The price is reduced by 20% in the sale.
Work out the cost of the jacket in the sale.

You can make up other percentages from 10%.

If you want to work out 40%, find 10% and then multiply by 4. 70% is 10% multiplied by 7.

50% of something is half of it. You can divide by 2 to find 50%. This is easier than finding 10% and then multiplying by 5.

You can find 25% by finding 50% and then dividing this by 2.

*Examples*  **1**  Find 40% of £24

10% of £24 = £2.40
40% of £24 = £2.40 × 4 = £9.60

**2**  Find 25% of £130

50% of £130 = £130 ÷ 2 = £65
25% of £130 = £65 ÷ 2 = £32.50

## Exercise 9:3

**1**  Find these percentages. You will need to work out 10% first.
 **a**  30% of £24
 **b**  40% of £30
 **c**  40% of £45
 **d**  60% of £150

**2**  Find:
 **a**  50% of £60
 **b**  50% of £46
 **c**  25% of £40
 **d**  25% of £170

**3**  A pair of jeans is reduced by 30% in a sale.
They normally cost £33
Work out the sale price of the jeans.

**4**  There are 225 pupils in Year 9.
20% have brown eyes.
How many pupils have brown eyes?

**5**  In an election 22 000 people voted.
35% of them voted Conservative.
 **a**  Find 10% of 22 000.
 **b**  Use your answer to **a** to find 5% of 22 000.
 **c**  Find the number of people who
voted Conservative.

**6**  In a trial of 2300 dogs, 65% preferred Dogidins.
 **a**  How many dogs preferred Dogidins?
 **b**  What percentage preferred another brand?

You can also work out 1% of an amount very easily.
To work out 1%, divide by 100. This moves all the numbers 2 places
to the right.

*Example*     1% of £27.00 = £2 7 . 0 0 ÷ 100

= £ 0 . 2 7

= 27 p

Once you have 1% and 10% you can build up any other percentage.
Sometimes you can do this mentally.

James wants to work out 43% of £200
In his head, he works out 10% of £200
He multiplies this by 4 to find 40%.
He writes down this part of the answer.

Next he works out 1% of £200 in his head.
He multiplies this by 3 to find 3%.

To find 43% James adds the two parts together.

$$80 \\ + 6 \\ \overline{£86}$$

## Exercise 9:4

**1** Work out these percentages. Work out 10% and 1% first.
  **a** 23% of 700     **c** 82% of 600     **e** 68% of 900
  **b** 32% of 200     **d** 51% of 400   • **f** 42% of 750

**2** Kylie goes into a shop to buy some new clothes. There is a special
14-day sale. Everything is reduced by 14%.
Work out the price of these clothes that she buys in the sale.
Here is a list of the normal prices:
    Jeans £30     T-Shirt £5     Trainers £45

**3** There are 700 pupils at Mill Road School.
58% have school meals.
23% take a packed lunch.
19% go home.
  **a** How many pupils have school meals?
  **b** How many pupils take a packed lunch?

**4** This pie-chart shows the types of casualties in road accidents in one year in Derbyshire.

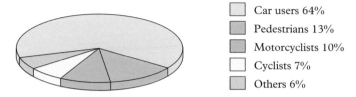

☐ Car users 64%
☐ Pedestrians 13%
☐ Motorcyclists 10%
☐ Cyclists 7%
☐ Others 6%

There were 1100 casualties altogether.
Work out the number of casualties in each group.

**5** Here are 6 question cards and 6 answer cards.
*Estimate* the answer to each question.
Match each question with its answer.
Write the questions and answers in your book.

| | | |
|---|---|---|
| **23% of 300** | **53% of 450** | **61% of 820** |
| **35% of 400** | **69** | **23% of 160** |
| **42% of 710** | **140** | **238.5** |
| **36.8** | **500.2** | **298.2** |

## 2   Calculating percentages

These opinion poll results are given as percentages.
We can work them out with a calculator.

---

To work out a percentage on a calculator:

(1) Turn the percentage into a decimal.
    To do this, divide it by 100.

(2) Multiply the amount by the decimal.

*Examples*   **1**   Find 38% of 1200 people.

$$38\% = \frac{38}{100} = 38 \div 100 = 0.38$$

38% of 1200 = 0.38 × 1200 = 456 people

**2**   Find 47% of 1200 people.

$$47\% = \frac{47}{100} = 47 \div 100 = 0.47$$

47% of 1200 = 0.47 × 1200 = 564 people

---

## Exercise 9:5

**1** Copy and fill in:

**a** $56\% = \dfrac{?}{100} = 0.56$ 　　　　**d** $98\% = \dfrac{?}{100} = \ldots$

**b** $76\% = \dfrac{76}{100} = \ldots$ 　　　　**e** $9\% = \dfrac{?}{100} = 0.09$

**c** $32\% = \dfrac{?}{100} = \ldots$ 　　　　**f** $\ldots\% = \dfrac{8}{100} = \ldots$

**2** 1200 people take part in a survey about banks.
They are asked which bank they use.
　　　23% say Nat West 　　　　15% say Midland
　　　17% say Lloyds 　　　　9% say Yorkshire
　　　18% say Barclays 　　　　18% say another bank

Work out the number of people who use each bank.

**3** Class 8J have a Maths test. The total mark is 40.
The teacher gives them their marks as percentages.
　　　Terry 35%　　　Sian 65%　　　Lindsey 95%
They want to know how many marks they got.
Work out the marks for each person.

**4** Look at this advertisement.

> **Rob's Records**
>
> **CD Sale**
>
> 15% off Chart CDs
> Up to 33% off Rock CDs
> 12% off all Classical CDs

**a** Pritesh buys a Chart CD. It normally costs £13
How much does the CD cost in the sale?
**b** Glenn also buys a Chart CD. It normally costs £13.80
How much does the CD cost in the sale?
**c** Michelle buys a Rock CD. It normally costs £11
There is 26% off in the sale.
How much does the CD cost?
**d** Anne buys a Classical CD. It normally costs £15
How much does the CD cost in the sale?

**5** Ben works part-time in a shop. He earns £2.50 per hour.
**a** Ben gets a rise of 8%.
How much extra will he get per hour?
**b** How much will he earn per hour after his rise?

---

You can work out fractions of 1%.

*Examples*  **1**  $17\frac{1}{2}\% = 17.5 \div 100 = 0.175$

**2**  $12\frac{1}{4}\% = 12.25 \div 100 = 0.1225$

**3**  $33\frac{1}{3}\% = 33.\dot{3} \div 100 = 0.\dot{3}$  (This is the same as one-third)

---

**6**  VAT stands for Value Added Tax. You pay it on lots of things you buy.
VAT is charged at $17\frac{1}{2}\%$ on most things.
Work out the VAT on each of these items.
  **a**  Jeans costing £30 without VAT.
  **b**  A stereo costing £290 without VAT.
  **c**  A car costing £9950 without VAT.

**7**  Mandy earns £3.20 per hour as a waitress.
She gets a rise of $12\frac{1}{4}\%$.
Find her new hourly rate to the nearest penny.

**8**  School bus fares are increased by $3\frac{1}{3}\%$ due to increased fuel costs.
Find the new prices to the nearest penny for:
  **a**  Lynda who normally pays £1.30
  **b**  Dave who normally pays 95 p
  **c**  Harjit who normally pays £1.25

· · · · · · · · · · · · · · · · · · · · · · · · · · · · · · · · · · · · · · · · · · · · · · · · · · · · · · · · · · · ·

## Exercise 9:6  *Four in a row*

This is a game for two players.
You will need two colours of counters.
Each player uses a different colour.
You need one calculator between you.

Underneath the number 650 you can see a list of 36 percentages.
If you work out these percentages of 650 you get the answers shown in
the board underneath.

**Player 1:**

(1) Choose a square on the board.
(2) One percentage from the list will give the answer in the square. Choose the percentage that you think is correct.
(3) Calculate the percentage.
(4) Cover up the calculator answer on the board with a counter.

**Player 2:**

You do the same thing using your counters.

The winner is the first person to get four counters in a straight line. The line can be in any direction.

The better you are at predicting the answers, the more likely you are to win!

$$650$$

| 23% | 57% | 68% | 24% | 12% | 45% | 97% | 81% | 27% |
| 39% | 42% | 17% | 15% | 47% | 25% | 84% | 71% | 55% |
| 66% | 10% | 13% | 54% | 93% | 61% | 49% | 60% | 80% |
| 22% | 43% | 74% | 99% | 24% | 33% | 58% | 17% | 75% |

| | | | | | |
|---|---|---|---|---|---|
| 149.5 | 110.5 | 305.5 | 214.5 | 357.5 | 442 |
| 390 | 162.5 | 156 | 292.5 | 110.5 | 396.5 |
| 526.5 | 643.5 | 604.5 | 461.5 | 175.5 | 520 |
| 97.5 | 429 | 370.5 | 143 | 318.5 | 630.5 |
| 78 | 481 | 253.5 | 65 | 487.5 | 546 |
| 84.5 | 396.5 | 279.5 | 273 | 377 | 351 |

To work out what percentage one number is of another:

(1) Write the numbers as a fraction.

(2) Change the fraction to a decimal.

(3) Change the decimal to a percentage.

*Example*

Michael gets £80 for his birthday. He saves £15
What percentage does he save?
We need 15 as a percentage of 80.

$$\frac{15}{80} = 15 \div 80 = 0.1875$$

To change a decimal to a percentage, multiply by 100.

$$0.1875 = 18.75\%$$

### Exercise 9:7

**1** Copy this table. It shows the marks in a test out of 40.
Fill in the rest of the table.

| Pupil | Mark | Fraction | Decimal | Percentage |
|-------|------|----------|---------|------------|
| Sean | 34 | $\frac{34}{40}$ | 0.85 | |
| Gavla | 19 | | | |
| Shellene | 27 | | 0.675 | |
| Jamie | 37 | | | |
| Emma | 21 | | | |

**2** This table shows the number of people living in Australia who were
not born there.
The figures are in thousands.

| Year | Number born overseas | Total population |
|------|----------------------|------------------|
| 1947 | 744.2 | 7518.6 |
| 1954 | 1286.5 | 8900.3 |
| 1966 | 2130.9 | 11 500.6 |
| 1976 | 2718.8 | 14 033.1 |
| 1986 | 3427.4 | 16 018.4 |

**a** Work out the percentage of the population who were born overseas
in each year. Round your answers to 1 dp.

**b** Has emigrating to Australia become more or less popular?

**3** In this question round your answers to 2 dp where necessary.
Jonathan runs a record shop.
He keeps a note of how many CDs, tapes and records he sells each day.

|         | Mon | Tues | Wed | Fri | Sat | Total |
|---------|-----|------|-----|-----|-----|-------|
| CDs     | 34  | 38   | 42  | 41  | 95  | 250   |
| tapes   | 35  | 29   | 20  | 48  | 68  | 200   |
| records | 11  | 3    | 18  | 21  | 27  | 80    |
| Total   | 80  | 70   | 80  | 110 | 190 | 530   |

**a** How many items did he sell on Monday?
**b** (1) What percentage of Monday's sales were CDs?
  (2) Work out the percentages of tape and record sales for Monday.
**c** Look at the Saturday column.
  (1) What percentage of Saturday's sales were tapes?
  (2) Work out the percentages of CD and record sales for Saturday.
**d** How many CDs did he sell in the week?
**e** What percentage of these CDs did he sell on Friday?
**f** What percentage of total tape sales did he make on Friday?
**g** Look at the last column.
  (1) What percentage of the week's sales were CDs?
  (2) Work out the percentages of tape and record sales for the week.

**4** This table shows the number of people listening to radio stations in 1994 and 1995.
The figures are in millions per week.

| Station          | 1994 | 1995 |
|------------------|------|------|
| Radio 1          | 11.2 | 11.2 |
| Radio 2          | 8.4  | 8.6  |
| Radio 3          | 2.6  | 2.6  |
| Radio 4          | 8.4  | 8.7  |
| Radio 5 Live     | 4.4  | 4.8  |
| BBC local        | 9.5  | 9.1  |
| Atlantic 252     | 4.9  | 4.7  |
| Classic FM       | 4.9  | 4.6  |
| Talk Radio UK    | N/A  | 2.3  |
| Virgin           | 3.9  | 4.3  |
| Independent local| 22.1 | 23.2 |

**a** Find each station's percentage of the total audience in 1994 and 1995. Round your answers to the nearest whole number.
**b** Use your percentages to draw a pie-chart for each year.
**c** Write about any differences in the two years' figures.

## 3 Fractions

Bill is ordering some new stock.
Three-quarters of the ice creams that he sells are cornets.
One-quarter are lollies.

He has sold 1200 ice creams this week.
He wants to work out how many of each he has sold.

*Example*

Find one-quarter of 1200.

$1200 \div 4 = 300$
He has sold 300 lollies.

Find three-quarters of 1200.

$1200 \div 4 \times 3 = 900$
He has sold 900 cornets.

### Exercise 9:8

**1** Find:
  **a** $\frac{1}{4}$ of 240
  **b** $\frac{3}{4}$ of 240

**2** Find:
  **a** $\frac{1}{5}$ of 240
  **b** $\frac{2}{5}$ of 240
  **c** $\frac{3}{5}$ of 240

**3** Find:
  **a** $\frac{1}{7}$ of 168
  **b** $\frac{2}{7}$ of 168
  **c** $\frac{5}{7}$ of 168

**4** Find:
  **a** $\frac{1}{8}$ of 192
  **b** $\frac{3}{8}$ of 192
  **c** $\frac{7}{8}$ of 192

**5** In a box of apples, $\frac{2}{7}$ have gone bad.
There are 35 apples in the box.
How many apples have gone bad?

**6** $\frac{2}{5}$ of the cars sold by a garage are hatchbacks.
The garage sells 45 cars in August.
  **a** How many hatchbacks do they sell?
  **b** How many other cars do they sell?

---

*Examples*  **1** Change $\frac{3}{5}$ to a decimal and a percentage.

$$\frac{3}{5} = 3 \div 5 = 0.6$$
$$0.6 = 60\%$$

**2** Change 80% to a fraction.

$$80\% = \frac{80}{100}$$

Cancel this fraction to its simplest form

| 8 | 0 | $a\frac{b}{c}$ | 1 | 0 | 0 | = | $4 \rfloor 5$ |

Answer: $\frac{4}{5}$

---

## Exercise 9:9

You will need a set of Cuisenaire rods.
Each picture shows a pair of Cuisenaire rods. The table shows what fraction the smaller one is of the bigger one.

**1** Copy this table.
Fill it in.

| Picture | | Fraction | Decimal | Percentage |
|---|---|---|---|---|
| **a** |  | $\frac{1}{2}$ | | |
| **b** | 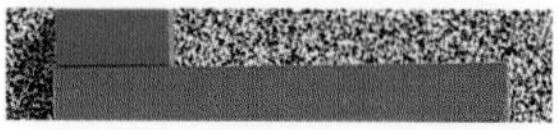 | | 0.25 | |
| **c** | 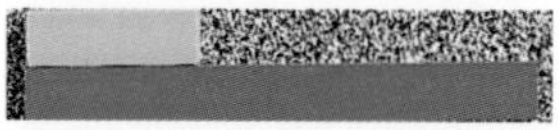 | $\frac{1}{3}$ | | |
| **d** | 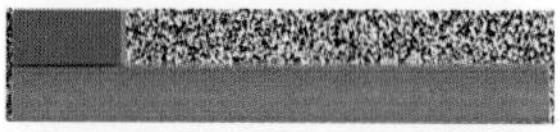 | | | 20% |
| **e** | | | 0.4 | |
| **f** |  | $\frac{3}{4}$ | | |

194

**2** Now choose pairs of rods for yourself.
Make a table like the one in question **1** to show the rods you choose.
Work out the fraction, decimal and percentage columns for each pair.

Some pairs will give you the same answers you saw in question **1**.
You do not have to do these again.

How many different sets of results can you find?

## Exercise 9:10

**1** Look at these televisions:

**a**                                           **b**

Which TV is the cheaper in the sale?

**2** Bhavini gets 40% in a Maths test.
Her friend in another class gets $\frac{26}{70}$ in the same test.
Whose score is higher?

**3** In Year 8 at Stanthorne High 54% of the pupils are girls.
In Year 9 there are 121 girls and 99 boys.
Which year has the bigger percentage of girls?

**4**  **a** Copy this table.

| | |
|---|---|
| $\frac{3}{8}$ | 39% |
| $\frac{4}{11}$ | 36% |
| $\frac{5}{8}$ | 64% |
| $\frac{8}{13}$ | 64% |
| $\frac{6}{7}$ | 87% |
| $\frac{3}{20}$ | 14% |
| $\frac{15}{28}$ | 51% |

 **b** Ring the bigger one in each row.

**1** Work out how much you would save on each of these in the sale.
  **a** A shirt costing £15
  **b** A coat costing £25
  **c** A book costing £9.50
  **d** A CD costing £13.50
  **e** A watch costing £14.80

**2** There are 220 pupils in Year 9 at Stanthorne High.
  **a** 65% of them have chips every day.
     How many pupils have chips every day?
  **b** 35% have a brother.
     How many pupils have a brother?
  **c** 40% have a sister.
     How many pupils have a sister?
  **d** 45% walk to school each day.
     How many pupils walk to school each day?
  **e** What percentage of pupils *do not* walk to school each day?

**3** Mrs Barton can earn £4500 before she pays tax.
Then she pays 20% on the next £3200 and 25% on the rest of her earnings.
In one year Mrs Barton earns £12 500
Copy and fill in:
  **a** Mrs Barton pays tax on £12 500 − £4500 = £...
  **b** Mrs Barton pays 20% tax on £...
  **c** Mrs Barton pays 25% tax on £... − £... = £...
  **d** Amount of tax
       20% of £... = £...
       25% of £... = £...
       Total tax    = £...
  **e** Mrs Barton keeps £12 500 − £... = £...

**4** Work these out.
  **a** 35% of 340 girls     **c** 27% of £500     **e** 78% of 5 metres
  **b** 65% of 8 hours     **d** 49% of £600     **f** 85% of 15 kilograms

**5** Work out the VAT at $17\frac{1}{2}$% on these items.
Give your answers correct to the nearest penny.
  **a** A video costing £9.99 without VAT.
  **b** A picture frame costing £29.99 without VAT.
  **c** Training shoes costing £44.99 without VAT.

**6** Work these out.
   **a** $64\frac{1}{2}\%$ of 4600 kilograms    **c** $17\frac{3}{4}\%$ of 3500 litres
   **b** $29\frac{1}{4}\%$ of 2400 people    **d** $37\frac{1}{2}\%$ of £2480

**7** Camille does a survey about favourite flavours of ice cream.
   She writes a report of her results.
   This is part of her report.

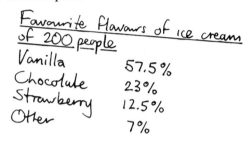

Favourite flavours of ice cream
of 200 people
Vanilla        57.5%
Chocolate      23%
Strawberry     12.5%
Other          7%

How many people like each flavour of ice cream the best?

**8** A bag contains 20 counters.
   $\frac{1}{4}$ of them are blue, $\frac{2}{5}$ are green and the rest are yellow.
   **a** How many counters of each colour are in the bag?
   **b** What percentage of the counters are yellow?

**9** A bag contains 36 beads.
   $\frac{1}{12}$ of them are orange, $\frac{2}{9}$ are black and the rest are white.
   **a** How many beads of each colour are in the bag?
   **b** What fraction of the counters are white?

**10** There are 32 teeth in a full adult set.
   $\frac{1}{8}$ are canines, $\frac{3}{8}$ are molars and $\frac{1}{4}$ are incisors.
   The rest are called pre-molars.
   **a** How many canines are there?
   **b** How many molars are there?
   **c** What percentage of the teeth are pre-molars?

**1** A market research company asks 1024 people in a city which supermarket they use. Here are the results.
Asda 24.8%    Tesco 34.8%    Sainsbury's 30.5%    Other 9.9%
How many people use each supermarket for their shopping?
*Be careful, this question is about people – you need sensible answers.*

**2** A trade warehouse shows all of its prices without VAT.
Joseph buys:
a CD costing £9.98
a jumper costing £19.98
a pair of shoes costing £24.98

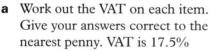

**a** Work out the VAT on each item. Give your answers correct to the nearest penny. VAT is 17.5%
**b** Work out the cost of each item to the nearest penny.
**c** In the warehouse, the total cost is calculated by adding all the prices without VAT and then adding the VAT at the end. Does this method give the same total cost?

**3** The word 'carat' describes the purity of gold.
9 carat gold means that 9 parts out of every 24 parts are gold.
**a** What fraction of a 9 carat gold bracelet is gold?
**b** What percentage of a 9 carat gold bracelet is gold?

Gold is also sold as 18 carat and 22 carat. These are much more expensive than 9 carat gold because they contain more gold.
**c** What fraction of 18 carat gold is gold?
**d** What percentage of 18 carat gold is gold?
**e** What percentage of 22 carat gold is *not* gold?

**4** Ms Crossley can earn £4500 before she pays tax.
Then she pays 20% on the next £3200 and 25% on the rest of her earnings.
In one year Ms Crossley earns £19 500
**a** How much does Ms Crossley pay in tax?
**b** What percentage of her income does she keep?

**5** Work these out.
Give your answers correct to 2 dp.
**a** $\frac{4}{7}$ of 354    **b** $\frac{5}{8}$ of 649    **c** $\frac{7}{12}$ of 2560    **d** $\frac{5}{11}$ of 287

- To find 10% of an amount divide the amount by 10.

*Example*   10% of £6.50 = £6 . 5   0 ÷ 10

$$= £0 . 6 \quad 5$$
$$= 65\,p$$

- You can make up other percentages from 10%.

  If you want to work out 40%, find 10% and then multiply by 4.
  70% is 10% multiplied by 7.

  50% of something is half of it. You can divide by 2 to find 50%.
  This is easier than finding 10% and then multiplying by 5.

  You can find 25% by finding 50% and then dividing this by 2.

*Example*   Find 40% of £24

10% of £24 = £2.40
40% of £24 = £2.40 × 4 = £9.60

- To work out a percentage on a calculator:

  (1) Turn the percentage into a decimal.

  (2) Multiply by the decimal.

*Example*   Find 38% of 1200 people.

$$38\% = \frac{38}{100} = 38 \div 100 = 0.38$$

38% of 1200 = 0.38 × 1200 = 456 people

- To work out what percentage one number is of another:

  (1) Write the numbers as a fraction.

  (2) Change the fraction to a decimal.

  (3) Change the decimal to a percentage.

*Example*   What percentage is 15 of 80?

$$\frac{15}{80} = 15 \div 80 = 0.1875 = 18.75\%$$

- *Examples*   **1**   Change $\frac{3}{5}$ to a decimal and a percentage.

  $\frac{3}{5} = 3 \div 5 = 0.6$
  0.6 = 60%

  **2**   Change 80% to a fraction.

  $$80\% = \frac{80}{100} = \frac{4}{5}$$

**1** There are 50 bananas on a supermarket shelf.
12 of them are very ripe.
What percentage of the bananas are very ripe?

**2** In a sale everything is reduced by 10%.
Work out how much you could save on each of these in the sale.
**a** A tape costing £9.50
**b** A CD costing £12.50

**3** Work these out.
**a** 10% of £400
**b** 40% of £400
**c** 25% of £340

**4** Work these out.
**a** 48% of 6700 people
**b** 7% of £1327
**c** $67\frac{1}{2}$% of 750 grams
**d** $38\frac{1}{4}$% of 1200 centimetres

**5** Work out the VAT at $17\frac{1}{2}$% on these items.
**a** A computer game costing £30 without VAT.
**b** A tracksuit costing £40 without VAT.

**6** Tanya scores 26 out of 40 in a test.
What percentage is this?

**7** A garage sells 2400 cars in August.
In the rest of the year they sell another 3600 cars.
What percentage of their cars do they sell in August?

**8** Paul eats a lot of sweets. He has fillings in $\frac{2}{7}$ of his 28 teeth.
**a** How many fillings has Paul got?
**b** What fraction of his teeth are *not* filled?

**9** The table shows how many cakes Ahsan sells in one week.

| Monday | Tuesday | Wednesday | Thursday | Friday |
|--------|---------|-----------|----------|--------|
| 24 | 28 | 28 | 36 | 44 |

**a** What fraction of the cakes did he sell each day?
**b** What percentage of the cakes did he sell each day?

# 10 Straight lines

QUESTIONS

EXTENSION

SUMMARY

TEST YOURSELF

The co-ordinates we use to draw graphs are called Cartesian co-ordinates. They were named after a Frenchman called René Descartes (1596–1650). In 1619 he had a dream in which he realised that all the sciences were connected and that physics could be expressed using the language of geometry. One of Descartes' famous sayings was: '*Cogito ergo sum*' which is Latin for '*Je pense, donc je suis*'.

# 1    Lines of the grid

Bill is on holiday in New York.
He wants to visit the World Trade Center Building.
It is at the intersection of Liberty Street with West Street.

◄◄ **REPLAY** ►

## *Exercise 10:1*

**1**  Look at the red line.
The co-ordinates of the point P
are (2, 3).

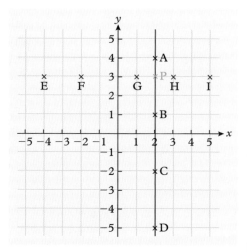

   **a**  Write down the co-ordinates of
the points A, B, C and D.

   All these points have
$x$ co-ordinate = 2
In algebra this is $x = 2$
The rule for the line is $x = 2$

   **b**  Write down the co-ordinates of
the points E, F, G, H and I on the
blue line.

   All these points have
$y$ co-ordinate = 3
The rule for the line is $y = 3$

**2** Write down the rules for these lines.

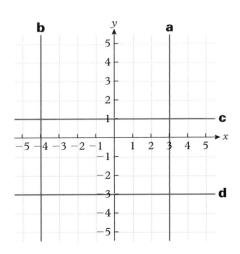

**3** Write down the rules for these lines.

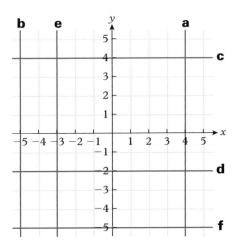

**4 a** Copy the diagram on to squared paper.
  **b** Label each line with its rule.
  **c** The lines cross at a point. Write down the co-ordinates of this point. Remember to use brackets (…, …)

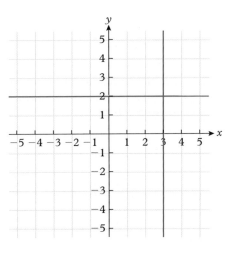

5 **a** Draw a new set of axes like the ones in question 4.
  **b** Draw a vertical line and a horizontal line.
   They must cross at the point (2, 5).
  **c** Copy and fill in the rules for these two lines.
   $$x = \ldots \qquad y = \ldots$$

6 Which vertical and horizontal lines cross at each point?
  **a** (3, 6)          **b** (5, 2)          **c** (6, 1)

---

| Point of intersection | The point where two lines cross is called a **point of intersection**. |
| --- | --- |

## Exercise 10:2

1 Write down the co-ordinates of the point of intersection of these lines.
  **a** $x = 1$ and $y = 6$          **c** $x = 5$ and $y = -7$
  **b** $x = -4$ and $y = 3$          **d** $x = 0$ and $y = 1$

2 Which vertical and horizontal lines have the point of intersection:
  **a** (8, 0)          **c** (-3, -4)          **e** (5, 0)
  **b** (-2, 1)          **d** (5, -1)          **f** (0, 3)

3 Write down the rule for:
  **a** the $x$ axis
  **b** the $y$ axis
  **c** Write down the co-ordinates of the point of intersection of these two lines.
  **d** What do we call this point?

4 The diagram shows a square.
  Write down the rule for each side of the square.

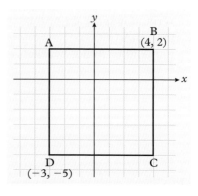

## 2   Patterns of lines

Matthew and Katy are looking for patterns on a grid.

### *Exercise 10:3*

You will need some counters and a grid.

**1  a**  Copy the axes on to the grid.
Use it for all the questions in this Exercise.

**b**  Matthew has put counters on points of the grid. He wants the *y* co-ordinate to be the same as the *x* co-ordinate.
Katy sees that they are in a straight line.

Mark the points on your grid where
$y$ co-ordinate = $x$ co-ordinate
In algebra this is $y = x$
Join the points with a straight line.
The rule for the line is $y = x$

**c**  Label the line with its rule  $y = x$

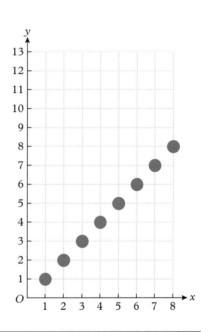

| **Equation** | The rule of a line is called the **equation** of the line. The equation of this line is $y = x$ |
|---|---|

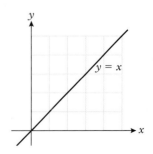

**2** Katy puts counters on the grid where
the **y** co-ordinate is 2 × the **x** co-ordinate.
She marks the points on her grid.
She joins the points with a straight line.
  **a** Mark the points on your grid.
    Join them with a straight line.
  **b** Copy:
      The equation of the line is $y = 2 \times x$
      In algebra this is        $y = 2x$
  **c** Label the line with its equation.

**3** **a** Put counters on your grid where
    the **y** co-ordinate is 3 × the **x** co-ordinate.
  **b** Mark the points.
    Join them with a straight line.
  **c** Copy and fill in the equation of the line.
      $y = \ldots x$
  **d** Label the line with its equation.

**4** You have drawn the lines   $y = x$
                $y = 2x$
                $y = 3x$
  **a** Which line is the steepest?
  **b** Which line is the least steep?
  **c** Which part of the equation tells you how steep the line is?

· · · · · · · · · · · · · · · · · · · · · · · · · · · · · · · · · · · · · · · · · · · · · · · · · · · · · · · · · ·

*Example*    Which line will be steeper $y = 3x$ or $y = 4x$?

We can use robots to help us draw lines.
To draw the line $y = 4x$ we use the
'×4' robot.

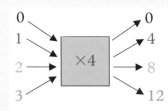

Put the          You get the
x co-ordinate      y co-ordinate
in.            out.

We now plot the points (0, 0) (1, 4)
(2, 8) (3, 12)
We join the points with a straight line.
We label the line with its equation
$$y = 4x$$

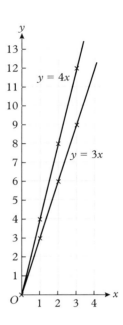

The line $y = 4x$ is steeper.

---

**5** Which line is the steeper in each of these pairs?

**a** $y = x$   or   $y = 4x$

**b** $y = 2x$  or  $y = 6x$

**c** $y = 5x$  or  $y = 4x$

**d** $y = 3x$  or  $y = 7x$

**e** $y = x$   or   $y = 2\frac{1}{2}x$

**f** $y = 5x$  or  $y = 3\frac{1}{2}x$

**g** $y = 4\frac{1}{2}x$  or  $y = 7\frac{1}{2}x$

**h** $y = 3\frac{1}{2}x$  or  $y = 3\frac{1}{4}x$

**6** The diagram shows three graphs.
Write down the equation of each graph.
Choose from these equations:
$y = 3x$      $y = \frac{1}{2}x$      $y = 5x$

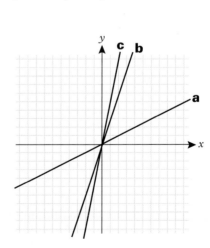

Marcus is looking at some patterns on a grid.
He has put his counters on the grid where
$y$ co-ordinate = $x$ co-ordinate + 1
The equation is:
$y = x + 1$

## Exercise 10:4

You will need some counters.

**1**  **a**  Make a new grid like the one that you used in Exercise 10.3.
Use it for all the questions in this Exercise.
   **b**  Draw the line $y = x$
Label the line with its equation.
   **c**  Now put the counters on the grid like Marcus did.
*Remember:*  $y$ co-ordinate = $x$ co-ordinate + 1
Your counters should be in a straight line.
   **d**  Mark the points.
Join them with a straight line.
   **e**  Copy and fill in the equation of the line.
$y = ... + ...$
   **f**  Label the line with its equation.

**2**  **a**  Put counters on your grid where
$y$ co-ordinate = $x$ co-ordinate + 2
   **b**  Mark the points.
Join them with a straight line.
   **c**  Copy and fill in the equation of the line.
$y = ... + ...$
   **f**  Label the line with its equation.

**3**  You have drawn the lines  $y = x$
$y = x + 1$
$y = x + 2$
   **a**  Copy and fill in:
The lines are all p....................
   **b**  Which line is higher up the grid?
   **c**  Where do you think the line $y = x + 3$ will go?
   **d**  Use counters to help you draw the line $y = x + 3$ on your grid.
Label the line with its equation.
Was your answer to **c** correct?

**4** Look at your grid. You have drawn four lines on it.
  **a** Copy and fill in these sentences.
    The line $y = x$ crosses the $y$ axis at 0.
    The line $y = x + 1$ crosses the $y$ axis at 1.
    The line $y = x + 2$ crosses the $y$ axis at ….
    The line $y = x + 3$ crosses the $y$ axis at ….
  **b** Where will the line $y = x + 4$ cross the $y$ axis?
  **c** Use counters to help you draw the line $y = x + 4$ on your grid.
    Label the line with its equation.
  **d** Was your answer to **b** correct?

**5** Where will these lines cross the $y$ axis?
  **a** $y = x + 5$    **c** $y = x + 8$    **e** $y = x + \frac{1}{2}$
  **b** $y = x + 7$    **d** $y = x + 12$    **f** $y = x + 3\frac{1}{2}$

**6** **a** Where will the line $y = x - 2$ cross the $y$ axis?
  **b** Copy the axes on to squared paper.
  **c** Draw the line $y = x - 2$
    Use this robot to help you.
    Copy and fill in:

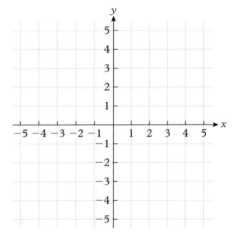

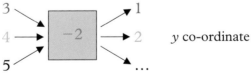

$x$ co-ordinate          $y$ co-ordinate

The points to plot are
$(3, 1)$ $(4, 2)$ $(5, …)$
Join them with a straight line.
Label the line with its equation
$y = x - 2$
  **d** Was your answer to **a** correct?

**7** Where will these lines cross the $y$ axis?

   **a** $y = x - 3$                   **d** $y = x + 6$

   **b** $y = x - 7$                   **e** $y = x - 6$

   **c** $y = x - 4$                   **f** $y = x$

**8** Matthew knows that the line $y = x + 3$ crosses the $y$ axis at $3$.
He wants to know if the rule still works for $y = 2x + 3$.
He uses robot screens to help him draw the line.

   **a** Copy and fill in:

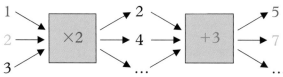

   **b** Copy the axes on to squared paper.

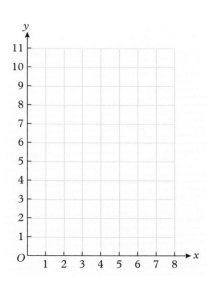

     Plot the points $(1, 5)$ $(2, 7)$ $(3, \dots)$
     Join them with a straight line.
     Label the line with the equation
     $y = 2x + 3$

     Does the rule still work?

**9** Where will these lines cross the $y$ axis?

   **a** $y = 2x - 4$                 **c** $y = 3x - 5$

   **b** $y = 3x + 7$                 **d** $y = 5x + 2$

**10** Katy knows that the lines $y = x + 1$ and $y = x + 2$ are parallel.
She wants to know if the lines $y = 2x + 1$ and $y = 2x + 2$ will be parallel.

   **a** Copy the axes from question **8** again.

   **b** Draw and label the line $y = 2x + 1$
     Use robot screens to help you.

   **c** Draw and label the line $y = 2x + 2$
     Use robot screens to help you.

   **d** Are the lines parallel?

**11** Look at each set of three lines.
Write down the two that are parallel.

a $y = 3x + 5$     $y = 4x - 3$     $y = 3x - 1$
b $y = 2x + 8$     $y = 3x - 5$     $y = 3x + 8$
c $y = 5x - 4$     $y = 4x - 5$     $y = 4x - 4$
d $y = 7x + 5$     $y = 5x - 3$     $y = 7x - 8$

· · · · · · · · · · · · · · · · · · · · · · · · · · · · · · · · · · · · · · · · · · · · · · · · ·

We can use robots to see if a point lies on a line.

---

*Example 1*

Does the point (3, 7) lie on the line $y = 2x$?

We put the $x$ co-ordinate into the '×2' robot.

$$3 \longrightarrow \boxed{\times 2} \longrightarrow 6$$

$x$ co-ordinate       $y$ co-ordinate

The robot tells us that the $y$ co-ordinate is 6.
The point (3, 6) lies on the line.
So the point (3, 7) does not lie on the line.

*Example 2*

Does the point (6, 19) lie on the line $y = 3x + 1$?

We put the $x$ co-ordinate into the robot:

$$6 \longrightarrow \boxed{\times 3} \xrightarrow{18} \boxed{+ 1} \longrightarrow 19$$

The robot tells us that the $y$ co-ordinate is 19.
The point (6, 19) lies on the line.

---

### Exercise 10:5

Each of these questions has a point and a line.
Find out if the point lies on the line.

**1** (3, 5)     $y = x + 1$
**2** (4, 3)     $y = x - 1$
**3** (3, 7)     $y = 3x - 1$
**4** (5, 8)     $y = 2x - 2$
**5** (3, 1)     $y = 3x - 8$
**6** (4, 11)     $y = 4x - 6$

Each of these questions has a line and some points.
The points lie on the line.
Find the missing co-ordinates.

**7**  $y = x + 3$       $(5, ...)$      $(3, ...)$      $(..., 5)$

**8**  $y = 2x + 5$      $(4, ...)$      $(7, ...)$      $(..., 25)$

**9**  $y = 3x - 2$      $(2, ...)$      $(8, ...)$      $(..., 7)$

**10**  $y = 5x - 4$     $(6, ...)$      $(9, ...)$      $(..., 16)$

· · · · · · · · · · · · · · · · · · · · · · · · · · · · · · · · · · · · · · · · · · · · · · · · · · · · · ·

We can use tables to plot graphs instead of robots.

---

*Example 1*

Draw the graph of $y = -2x + 3$

We can find the value of $y$ when $x = 1$

$$y = -2 \times \mathbf{1} + 3$$
$$= -2 \qquad + 3$$
$$= 1$$

Similarly when $x = \mathbf{2}$

$$y = -2 \times \mathbf{2} + 3$$
$$= -4 \qquad + 3$$
$$= -1$$

when $x = \mathbf{3}$

$$y = -2 \times \mathbf{3} + 3$$
$$= -6 \qquad + 3$$
$$= -3$$

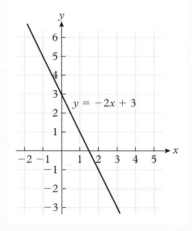

To save all this writing we can make a table:

| $x$ | 1 | 2 | 3 |
|---|---|---|---|
| $y$ | 1 | −1 | −3 |

We can now draw the graph.
The points to plot are $(1, 1)$ $(2, -1)$ $(3, -3)$

*Example 2*  Plot the graph $y = 3x - 2$

The table is:

| $x$ | 1 | 2 | 3 |
|---|---|---|---|
| $y$ | 1 | 4 | 7 |

We can now draw the graph.
The points to plot are
(1, 1) (2, 4) (3, 7)

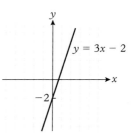

## Exercise 10:6

**1** Draw the graph of $y = -x + 7$
   **a** Copy and fill in the table.

| $x$ | 1 | 2 | 3 |
|---|---|---|---|
| $y$ | 6 | | |

   **b** Copy these axes on to squared paper.
   Draw your graph and label it.

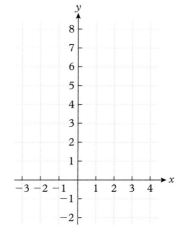

**2** Draw the graph of $y = -2x + 6$
Use a table.
Label your graph.

**3** Draw the graph of $y = -3x + 8$
Use a table.
Label your graph.

**4** The lines you have drawn in this Exercise are different from the lines
that you have drawn before.
   **a** Write down what is different about the lines.
   **b** What is different about the equations?

## *Exercise 10:7*

**1** Copy the axes on to squared paper.
Draw these three lines on the axes.
Remember to label your lines.
  **a** $y = -x$
  **b** $y = -2x$
  **c** $y = -3x$
  **d** Does the rule for steepness still work?

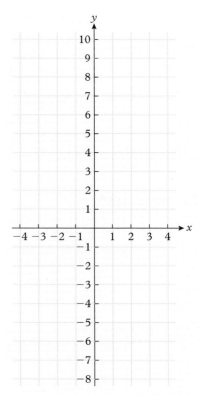

**2** Copy the axes from question **1** again.
Draw these three lines on the axes.
Remember to label your lines.
  **a** $y = -x + 1$
  **b** $y = -x + 2$
  **c** $y = -x + 3$
  **d** Does the rule for crossing the $y$ axis still work?

**3** Which line is the steeper in each of these pairs?
  **a** $y = -3x$ and $y = -5x$
  **b** $y = -2x$ and $y = -x$
  **c** $y = -3x + 5$ and $y = -4x$
  **d** $y = -5x + 7$ and $y = -3x - 5$

**4** Where will these lines cross the $y$ axis?
  **a** $y = -x + 7$
  **b** $y = -4x - 8$
  **c** $y = -6x + 2$
  **d** $y = -3x - 1$

# 3 Finding the equation

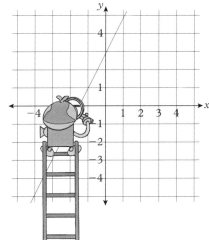

This is the line $y = 2x + 3$

The **2** tells us how steep the line is.
The **3** tells us where the line will cross the $y$ axis.

This is the line $y = 3x - 4$

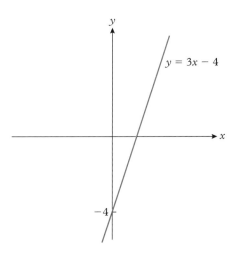

The **3** tells us how steep the line is.
The $-4$ tells us where the line crosses the $y$ axis.

This is the line $y = x + 7$
In algebra $x$ means $1x$
So the equation is $y = 1x + 7$

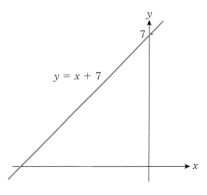

The **1** tells us how steep the line is.
The $+7$ tells us where the line crosses the $y$ axis.

Look at these two equations.    $y = 2x + 3$
$y = 2x + 5$

They both have a 2 telling us how steep they are.
The lines are parallel.

*Example*    Robot wants to find the equation of the red line.

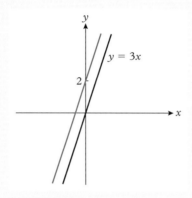

It is parallel to the line $y = 3x$
He knows part of the equation is $y = 3x + ...$

The red line crosses the $y$ axis at 2
The equation must be $y = 3x + 2$

### Exercise 10:8

Write down the equation of each red line.

**1**

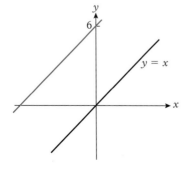

**2**

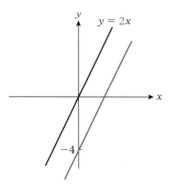

**3**

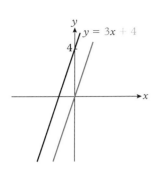

$y = 3x + 4$

**6**

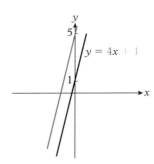

$y = 4x + 1$

**4**

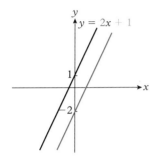

$y = 2x + 1$

**7**

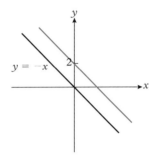

$y = -x$

**5**

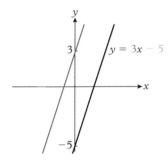

$y = 3x - 5$

**8**

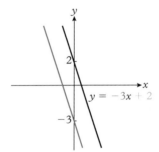

$y = -3x + 2$

**9**  Look at these diagrams.
The red line is going to be reflected in the $y$ axis.
What will be the equation of the new line?

**a**

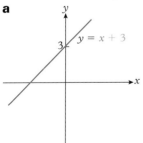

$y = x + 3$

**b**

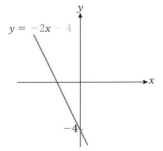

$y = -2x - 4$

In these questions there are 4 graphs and 4 equations.
Match the equation to the graph.

**10**  **a**

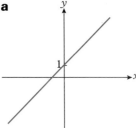

**c**

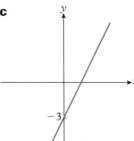

**b**

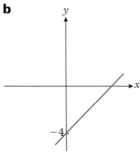

**d**

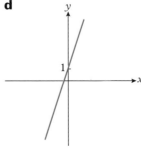

$$y = 3x + 1 \qquad y = x + 1 \qquad y = 2x - 3 \qquad y = x - 4$$

**11**  **a**

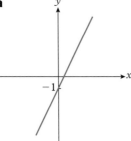

**c**

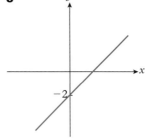

**b**

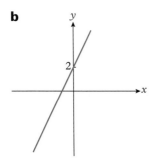

**d**

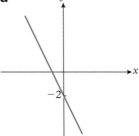

$$y = -2x - 2 \qquad y = 2x + 2 \qquad y = 2x - 1 \qquad y = x - 2$$

## Can't see the wood for the trees

The Forestry Commission has planted a new forest.
A tree is planted at each of the crossing points of a grid.

Look at the diagram showing part of the forest. It shows 25 trees on a 5 by 5 grid.
John is standing at the origin.
He can see the tree at (1, 1)
He can't see the trees at (2, 2), (3, 3), (4, 4) and (5, 5) because they are directly in line with (1, 1)

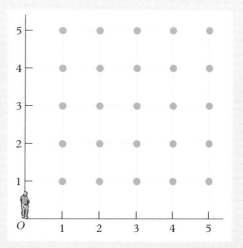

**1  a**  Which other trees can't he see?
　**b**  How many trees can't he see?

**2  a**  Draw a 6 by 6 grid.
　**b**  Mark on your grid the trees that John can't see.
　**c**  How many trees can't he see?

**3  a**  Try to predict how many trees John can't see on a 7 by 7 grid. Explain how you get this number.
　**b**  Draw the 7 by 7 grid to check.

**4**  Investigate other grids. Write a report about what you find out.

**1**   Write down the co-ordinates of the point of intersection of these lines.
   **a**   $x = 5$ and $y = 7$          **c**   $x = -5$ and $y = -1$
   **b**   $x = 4$ and $y = -5$        **d**   $x = -2$ and $y = 0$

**2**   Which vertical and horizontal lines have the point of intersection:
   **a**   $(5, 8)$        **b**   $(0, 4)$        **c**   $(-5, 5)$        **d**   $(7, -1)$

**3**   The vertices of a rectangle have co-ordinates
   $(-1, -2)$     $(-1, 6)$     $(3, 6)$     $(3, -2)$
   Write down the rules for the four sides of the rectangle.

**4**   Three sides of a square have the rules
   $x = -1$      $y = 3$      $x = 6$
   There are two possible squares.
   **a**   Write down the rule for the missing side of each square.
   **b**   Write down the co-ordinates of the vertices of each square.

**5**   **a**   Copy the axes on to squared paper.
     **b**   Plot these points in order:
       $(1, 4)$ $(3, 6)$ $(6, 6)$ $(6, 5)$ $(4, 5)$ $(4, 4)$
       Join them with a ruler as you go.
     **c**   Draw the line $y = 4$ on your axes.
     **d**   Reflect the shape in the line $y = 4$
     **e**   Write down the co-ordinates of the
       vertices of the new shape.

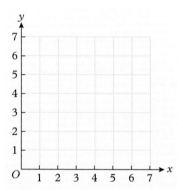

**6**   Which line is the steeper in each of these pairs?
   **a**   $y = 7x$ or $y = 4x$          **b**   $y = x$ or $y = 3x$

**7**   Where will these lines cross the $y$ axis?
   **a**   $y = x + 3$        **c**   $y = x + 1$        **e**   $y = 2x + 5$
   **b**   $y = x + 6$        **d**   $y = x - 9$        **f**   $y = 5x - 3$

**8**   Look at each set of three lines.
   Write down the two that are parallel.
   **a**   $y = 2x + 1$         $y = x - 1$         $y = 2x - 1$
   **b**   $y = 7x + 3$        $y = 4x + 3$       $y = 4x - 7$
   **c**   $y = 8x + 9$        $y = 9x - 8$       $y = 8x + 8$
   **d**   $y = 4x - 7$        $y = 7x - 4$       $y = 4x + 7$

**9** Look at each set of three lines.
Which line is the odd one out?
Give the reason why.

**a** $y = 3x - 1$     $y = 7x - 1$     $y = 6x + 1$
**b** $y = 4x - 5$     $y = 5x + 4$     $y = 4x + 5$
**c** $y = 7x - 1$     $y = x - 7$     $y = 7x + 7$

**10** Each of these questions has a point and a line.
Find out if the point lies on the line.

**a** $(2, 3)$    $y = x - 1$      **d** $(4, 12)$    $y = 2x + 3$
**b** $(5, 13)$    $y = 2x + 3$      **e** $(6, 24)$    $y = 5x - 4$
**c** $(3, 7)$    $y = 4x - 5$      **f** $(8, 31)$    $y = 3x + 7$

**11** Each of these questions has a line and some points.
The points lie on the line.
Find the missing co-ordinates.

**a** $y = x - 2$    $(4, \dots)$    $(\dots, 6)$    $(\dots, 0)$
**b** $y = 3x + 4$    $(5, \dots)$    $(2, \dots)$    $(\dots, 22)$
**c** $y = 6x - 5$    $(3, \dots)$    $(\dots, 7)$    $(\dots, 1)$
**d** $y = 2x - 8$    $(4, \dots)$    $(0, \dots)$    $(\dots, -10)$

Write down the equation of each red line.

**12**

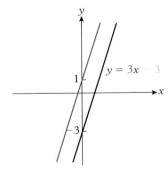

$y = 3x - 3$

**14**

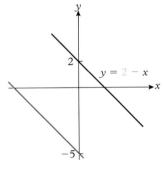

$y = 2 - x$

**13**

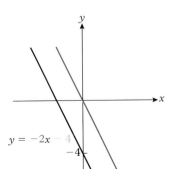

$y = -2x - 4$

**15**

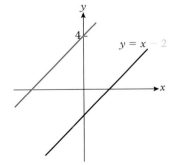

$y = x - 2$

1  **a**  Draw a set of axes with $x$ and $y$ from $-6$ to $+6$.
   **b**  Draw and label the three lines
       $$y = x + 1 \qquad y = 2x - 1 \qquad y = -3$$
   **c**  The three lines form a triangle.
       Write down the co-ordinates of the vertices of the triangle.
   **d**  Find the area of the triangle.

2  These three lines all cross at the same point.
   $$y = 2x - 9 \qquad y = 3 - x \qquad y = x - a$$
   Find the value of $a$.

3  The point $(3, -1)$ lies on some of these lines.
   Which lines does it lie on?
   $$y = 2x + 5 \qquad y = x - 4 \qquad y = 4x - 17 \qquad y = 11 - 4x$$

4  Find the equation of a line that is:
   **a**  parallel to the line $y = 3x - 5$ and crosses the $y$ axis at $+6$.
   **b**  parallel to the line $y = 4x + 2$ and goes through the origin.
   **c**  parallel to the line $y = 12 - 6x$ and crosses the $y$ axis at $7$.

5  Write down the equation of the line that is parallel to $y = 4x - 5$ and
   passes through the point:
   **a**  $(0, 3)$ **b**  $(0, -7)$ **c**  $(0, 0)$

6  **a**  Draw a set of axes with $x$ and $y$ from $-6$ to $+6$.
   **b**  Draw the line $y = 5 - x$
   **c**  Plot the points $(-3, 5)$ and $(4, -2)$
       Join them with a straight line.
   **d**  Write down the equation of the line joining the two points.

7  **a**  Draw a set of axes with $x$ and $y$ from $-6$ to $+6$.
   **b**  Plot the graph of $y + x = 4$
   **c**  Plot the graph of $y = 5x - 2$
   **d**  Write down the co-ordinates of the point of intersection.

- **Point of intersection**
  The point where two lines cross is
  called a **point of intersection**.

  The point of intersection of the
  lines $x = 3$ and $y = 1$ is $(3, 1)$.

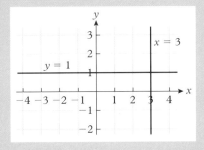

- **Equation**
  The rule of a line is called the **equation** of
  the line.

  The equation of this line is $y = x$

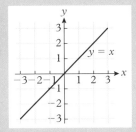

- Look at these equations
  $$y = 1x \qquad y = 2x - 1 \qquad y = 3x + 5 \qquad y = 4x + 2 \qquad y = 5x$$
  The red number tells us how steep the line is.
  The bigger the number the steeper the line.

  If two lines have the same red number they are parallel.
  The lines $y = 2x + 3$ and $y = 2x + 5$ are parallel.

  Look at these equations
  $$y = x + 1 \qquad y = 3x - 2 \qquad y = 5x + 3 \qquad y = x + 4 \qquad y = 2x + 5$$
  The blue number tells us where the line crosses the $y$ axis.
  The line $y = 5x + 2$ crosses the $y$ axis at $2$
  The line $y = x + 5$ crosses the $y$ axis at $5$

- We can use robots to see if a point lies on a line.

  *Example*    Does the point $(3, 7)$ lie on the line $y = 2x$?

  We put the $x$ co-ordinate into the '×2' robot.

  The robot tells us that the $y$ co-ordinate is 6.
  The point $(3, 6)$ lies on the line.
  So the point $(3, 7)$ does not lie on the line.

223

**1** Write down the rules for these lines.

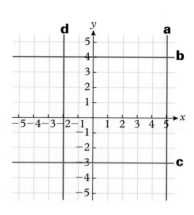

**2** Which vertical and horizontal lines cross at the point (5, 3)?

**3** Look at these equations of lines.
$y = 3x - 3$    $y = x + 7$    $y = 5x + 1$
**a** Which line is the steepest?
**b** Which line is the least steep?

**4** Look at these three lines.
$y = x + 4$    $y = x + 7$    $y = x$
**a** What can you say about these lines?
**b** Where does the line $y = x + 7$ cross the $y$ axis?
**c** Which line is highest up the grid?
**d** Which line is lowest on the grid?
**e** Which two lines would the line $y = x + 2$ be between?

**5** Does the point (4, 6) lie on the line $y = 2x - 2$?

**6** These points lie on the line $y = 3x - 2$
Fill in the missing co-ordinates.
(4, ...)   (0, ...)   (..., 16)

**7** Write down the equation of each red line.

**a**

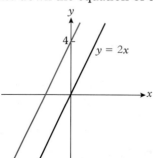

**b**

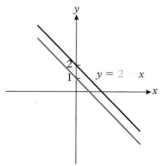

# 11 Ratio

QUESTIONS

EXTENSION

SUMMARY

TEST YOURSELF

Most maps of the UK are produced from the Ordnance Survey. The Board of Ordnance used to be in charge of defending Britain. (Ordnance means military supplies.) They wanted good maps for soldiers to use so they began the Ordnance Survey.

The Ordnance Survey put 'bench marks' in places like the stone of bridges or on the tops of hills. They use these points to measure from.

*A bench mark*

*A large-scale Ordnance Survey map*

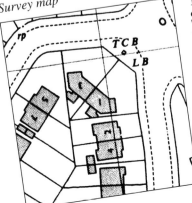

The Ordnance Survey bring maps up to date from time to time. They mark new buildings and roads.

They produce large-scale maps and smaller-scale maps.

# 1 The metric system

Jane and Andy have broken a window.
Their father is measuring to find the size of glass that is needed to repair the window.
His tape measure has one side marked in feet and inches. The other side is marked in metric units.

Jane has a pencil and paper to write down the measurements.
Jane asks her father what units he is using.
He says he is using millimetres.

## ◄◄ REPLAY ►

### Units of length

$$10 \text{ millimetres (mm)} = 1 \text{ centimetre (cm)}$$
$$100 \text{ centimetres} = 1 \text{ metre (m)}$$
$$1000 \text{ metres} = 1 \text{ kilometre (km)}$$

*Example*

| 0mm 10 | 20 | 30 | 40 | 50 | 60 | 70 | 80 |
| 0cm 1 | 2 | 3 | 4 | 5 | 6 | 7 | 8 |

This line measures 5.7 cm (or 57 mm).

### Converting units within the metric system

*Examples*

**1** Convert 6.75 m to cm

$$6.75 \text{ m} = 6.75 \times 100 \text{ cm}$$
$$= 675 \text{ cm}$$

**2** Convert 6400 m to km

$$6400 \text{ m} = 6400 \div 1000 \text{ km}$$
$$= 6.4 \text{ km}$$

## Exercise 11:1

**1** Convert the units in each of these.
   **a** 4 km to m     **d** 6 cm to mm     **g** 30 mm to cm
   **b** 400 cm to m    **e** 15 km to m    **h** 5000 m to km
   **c** 20 mm to cm   **f** 2 m to cm      **i** 5 m to mm

**2** Convert the units in each of these.
   **a** 285 cm to m    **d** 0.6 cm to mm   **g** 65 mm to cm
   **b** 5500 m to km   **e** 7.4 km to m    **h** 0.9 km to m
   **c** 8.7 cm to mm   **f** 3.75 m to cm   **i** 0.15 m to mm

**3** Write down the unit that completes each sentence.
Choose from mm, cm, m, km.
   **a** A paperclip is about 30 ... long.
   **b** A door is about 2 ... high.
   **c** A teaspoon is about 13 ... long.
   **d** The distance from London to Cardiff is about 240 ...
   **e** A filing cabinet is about 45 ... wide.
   **f** A football pitch is about 70 ... wide.
   **g** A fingernail is about 10 ... wide.
   **h** The English Channel is about 33 ... across.

## Converting Imperial units of length to metric units

1 in = 2.5 cm      1 yd = 0.9 m      1 mile = 1.6 km

*Examples*

**1** Convert 3 in to cm
   1 in = 2.5 cm
   3 in = 3 × 2.5 cm
       = 7.5 cm

**2** Convert 3.5 yd to m
   1 yd = 0.9 m
   3.5 yd = 3.5 × 0.9 m
        = 3.15 m

**3** Convert 4 miles to km
   1 mile = 1.6 km
   4 miles = 4 × 1.6 km
        = 6.4 km

## Exercise 11:2

**1** Convert the units in each of these.
   **a** 2 in to cm     **c** 7 miles to km    **e** 20 miles to km
   **b** 6 yd to m     **d** 10 yd to m      **f** 12 inches (1 foot) to cm

**2** Convert the red lengths into metric units.
   **a** Julie's book is 8 in by 6.5 in.
   **b** Deepal's bedroom door is 30 in wide.
   **c** A cricket pitch is 22 yd long.
   **d** Allison has a 1 foot ruler.
      She also has a smaller ruler 6 in long.
   **e** Paul runs the London
      marathon, which is 26.2 miles.
   **f** Stanthorne High's tennis court
      is 26 yd by 12 yd.

1 inch is about $2\frac{1}{2}$ cm.
1 yard is a bit less than 1 metre.
1 mile is a bit more than $1\frac{1}{2}$ km.

**3** Estimate these in metric units.

| | | | | | | | |
|---|---|---|---|---|---|---|---|
| **a** | 6 inches | **e** | 2 yd | **i** | 2 miles | **m** | 15 inches |
| **b** | 8 inches | **f** | 12 yd | **j** | 30 miles | **n** | 27 inches |
| **c** | 10 inches | **g** | 25 yd | **k** | 1000 miles | **o** | 17 miles |
| **d** | 20 inches | **h** | 100 yd | **l** | 16 miles | **p** | 55 miles |

**4** **a** 1 in = 2.5 cm, 1 yd = 0.9 m, 1 mile = 1.6 km
      Use these and multiplication to convert the lengths in question **3**
      into metric units.
   **b** Use your answers to **a** to check your estimates in question **3**.

**Units of mass**

Units of mass have similar names to units of length.
   1000 milligrams (mg) = 1 gram (g)
      1000 grams = 1 kilogram (kg)
         1000 kg = 1 tonne (t)

A quarter teaspoon of sugar weighs about 1 gram.
An ordinary bag of sugar weighs 1 kilogram.

## Converting units within the metric system

*Examples*

**1** Convert 2.5 kg to g

$$2.5 \, kg = 2.5 \times 1000 \, g$$
$$= 2500 \, g$$

**2** Convert 5000 g to kg

$$5000 \, g = 5000 \div 1000 \, kg$$
$$= 5 \, kg$$

## Exercise 11:3

**1** Convert the units in each of these.

| | | | | | |
|---|---|---|---|---|---|
| **a** | 4 kg to g | **e** | 6 kg to g | **i** | 125 mg to g |
| **b** | 7000 mg to g | **f** | 55 kg to g | **j** | 0.3 g to mg |
| **c** | 2000 g to kg | **g** | 85 mg to g | **k** | 650 g to kg |
| **d** | 8000 kg to t | **h** | 0.6 kg to g | **l** | 1.5 t to kg |

## Converting Imperial units of mass to metric units

1 ounce is about 30 grams.                    (16 ounces = 1 pound)

1 pound is a bit less than half a kilogram.   (14 pounds = 1 stone)

1 ton is a bit more than 1 tonne.

**2** Estimate the red amounts in metric units.

  **a** A newborn baby boy weighs about 8 pounds.

  **b** An egg weighs about 2 ounces.

  **c** A woman weighs about 140 pounds.

  **d** A small car weighs about 2 tons.

  **e** An orange weighs about 6 ounces.

  **f** A large roast turkey weighs about 20 pounds.

Sometimes we need to be more accurate.

1 ounce (oz) = 28 g    1 pound (lb) = 450 g = 0.45 kg    1 kg = 2.2 lb

*Examples*

**1**  Convert 3 ounces to g

1 oz = 28 g
3 ounces = 3 × 28 g
= 84 g

**2**  Convert 5 pounds to kg

1 pound = 0.45 kg
5 pounds = 5 × 0.45 kg
= 2.25 kg

**3**  Convert the units in each of these.
   **a**  4 ounces to g
   **b**  0.5 ounces to g
   **c**  3 pounds to kg
   **d**  6.5 pounds to kg
   **e**  8 ounces to g
   **f**  14 pounds to kg
   **g**  100 pounds to kg
   **h**  12 ounces to g
   **i**  7 pounds to kg

**4**  One Imperial ton equals 2240 pounds.
   **a**  Convert one ton to kilograms using 1 pound = 0.4536 kg
   Give your answer correct to the nearest whole number.
   **b**  An Imperial ton is larger than a metric tonne.
   Find the percentage extra in an Imperial ton.

## Units of capacity

Units of capacity have similar names to units of length.
1000 millilitres (m*l*) = 1 litre (*l*)
100 centilitres (c*l*) = 1 litre

5 m*l*       75 c*l*       1 litre

The plastic medicine spoon holds 5 m*l*.
The bottle holds 75 c*l*.
The carton of fruit juice holds 1 litre.

We can convert units of capacity in the same way as units of length or mass.

## Exercise 11:4

**1** Convert the units in each of these.
   **a** 3000 ml to *l*       **d** 4.5 *l* to ml       **g** 800 ml to *l*
   **b** 75 cl to *l*         **e** 0.5 *l* to ml       **h** 5600 ml to *l*
   **c** 7 *l* to ml          **f** 9000 ml to *l*      **i** 0.25 *l* to ml

## Converting Imperial units of capacity to metric units

One pint is a bit more than half a litre.
One gallon is about $4\frac{1}{2}$ litres.

**2** Estimate the red quantities in metric units.
   **a** A washing-up bowl holds about
      12 pints of water.
   **b** A household bucket holds about
      2 gallons of water.
   **c** A dustbin would hold about
      20 gallons of water.
   **d** A classroom waste bin would
      hold about 7 gallons of water.

Sometimes we need to be more accurate.
1 pint = 0.57 *l*     1 gallon = 4.5 *l*     (8 pints = 1 gallon)

*Examples*    **1** Convert 4 pints to litres.   **2** Convert 3 gallons to litres.
               1 pint = 0.57 *l*             1 gallon = 4.5 *l*
               4 pints = 4 × 0.57 *l*         3 gallons = 3 × 4.5 *l*
                     = 2.28 *l*                  = 13.5 *l*

**3** Convert each of these quantities to litres.
   **a** 7 pints     **c** 0.5 pints     **e** 5 pints     **g** 3.5 pints
   **b** 15 gallons  **d** 5.6 gallons  **f** 9 gallons   **h** 1.4 gallons

**4** An Imperial gallon is 4.546 litres.
   An American gallon is smaller. It is 3.785 litres.
   **a** Find the difference between an Imperial and an American gallon in
      millilitres.
   **b** Find the percentage more in an Imperial gallon than in an
      American gallon.

# 2   Introduction to ratio

4 cm

8 cm

← 3 cm → ← 6 cm →

Year 8 have had their photographs taken.
Sonya has bought the large size for her mother.
The small size is for her school record.

The width of the small photograph is half the width of the
large photograph.
Also, the length of the small photograph is half the length of the
large one.

We can write this fraction another way: **1 : 2** (said as 'one *to* two').

| Ratio | **Ratio** is a measure of the relative size of two things. |
|---|---|
| *Example* | The ratio of the width of the small photograph to the width of the large photograph is 3 cm : 6 cm (said as 3 cm *to* 6 cm). |
| | We can write ratios without units.    3 cm : 6 cm = 3 : 6 |
| | We can simplify ratios like fractions.    $\frac{3}{6} = \frac{1}{2}$ so 3 : 6 = 1 : 2 |

## Exercise 11:5

1  **a**  Measure this square.
      Copy it into your book.
   **b**  Draw a new square with sides half as long.
   **c**  Write down these ratios.
      Give your answers in their simplest form.
      (1) The ratio of the sides of the *small* square to
          the sides of the *large* square.
      (2) The ratio of the sides of the *large* square to
          the sides of the *small* square.

2  **a**  Measure this rectangle.
      Copy it into your book.
   **b**  Draw a new rectangle with sides three times as long.
   **c**  Write down these ratios.
      Give your answers in their simplest form.
      (1) The ratio of the width of the *small* rectangle
          to the width of the *large* rectangle.
      (2) The ratio of the length of the *large* rectangle
          to the length of the *small* rectangle.

3  **a**  Measure the length and width of each rectangle.

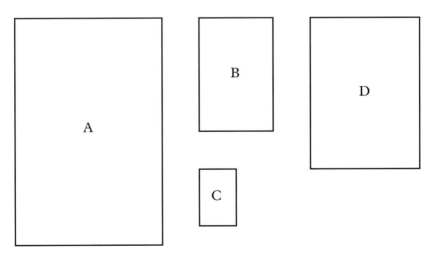

   **b**  Which rectangle does not have its width and length in the
      same ratio as the others?

*Example*

A car-hire company has 8 cars and 4 vans for hire.
Find:
**a** the ratio of cars to vans
**b** the ratio of vans to cars
Give your answers in their simplest form.

**a** cars : vans $= 8 : 4$
$= 2 : 1$

**b** vans : cars $= 4 : 8$    (simplify like the fraction $\frac{4}{8} = \frac{1}{2}$)
$= 1 : 2$

## Exercise 11:6

Give all the ratios in this exercise in their simplest form.

**1** Laura works 4 hours a week. Nancy works 3 hours.
  **a** What is the ratio of Nancy's work time to Laura's work time?
  **b** What is the ratio of Laura's work time to Nancy's work time?

**2** Alan is 12 years old. His little sister Claire is 6 years old.
  **a** What is the ratio of Alan's age to Claire's age?
  **b** What is the ratio of Claire's age to Alan's age?

**3** Gurjeet has £8 pocket money. His friend Dale has £6.
  **a** What is the ratio of Gurjeet's pocket money to Dale's pocket money?
  **b** What is the ratio of Dale's pocket money to Gurjeet's pocket money?

**4** There are 30 pupils in 8L. 10 of them are girls.
  **a** What is the ratio of girls to boys?
  **b** What is the ratio of boys to girls?

**5**  **a** What is the ratio of girls to boys?
  **b** What is the ratio of boys to girls?
  **c** What fraction of the children are girls?
  **d** What fraction of the children are boys?

**6** Here are some patterns made with red and blue cubes.
For each pattern write down the ratio of red cubes to blue cubes.
Give your answers in their simplest forms.

**a**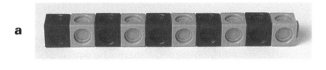

**b**

**c**

**d** Make up some patterns of your own.
Write down the ratio of red cubes to blue cubes for your patterns.

**7 a** 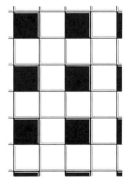     **b**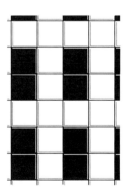

The diagrams show two repeated patterns which are parts of
floor tilings.
In each case write down the ratio of black tiles to white tiles.
**c** Make up a pattern of your own.
Write down the ratio for your pattern.

# 3 Proportion

Robert is cooking some fruit buns. The recipe is for 20 buns but Robert only wants to make 10. He needs to change the amounts in the recipe.

### Exercise 11:7

**1** Here are the ingredients to make 20 fruit buns.

     14 oz self-raising flour
     4 oz sultanas
     2 oz raisins
     6 oz sugar
     7 oz margarine
     1 teaspoon mixed spice
     2 small eggs

  **a** Write down the ingredients that you need to make 10 buns.
  **b** What is the ratio of the amounts of ingredients for 10 buns to the amounts for 20 buns? Give the ratio in its simplest form.
  **c** Write down the ingredients that you need to make 30 buns.
  **d** What is the ratio of the amounts of ingredients for 30 buns to the amounts for 20 buns? Give the ratio in its simplest form.

**2** The instructions on a bottle of orange squash say
'One part squash to five parts water.'
Louise is making a jug of the orange drink.
  **a** Write down, in figures, the ratio of squash to water in the diluted drink.
  **b** Louise dilutes 200 ml of the squash.
    How much water does she use?
  **c** How much of the orange drink does Louise have in her jug?

**3** The instructions on a bottle of carpet shampoo say
'One part shampoo to 30 parts water.'
  **a** Write down, in figures, the ratio of shampoo to water.
  **b** The bottle of shampoo contains 500 m*l*.
    How much water do you add if you use the whole bottle?
  **c** How much diluted shampoo will you have altogether?

**4** Mr Bean uses three parts sand to one part cement to make mortar.
  **a** Write down the ratio of sand to cement in figures.
  **b** (1) How much sand does Mr Bean mix with 6 kg cement?
     (2) How much mortar does this make altogether?
  **c** (1) How much cement does Mr Bean mix with 30 kg of sand?
     (2) How much mortar does this make altogether?

**5** The instructions on a medicine bottle are
'Dilute with two parts water.'
  **a** Write down the ratio of medicine to water.
  **b** (1) How much water is needed to dilute 5 m*l* of medicine?
     (2) How much diluted medicine is there altogether?
  **c** A nurse measures 30 m*l* of water to mix with some of the medicine.
    How much of the medicine is she using?

**6** A photograph is 7 cm long and 4.5 cm wide.
It is enlarged to give a photograph
21 cm long.
  **a** Write down the ratio of the small
    photograph to the large one.
  **b** Work out the width of the large
    photograph.

7 cm

4.5 cm

21 cm

**7** A photograph is 5 cm wide and 8 cm long.
It is enlarged to give a photograph 20 cm long.
Work out the width of the enlarged photograph.

?

## More simplifying of ratios

*Example*    Simplify these ratios.  **a** $8 : 12$    **b** $24 : 6$

  **a** 4 goes into 8 and 12    $8 : 12 = \dfrac{8}{4} : \dfrac{12}{4} = 2 : 3$

  **b** 6 goes into 24 and 6    $24 : 6 = \dfrac{24}{6} : \dfrac{6}{6} = 4 : 1$

**1**  Simplify these ratios.

| | | | | |
|---|---|---|---|---|
| **a** 5:15 | **d** 18:30 | **g** 100:20 | **j** 9:27 |
| **b** 14:21 | **e** 25:10 | **h** 88:55 | **k** 36:24 |
| **c** 16:20 | **f** 30:20 | **i** 12:18 | **l** 30:25 |

. . . . . . . . . . . . . . . . . . . . . . . . . . . . . . . . . . . . . . . . . . . . . . . . . . . . . . . .

## Sharing in ratios

*Example*    Carl and his sister Sian win a prize of £20. They decide to share the prize in the ratio of their ages.
Carl is 15 and Sian is 10.
How much do they each receive?

The ratio of Carl's age to Sian's age is $15:10 = 3:2$
Carl gets 3 shares and Sian gets 2 shares.
$3 + 2 = 5$ shares are needed.
One share is £20 ÷ 5 = £4
Carl gets £4 × 3 = £12
Sian gets £4 × 2 = £8
*Check:* £12 + £8 = £20

**2**  Share these amounts of money in the ratios given.
Check your answer each time.

| | | | | | | |
|---|---|---|---|---|---|---|
| **a** £12 | 2:1 | **e** £18 | 5:4 | **i** £27 | 20:4 |
| **b** £15 | 1:4 | **f** £30 | 7:3 | **j** £24 | 2:1:1 |
| **c** £24 | 3:5 | **g** £100 | 15:35 | **k** £36 | 3:2:1 |
| **d** £28 | 3:4 | **h** £30 | 10:14 | **l** £40 | 5:2:3 |

**3**  Charmaine makes some lemon drink.
She uses five parts water to one part lemon squash.
How much water and how much squash are there in 3 litres of the drink?

**4**  A ready-mix concrete has one part cement, two parts sand and three parts gravel.
How much of each is there in 60 kg of the mix?

. . . . . . . . . . . . . . . . . . . . . . . . . . . . . . . . . . . . . . . . . . . . . . . . . . . . . . . .

These two statues are made of bronze. The leopard contains two parts tin to fifteen parts copper, so the ratio of tin to copper is $2:15$
The horse contains three parts tin to twenty parts copper, so the ratio of tin to copper is $3:20$
Which statue has the higher proportion of copper?

*Example*

Convert these ratios into the form $1:n$
**a** $2:15$    **b** $3:20$

**a** To convert $2:15$ into the form $1:n$ we need to divide by 2.

$$2:15 = \frac{2}{2} : \frac{15}{2} = 1:7.5$$

**b** To convert $3:20$ into the form $1:n$ we need to divide by 3.

$$3:20 = \frac{3}{3} : \frac{20}{3} = 1:7.33 \text{ (correct to 2 dp)}$$

The ratio of tin to copper in the leopard is $1:7.5$
The ratio of tin to copper in the horse is $1:7.33$
7.5 is larger than 7.33
The statue of the leopard has the higher proportion of copper.

## Exercise 11:9

**1** Convert these ratios into the form $1:n$
Where necessary round to 2 dp.

| | | | | |
|---|---|---|---|---|
| **a** $2:8$ | **d** $3:18$ | **g** $2.5:5$ | **j** $7:25$ | **m** $4:2$ |
| **b** $2:11$ | **e** $3:25$ | **h** $1.5:6$ | **k** $0.2:0.72$ | **n** $5.6:2.8$ |
| **c** $4:14$ | **f** $5:16$ | **i** $0.8:22$ | **l** $0.6:0.39$ | **o** $10.8:2.4$ |

**2** A disinfectant has 'Active ingredient 12.5%' on its label. The rest is water.
   **a** Write down the percentage of water.
   **b** Write down the ratio of active ingredient to water.
   **c** Convert the ratio into the form $1:n$
   **d** What fraction of the disinfectant is the active ingredient?

**3** Peter does not like to eat too much fat.
Cake mix A uses seven parts fat to eleven parts flour.
Cake mix B uses five parts fat to eight parts flour.
Use the method of ratios to decide which cake mix Peter should choose.

# 4 Maps and scales

Tony wants to draw a plan of his room.
Denis helps Tony measure the room.
Tony has to choose a scale before he can draw his plan.

◀◀ **REPLAY** ▶

**Scale**    The **scale** of a drawing gives the relative size of the actual length to the drawn length.

## Exercise 11:10

**1**   Tony makes a scale drawing of his room. He uses a scale of 1 cm to 1 metre.
  **a** (1) Measure the length of the drawing in centimetres.
     (2) Write down the actual length of the room in metres.
  **b** (1) Measure the width of the drawing in centimetres.
     (2) Write down the actual width of the room in metres.

*Scale:* 1 cm to 1 m

**2**   Tony decides his drawing is too small.
   He draws a new rectangle with sides twice as long.
  **a** Write down the length and width of the new rectangle in centimetres.
  **b** How many centimetres represent 1 metre on the new scale?

We can find the length of a curved line.
We use a piece of string.
Place the string on top of the curved line.
Mark the length of the line on the string.
Measure the marked length of the string
with a ruler.

We can use this method for finding
distances on maps.

Tracey and Drew are planning a
walk. They are going from Cark
and Cartmel station south along
the road to West Plain Farm.
They will then turn west to
Cowpren Point along the
footpath.
From there they will walk back to
the station through Canon
Winder, Sand Gate and
Flookburgh.
Tracey and Drew can find out
how far they will walk using
the scale.

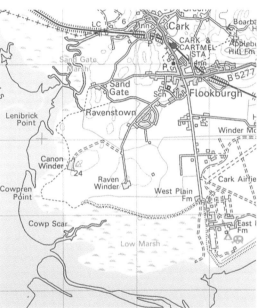

*Scale:* 2 cm to 1 km

**3** **a** (1) Measure the length on the map of the wide runway at
  Cark Airfield.
  (2) Write down this distance in kilometres.
  **b** (1) Measure the distance on the map going south from Cark and
  Cartmel station to West Plain Farm.
  (2) Write down this distance in kilometres.
  **c** (1) Measure the distance on the map that a seagull flies from
  Cowpren Point to Flookburgh crossroads.
  (2) Write down this distance in kilometres.
  **d** (1) Estimate the length on the map of Tracey and Drew's walk.
  Use your string to help you.
  (2) Give the length of their walk in kilometres.

We can write map scales as a ratio of numbers.

---

*Example*     Express the scale 2 cm to 1 km as a ratio in the form $1:n$

We need to convert 1 km to cm.     1 km = 1000 m
$$1000\,m = 1000 \times 100\,cm$$
$$= 100\,000\,cm$$
The scale is 2 cm to 100 000 cm or 2 : 100 000 = 1 : 50 000
Answer: 2 cm to 1 km can be written as 1 : 50 000

---

### Exercise 11:11

**1**  Copy and fill in:
A scale of 1 cm to 1 km = 1 : ?
A scale of 2 cm to 1 km = 2 : ? = 1 : ?
A scale of 4 cm to 1 km = 4 : ? = 1 : ?

**2**  Express the scale 1 cm to 2 km as a ratio in the form 1 : ?

**3**  Express the scale 1 inch to 1 mile as a ratio in the form $1:n$
12 in = 1 foot,  3 ft = 1 yd,  1760 yd = 1 mile

---

*Example*     Sharon is drawing a plan of the school field.
She is using a scale of 1 : 500
**a**  What actual length does 4 cm on her plan represent?
**b**  The football pitch is 90 m long.
How long will it be on Sharon's plan?

**a**  4 cm represents $4 \times 500$ cm = 2000 cm
$$2000\,cm = 2000 \div 100\,m$$
$$= 20\,m$$

**b**  An actual length of 90 m is $90 \times 100$ cm = 9000 cm
$$9000\,cm \div 500 = 18\,cm$$
The pitch will be 18 cm long on Sharon's plan.

*Remember:* Always check to see if your answers are sensible.

---

**4**  John has drawn a plan of his form room. He has used a scale of 1 : 100
**a**  The plan is 7 cm wide.
How wide is John's form room?
**b**  John's form room is 9 m long.
How long is the plan?

**5**   Mr Turner is making a play house for his daughter's fourth birthday.
It is a copy of Mr Turner's own house. The scale is 1 : 5
  **a**   Mr Turner's house is 10 m high.
   How high is the play house?
  **b**   The play house is 3 m long.
   How long is the actual house?

**6**   Nicholas is making a scale model
of an aeroplane.
The ratio of lengths on the
model plane to lengths on the
actual plane is 1 : 10
Copy the table.
Fill it in.

| Part of plane | Model plane | Actual plane |
|---|---|---|
| length of wing | 1 m | |
| door height | 20 cm | |
| door width | | 90 cm |
| tail height | 15 cm | |
| overall length | | 20 m |
| number of seats | | 60 |

**7**   This street map is of part of
Runcorn in Cheshire. It has a scale
of 1 : 12 000
  **a**   Measure the length of Park Road
   on the map.
  **b**   Work out the actual length of
   Park Road.
  **c**   Part of Heath Road is shown on
   the map.
   Heath Road has an actual length
   of 2.4 km.
   Work out the length of the whole
   of Heath Road on this map.

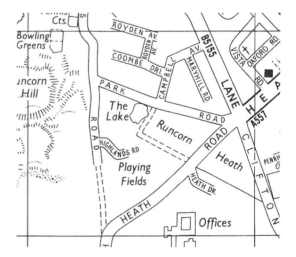

**8**   Mr Singh has a road map with a scale of 1 : 300 000
  **a**   Two towns are 8 cm apart on the map.
   What is their actual distance apart?
  **b**   Two other towns are an actual distance of 60 km apart.
   How many centimetres apart are they on Mr Singh's map?

243

**1** Convert the units in each of these.
  **a** 380 cm to m       **e** 7250 g to kg       **i** 17.9 cm to mm
  **b** 1.7 kg to g        **f** 8.6 km to m        **j** 0.35 g to mg
  **c** 0.6 *l* to m*l*     **g** 50 000 m*l* to *l*   **k** 95 cm to m
  **d** 1900 mg to g       **h** 14.7 m to cm       **l** 0.25 m to mm

**2** Give an estimate of these Imperial quantities.
  Use the metric unit given.
  **a** 12 inches or 1 foot (cm)   **d** 4 ounces (g)      **g** 4 pints (*l*)
  **b** 5 miles (km)               **e** 2 pounds (kg)     **h** 2 gallons (*l*)
  **c** 20 yd (m)                  **f** 1 pound (g)

**3** **a** Measure the sides of this rectangle.
  **b** Draw a larger rectangle so that the ratio
     of the sides of the small rectangle to the
     sides of the large rectangle is 1 : 4

**4** Give each answer in its simplest form.
  **a** What is the ratio of dogs to cats?
  **b** What is the ratio of cats to dogs?
  **c** What fraction of the animals are cats?
  **d** What fraction of the animals are dogs?

**5** A cake recipe uses one part sugar to four parts flour.
  **a** How much flour do you need when you use 150 g of sugar?
  **b** How much sugar do you need when you use 1 kg of flour?

**6** Convert these ratios in the form 1 : *n*
  Where necessary round to 2 dp.
  **a** 2 : 3. 4       **b** 9 : 25       **c** 14 : 8       **d** 0.77 : 0.35

**7** Share these amounts of money in the ratios given.
  Check your answer each time.
  **a** £50  3 : 7     **b** £15  15 : 10     **c** £240  16 : 8     **d** £90  2 : 3 : 4

**8** Express these scales as ratios in the form 1 : *n*
  **a** 1 cm to 1 m       **b** 1 cm to 2 m       **c** 2 cm to 1 m

**9** Mr Brick the builder has a plan of a new housing estate.
  The scale is 1 : 1000
  **a** The actual road through the estate is 500 m long.
     How long is the road on the plan?
  **b** A bungalow is 1.2 cm wide on the plan.
     How wide is the actual bungalow?

244

**1** Learn these to help you remember the size of some Imperial units.
- Two and a quarter pounds of jam weigh about a kilogram.
- A litre of water's a pint and three quarters.
- A metre measures three foot three, it's longer than a yard you see.

Can you think of any more helpful rhymes?

**2** These are sayings, phrases and names of people.
The words that complete the sayings have been converted to metric units.
Write down the correct words.
- **a** 30 cm in the grave
- **b** 45 l hat
- **c** Sharon 6.4 kg
- **d** New Scotland 0.9 metres
- **e** 0.57 l sized
- **f** 0.45 kg of flesh
- **g** Give him 2.5 cm and he will take 1.6 km
- **h** A miss is as good as 1.6 km
- **i** It went down like 1016 kg of bricks
- **j** She hasn't got 28 g of common sense
- **k** Full 183 cm five thy father lies …
- **l** Pooh wandered into the 0.405 km² Wood
- **m** Spare the 5.03 m and spoil the child
- **n** A 20 m gang
- **o** Jack and 0.14 l went up the …

Can you make up some more of these yourself?

**3** The instructions on a bottle of lemon squash say
'Dilute with six parts water.'
- **a** (1) Gemma makes a jug of the drink. She measures 150 ml of squash. How much water does she need?
  - (2) How much diluted squash does Gemma have altogether?
- **b** Gemma makes a second jug of the drink. She dilutes the squash in the same ratio as before to get 1.575 l of drink altogether. How much water does the diluted drink contain?

**4** Which is the bigger ratio, $1.4 : 1.8$ or $8 : 11$?

**5** Find $x$ and $y$    **a** $2 : 9 = 11 : x$    **b** $4 : y + 3 = 5 : 17$

**6** The angles of a quadrilateral are in the ratio $3 : 4 : 5 : 6$
Work out the angles of the quadrilateral.

**7** A cake weighs 550 g.
There is twice as much flour as sugar and one and a half times as much sugar as fat. There are no other ingredients.
How much of each ingredient is there in the cake?

**8**

1          2          3

**a** Write down the ratio of white counters to black counters for each pattern.
Give your answers in the simplest form.

**b** Predict the answer for the fourth pattern.
Draw the fourth pattern to see if you are right.

**c** Copy this table.
Use the pattern to fill it in.

| Number of pattern | 1 | 2 | 3 | 4 | 5 | 6 |
|---|---|---|---|---|---|---|
| Number of black counters | | | | | | |
| Number of white counters | | | | | | |

**d** Write down the ratio of white counters to black counters for the $n$th pattern, where $n$ is the $n$umber of the pattern.

**e** (1) How many white counters will there be in the 20th pattern?
(2) Explain in words how you got this answer.

**f** Write a rule in algebra to find the number of *white* counters if you know the $n$umber of the pattern.

**9** The A series of paper sizes is used for standard book printing and stationery. Here is part of the series.
The measurements are given in millimetres.

| A2 | $420 \times 594$ |
|---|---|
| A3 | $297 \times 420$ |
| A4 | $210 \times 297$ |
| A5 | $148 \times 210$ |

**a** (1) For A2 paper, write down the ratio of the width to the length.
(2) Convert the ratio into the form $1 : n$
Write down all the figures on the calculator display for $n$.

**b** Repeat part **a** for A3, A4 and A5 paper.

**c** Write down all the figures on the calculator display for $\sqrt{2}$
Compare your answer for $\sqrt{2}$ with the values of $n$ in parts **a** and **b**.
Why do you think the ratio varies slightly?

**d** Work out the size of A6 paper.

**10** A map of North America uses a scale of $1 : 7\,500\,000$

**a** On this map New York and Pittsburgh are 7 cm apart.
Estimate their actual distance apart.

**b** Detroit is about 825 km from New York.
Write down their distance apart on the map in centimetres.

- **Length**     1 inch is about $2\frac{1}{2}$ cm.           1 in = 2.5 cm
  1 yard is a bit less than 1 metre.     1 yd = 0.9 m
  1 mile is a bit more than $1\frac{1}{2}$ km.     1 mile = 1.6 km

- **Mass**     1000 mg = 1 g     1000 g = 1 kg     1000 kg = 1 t
  1 ounce is about 30 grams.               1 ounce (oz) = 28 g
  1 pound is a bit less than half a kilogram.     1 pound (lb) = 450 g = 0.45 kg
  1 ton is a bit more than 1 tonne          1 kg = 2.2 pounds

- **Capacity**     1000 m$l$ = 1 $l$     100 c$l$ = 1 $l$
  One pint is a bit more than half a litre.     1 pint = 0.57 $l$
  One gallon is about $4\frac{1}{2}$ litres.     1 gallon = 4.5 $l$

- **Ratio**     **Ratio** is a measure of the relative size of two things.

  *Example*     Simplify the ratio 8 : 12

  4 goes into 8 and 12          $8 : 12 = \dfrac{8}{4} : \dfrac{12}{4} = 2 : 3$

- *Example*     Carl and his sister Sian win a prize of £20. They decide to share the prize in the ratio of their ages.
  Carl is 15 and Sian is 10.
  How much do they each receive?

  The ratio of Carl's age to Sian's age is 15 : 10 = 3 : 2
  Carl gets 3 shares and Sian gets 2 shares.
  3 + 2 = 5 shares are needed.
  One share is £20 ÷ 5 = £4
  Carl gets £4 × 3 = £12
  Sian gets £4 × 2 = £8     *Check:* £12 + £8 = £20

- *Example*     Convert the ratio 2 : 15 into the form 1 : $n$

  We need to divide by 2.     $2 : 15 = \dfrac{2}{2} : \dfrac{15}{2} = 1 : 7.5$

- *Example*     Express the scale 2 cm to 1 km as a ratio in the form 1 : $n$
  We need to convert 1 km to cm.     1 km = 1000 m
  1000 m = 1000 × 100 cm
  = 100 000 cm
  The scale is 2 cm to 100 000 cm or 2 : 100 000 = 1 : 50 000

- *Example*     Sharon is drawing a plan of the school field.
  She is using a scale of 1 : 500
  What actual length does 4 cm on her plan represent?

  4 cm represents 4 × 500 cm = 2000 cm
  2000 cm = 2000 ÷ 100 m = 20 m

**1**   Convert the units in each of these.
- **a**   300 cm to m     **c**   8.6 m to cm     **e**   7.2 kg to g     **g**   3000 ml to l
- **b**   7 km to m        **d**   4500 g to kg     **f**   0.4 t to kg     **h**   4.8 l to ml

**2**   Estimate the red quantities in the metric unit given in brackets.
- **a**   Your middle finger is about 3 inches long. (cm)
- **b**   The Tyne bridge in Newcastle is 177 yd long. (m)
- **c**   The speed limit in towns is 30 miles an hour. (km)
- **d**   A medium sized apple weighs about 4 ounces. (g)
- **e**   A man weighs about 165 pounds. (kg)
- **f**   A large watering can holds about 3 gallons. (l)
- **g**   Two mugs of coffee make about a pint. (l)

**3**   **a**   Use multiplication to convert the red quantities accurately to metric units in question **2**.
-      **b**   Use the answers to check your estimates in question **2**.

**4**   Melanie is 6 years old. Her brother Keith is 18 years old.
- **a**   What is the ratio of Melanie's age to Keith's age? Give your answer in its simplest form.
- **b**   Share a prize of £60 between Melanie and Keith in the ratio of their ages.

**5**   The instructions on a tin of concentrated orange juice say 'add three parts water to one part orange juice'.
- **a**   A tin holds 250 ml of juice. How much water do you add?
- **b**   How much orange drink does this make altogether?

**6**   Simplify these ratios.
- **a**   12 : 20       **b**   15 : 10       **c**   50 : 45       **d**   10 : 1000

**7**   Express these as ratios in the form $1 : n$
- **a**   A map scale of 5 cm to 1 km       **b**   7 : 20   (correct to 2 dp)

**8**   A map has a scale of 4 cm to 1 km.
- **a**   A road on the map is 24 cm long. How long is the actual road?
- **b**   A lake is 2.5 km wide. How wide is the lake on the map?

**9**   Helen makes a model aircraft carrier to a scale of 1 : 500
- **a**   The aircraft carrier is 300 m long. How long is the model?
- **b**   The model is 15 cm wide. How wide is the carrier?

# 12 Area

*The surface area of a human lung is approximately the same as the area of a tennis court.*

# 1 Perimeter and area

◀◀REPLAY▶

This is a picture of York.
It shows the old perimeter wall.
This goes all the way round
the outside of the old part of
the city.

| Perimeter | The total distance around the outside of a shape is called its **perimeter**. |
|---|---|

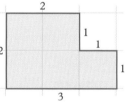

The red line is the perimeter of
this shape.
The perimeter is
$2 + 2 + 1 + 1 + 1 + 3 = 10$ cm

Each square has
an area of 1 cm$^2$

| Area | The amount of space inside the shape is called its **area**. |
|---|---|

The area of this shape is shaded green.
We use squares to measure area.

The area of this shape is 5 cm$^2$.

### Exercise 12:1

Copy these shapes on to squared paper.
Find their perimeters and areas.

**1**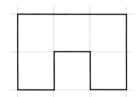

**2**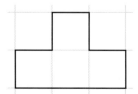

**3** 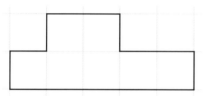    **4**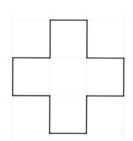

---

| **Area of a rectangle** | **Area of a rectangle** = *l*ength × *w*idth |
|---|---|
| | = *lw* |

*Example*    Calculate the area of this rectangle.

Area = *lw*
     = 4 × 3
     = 12 cm²

3 cm

4 cm

---

## Exercise 12:2

Find the perimeters and areas of these rectangles.

**1** 

5 cm

6 cm

**2**

1 cm

8 cm

**3** A picture measures 30 cm by 25 cm.
What is the perimeter of the picture?

**4** The front of a Bran Flakes packet
measures 190 cm by 270 cm.
Find its area.

**5** Peter wants to cover his back garden with grass.
  **a** What is the area of his back garden?
  **b** Grass seed costs 25 p for every m².
    How much will the grass seed cost?

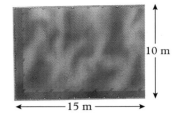

10 m

15 m

**6** Sinita is making new curtains for her bedroom.
  The material is 2 metres wide.
  She buys a length of 6 metres.
  **a** What area of material does she buy?
  **b** The material costs £5 per m².
    How much does Sinita's material cost?

**7** The area of a rectangle is 65 cm².
  The length is 13 cm.
  What is the width?

**8** The area of a wall is 48 m².
  The height of the wall is 1.5 m.
  What is the width?

**9** The area of a square is 256 cm².
  **a** What is the length of one side?
  **b** What is the perimeter of the square?

**10** The area of a square is 625 cm².
  What is its perimeter?

**11** The perimeter of a square is 60 cm².
  Find its area.

**12** A football pitch is 100 m by 72 m.
  Find the perimeter and area of the pitch.

**13** In a rectangle the length is 8 cm more than the width.
  The perimeter is 80 cm.
  Find the area.

*Example*

Estimate the area of this leaf.

Count whole squares first.
There are 17 whole squares.

Now count squares which
lie more than half inside the
outline.
There are 12 of these.

An estimate of the area of
the leaf is 29 squares

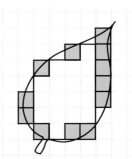

**14** Estimate the areas of these leaves.

**a**

**b**

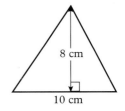

| **Area of a triangle** | **Area of a triangle** $= \dfrac{base \times height}{2} = \dfrac{bh}{2}$ |
| :--- | :--- |

*Example*

Find the area of this triangle.

$$\text{Area of triangle} = \frac{base \times height}{2}$$

$$= \frac{10 \times 8}{2}$$

$$= 40 \text{ cm}^2$$

8 cm

10 cm

## Exercise 12:3

Find the areas of these triangles.

**1**
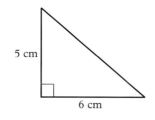

**3**
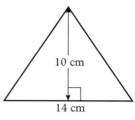

**5**
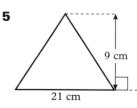

**2**
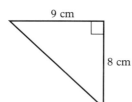

**4**
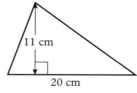

**6**
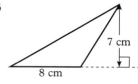

---

**Area of a parallelogram**

Area of a parallelogram $= base \times height$
$$= bh$$
$$= 8 \times 5$$
$$= 40 \text{ cm}^2$$

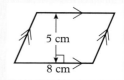

Find the areas of these parallelograms.

**7**
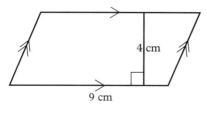

**9**
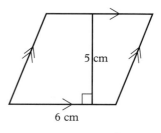

**8**
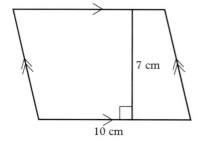

**10**
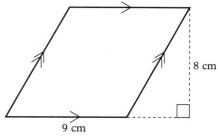

## 2 More areas

The O'Reilly family have moved into their new house.
They are going to grass the back garden which is a trapezium shape.
They need to work out the area of lawn to know how much turf to buy.

### Exercise 12:4

You will need 1 cm squared paper.

**1** Here is Mr O'Reilly's scale drawing of his back lawn.

**a** Copy the drawing on to 1 cm squared paper.

You are going to find the area of Mr O'Reilly's lawn.

**b** Mark the mid point of each of the sloping edges.
Draw the red rectangle.

**c** Write down the length of the rectangle.
Write down its width.
Find the area of the rectangle.

**d** Explain why the rectangle has the same area as the trapezium.

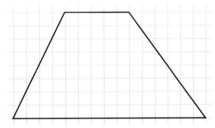

*Scale:* 1 square represents 1 m²

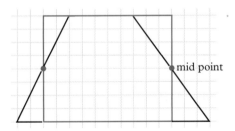

mid point

We do not always have a scale drawing.
We need a formula for finding the area of a trapezium.

Length of rectangle = mean (average) of side $a$ and side $b$

$$= \frac{a+b}{2}$$

**Area of a trapezium**  **Area of a trapezium** = Area of rectangle

$$= \frac{a+b}{2} \times h$$

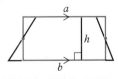

*Example*

Calculate the area of this trapezium.

$a = 4$ cm   $b = 12$ cm   $h = 6$ cm

Area of trapezium $= \dfrac{a + b}{2} \times h$

$= \dfrac{4 + 12}{2} \times 6$

$= 48$ cm$^2$

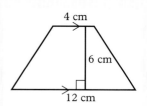

Use the formula to find the areas of these trapeziums.

**2**

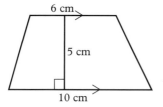

**5**

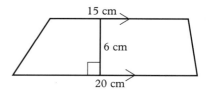

**3**

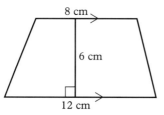

**6**

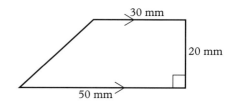

**4**

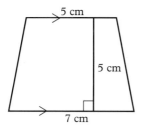

**7**

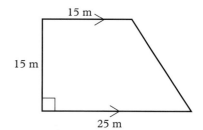

These trapeziums are drawn accurately.
Find their areas.

**8**

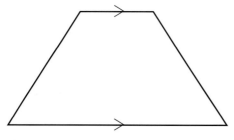

**9**

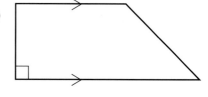

● **10** Find side *a* of this trapezium.

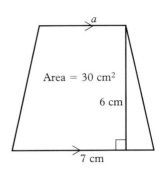

Area = 30 cm²

6 cm

7 cm

## Exercise 12:5

**1** The end of this drinking trough is a trapezium.
Find its area.

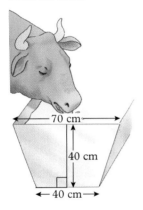

70 cm

40 cm

40 cm

**3** The side wall of this swimming pool is a trapezium.
Find its area.

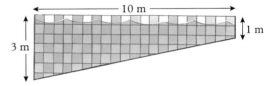

10 m

1 m

3 m

**2** The end wall of this shed is a trapezium.
Find the area of the wall.

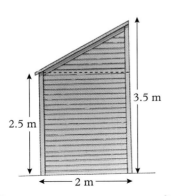

3.5 m

2.5 m

2 m

**4** This buttress holds up a church wall.
Find its area.

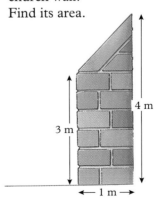

4 m

3 m

1 m

To find the area of a complicated shape, divide it into simple shapes.

(1) Decide how to divide the shape.

(2) Find any missing lengths.

(3) Calculate the area of each part of the shape.

(4) Add the areas of the parts together.

*Take extra care to show your working clearly.*

## Exercise 12:6

**1** Find the area of this shape by dividing it into a trapezium and a rectangle.
Copy and fill in:
Width of rectangle
$$8\,m - 2\,m = \ldots m$$

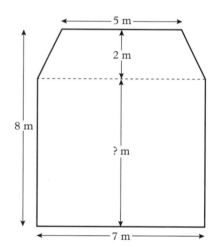

$$\text{Area of rectangle} = lw$$
$$= \ldots \times \ldots$$
$$= \ldots m^2$$

$$\text{Area of trapezium} = \frac{a+b}{2} \times h$$
$$= \frac{\ldots + \ldots}{2} \times \ldots$$
$$= \ldots m^2$$

$$\text{Total area of shape} = \ldots m^2 + \ldots m^2$$
$$= \ldots m^2$$

Find the areas of these shapes in the same way.

**2**

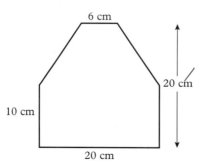

**3**

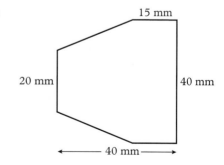

**4** A badge is in the form of a yacht. Find the area of the badge.

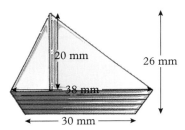

**5** This kitchen worktop can be divided into two trapeziums.
**a** Find its area in mm².
**b** Convert the area into m².

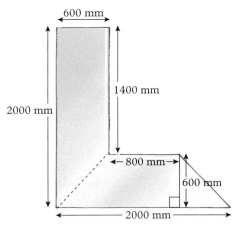

**6** This castle turret is a piece of stage scenery. Find its area.

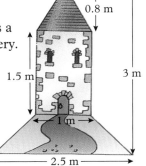

**7** The picture shows the side of a wooden shed with a rectangular window.
Find the area of wood in the side of the shed.

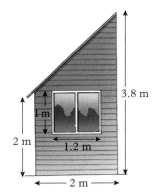

**8** Tony has made a truncated pyramid from card.
The solid has a square base and a square top and four congruent trapeziums as sides.
**a** Sketch a net of the solid.
**b** Work out the total area of card used to make the solid.

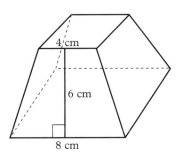

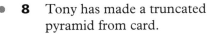

We can find the area of rhombuses and kites by dividing them into triangles.
Sometimes it is quicker to use the diagonals.

---

The kite and the rhombus are each half the area of a rectangle.
The length and width of each rectangle are equal to the diagonals.

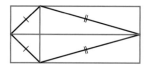 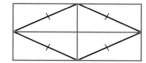

Area of kite or rhombus $= \dfrac{\text{the area of the surrounding rectangle}}{2}$

$= \dfrac{\text{the product of the diagonals}}{2}$

*Reminder:* the product of two numbers is the answer when you multiply the numbers.

*Example*    Work out the area of this kite.

Area of kite $= \dfrac{\text{the product of the diagonals}}{2}$

Area $= \dfrac{8 \times 3}{2}$

$= 12 \text{ cm}^2$

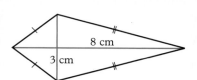

---

## Exercise 12:7

Work out the areas of these shapes.

**1**
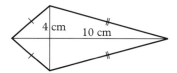

**3**
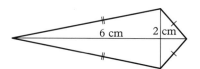

**2**
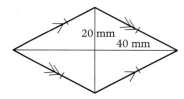

**4**
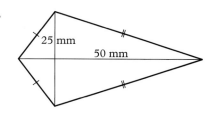

**5**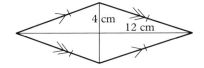

**6**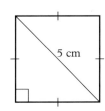

- **7** A rhombus has an area of 15 cm².
  Its diagonals are whole numbers.
  Make sketches of possible rhombuses.
  Mark the lengths of all the diagonals.

**8** Draw two different kites and a rhombus which all have the same area.

---

### Exercise 12:8  The largest triangle

All the triangles in this exercise have a perimeter of 24 cm.
You will investigate which one has the largest area.

You will need a pair of compasses.
A set square is helpful for drawing the heights of triangles.

**1** **a** Construct this triangle using your compasses.

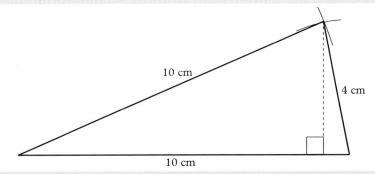

  **b** Draw and measure the height of the triangle.
  **c** Calculate the area of the triangle.
  **d** Calculate the perimeter of the triangle.

**2** Investigate the areas of other triangles with base 10 cm and perimeter 24 cm.
Which triangle has the *largest* area?

**3** Investigate the areas of triangles with bases of different lengths.
All your triangles should have a perimeter of 24 cm.

# 3 Enlargement and area

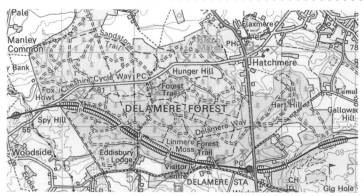

Alec needs to find the approximate area of this forest for his Geography homework.

### Exercise 12:9

You will need 1 cm squared paper.

**1** Copy this shape on to squared paper.
Label it A.
Work out the area of A.

**2** Enlarge shape A by a scale factor of 2.
Label it B.
Work out the area of B.

**3** Enlarge shape A by a scale factor of 3.
Label it C.
Work out the area of C.

**4** Copy and fill in this table.
Only draw diagrams of D and E if you need to.

| Shape | Area of A | Scale factor | New area |
|-------|-----------|--------------|----------|
| A | 4 | 1 | 4 |
| B | 4 | 2 | 16 |
| C | 4 | 3 | 36 |
| D | 4 | 4 | |
| E | 4 | 5 | |

**5** What is the rule for finding the new area?
*Hint:* It has something to do with the scale factor.

**6** What will be the new area for a scale factor of 8?

**7** What scale factor gives a new area of 400 cm²?

. . . . . . . . . . . . . . . . . . . . . . . . . . . . . . . . . . . . . . . . . . . . . . . . . . . . . . . . .

When a shape is enlarged, the area is multiplied by the square of the scale factor.

---

*Example*   The area of a rectangle is 8 cm².
The rectangle is enlarged by a scale factor of 3.
What is the new area?

Square of the scale factor is $3^2 = 9$
New area = original area × square of the scale factor
$$= 8 \times 9$$
$$= 72 \text{ cm}^2$$

---

## Exercise 12:10

In questions **1–6** you are given the area of a shape.
The shape is enlarged by the scale factor given.
Find the new area.

**1**   4 cm²   scale factor 2

**2**   7 cm²   scale factor 8

**3**   6 cm²   scale factor 5

**4**   9 cm²   scale factor 10

**5**   12 cm²   scale factor 6

**6**   11 cm²   scale factor 4

**7** The area of a patio is 9 m².
It is enlarged by a scale factor of 2.
What is the new area of the patio?

**8** A car park has an area of 75 m².
It is to be enlarged by a scale factor of 1.5
What will the new area be?

**9** The area of a vineyard is 950 m².
It is enlarged by a scale factor of 4.
What is the new area?

*Example*

A lawn has been enlarged by a scale factor of 2.
The new area is 36 m².
What was the original area?

Square of the scale factor is $2^2 = 4$

New area = original area × square of the scale factor
$$36 = ? × 4$$
Original area = $36 ÷ 4$
$$= 9$$

The original area was 9 m².

## Exercise 12:11

In questions **1–6** you are given the area of a shape.
The shape has been enlarged by the scale factor given.
Find the original area.

**1**  32 cm²   scale factor 2

**2**  45 cm²   scale factor 3

**3**  75 cm²   scale factor 5

**4**  64 cm²   scale factor 4

**5**  700 cm²   scale factor 10

**6**  640 cm²   scale factor 8

**7**  A farmer has enlarged his field by a scale factor of 2.
The area is now 12 hectares.
What was the original area of the field?

**8**  A Trading Estate has been enlarged by a scale factor of 3.
The new area is 1305 hectares.
What was the original area?

*Example*

This plan shows Stanthorne High School pond.
8P estimate that the plan of the pond has an area of 15 cm².

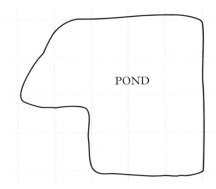

POND

The plan has a scale of 1 : 200
This means that the scale factor is 200.

Square of the scale factor is $200 \times 200 = 40\,000$
Approximate area of the pond $= 15 \times 40\,000$
$$= 600\,000 \text{ cm}^2$$
$(10\,000 \text{ cm}^2 = 1 \text{ m}^2)$ $\qquad = 60 \text{ m}^2$
The approximate area of the pond is 60 m².

## Exercise 12:12

**1** 8P estimate that a flower bed on the same plan has an area of 2 cm².
Find the actual area of the flower bed.

**2** Michelle has drawn a plan of her bedroom.
She has used a scale of 1 : 25
The floor has an area of 120 cm² on her plan.
What is the actual area of the floor in m²?

**3** The area of the bonnet on a model car is 10 cm².
The scale is 1 : 30
Find the actual area of the bonnet.

**4** Theo has a scale drawing of the holiday village he is going to visit.
The scale is 1 : 5000
The swimming pool covers an area of 1 cm².
What is the actual area of the swimming pool in m²?

**1** The end of the gutter on a house
is a trapezium.
Find its area.

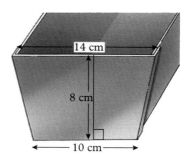

**2** Copy these axes on to squared paper.
  **a** Plot these points:
    A (1, 1) B (3, 1) C (6, 5)
    D (0, 5)
    Join the points to get trapezium
    ABCD.
  **b** Find the area of ABCD.

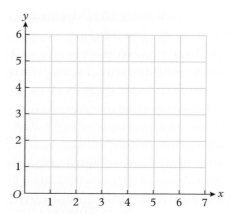

**3** The sides of this metal waste
paper bin are trapeziums.
The base is square.
  **a** Work out the area of one side.
  **b** Work out the area of the base.
  **c** Find the total area of metal
    used to make the bin.

**4** In parts **a**–**f** you are given the area of a shape.
The shape is enlarged by the scale factor given.
Find the new area.
  **a** 5 cm²    scale factor 4       **d** 7 cm²    scale factor 12
  **b** 6 cm²    scale factor 2       **e** 4 cm²    scale factor 1.5
  **c** 3 cm²    scale factor 5       **f** 8 cm²    scale factor 3.2

**5** In parts **a**–**f** you are given the area of a shape.
The shape has been enlarged by the scale factor given.
Find the original area.
  **a** 81 cm²    scale factor 3       **d** 175 cm²    scale factor 5
  **b** 48 cm²    scale factor 2       **e** 35.28 cm²    scale factor 2.1
  **c** 147 cm²    scale factor 7       **f** 57.8 cm²    scale factor 3.4

**6** A shape has an area of 15 cm².
It is enlarged by a scale factor of 5.
What is the new area?

**7** A play area has an area of 60 m².
It is enlarged to 540 m².
What scale factor is used?

**8** Pauline has enlarged her drawing by a scale factor of 3.
The new area is 396 cm².
What was the area of her original drawing?

**9** The diagram shows a side view of a swimming pool being filled.

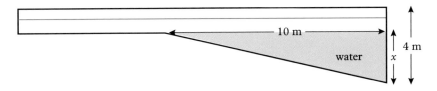

**a** The area of the shaded triangle is 13.5 m².
What is the value of $x$?
**b** The pool is now filled to the red line.
The area the water now covers is 32.7 m².
How far is the water level from the top?

**10** Copy these axes on to squared paper.
**a** Plot the points (1, 1) (1, 8) (7, 8)
These are three vertices of a rectangle.
Write down the co-ordinates of the
fourth vertex.
Draw the rectangle.
**b** Plot and label these points:
A (1, 4) B (4, 8) C (7, 6) D (5, 4) E (5, 1)
Join them with straight lines in order.
**c** Find the area of the shape ABCDE.
*Hint:* Find the area of the rectangle and
then subtract areas until you are left with
the shape ABCDE.

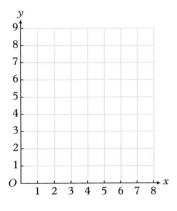

**1**

Area = 25.5 cm²                    Area = 82.62 cm²

Find the values of *a*, *b* and *c*.

**2**   What fraction of this shape is shaded?

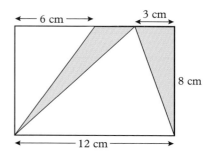

**3**   The area of a kite is 361 cm².
One diagonal is twice the length of the other.
What are the lengths of the diagonals?

**4**   The area of a trapezium is 154 cm².
The parallel sides are 7 cm apart.
The length of one of them is 26 cm.
Find the length of the other parallel side.

**5**   The area of this trapezium is 104 cm².
   **a**   Write down an equation for the area of
      the trapezium.
   **b**   Use algebra to solve the equation.
   **c**   Write down the lengths of the parallel sides.

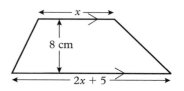

**6**   The area of this kite is 437 cm².
Use Trial and Improvement to find
the lengths of the diagonals of this kite.

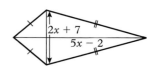

- **Perimeter**   The total distance around the outside of a shape is called its **perimeter**.

  **Area**   The amount of space inside the shape is called its **area**.

  **Area of a rectangle** = *l*ength × **w**idth = *lw*

  **Area of a triangle** = $\dfrac{base \times height}{2}$ = $\dfrac{bh}{2}$

  **Area of a parallelogram** = *base* × *height* = *bh*

  **Area of a trapezium** = $\dfrac{a+b}{2} \times h$

  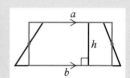

  **Area of a kite or rhombus** = $\dfrac{\text{the product of the diagonals}}{2}$

---

- *Example*   Calculate the area of this trapezium.

  $a = 4\,\text{cm}$   $b = 12\,\text{cm}$   $h = 6\,\text{cm}$

  Area of trapezium = $\dfrac{a+b}{2} \times h$

  $= \dfrac{4+12}{2} \times 6$

  $= 48\,\text{cm}^2$

  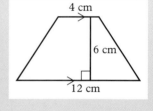

---

- *Example*   Work out the area of this kite.

  Area of kite = $\dfrac{\text{the product of the diagonals}}{2}$

  Area = $\dfrac{8 \times 3}{2}$

  $= 12\,\text{cm}^2$

  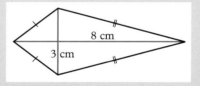

---

- When a shape is enlarged, the area is multiplied by the square of the scale factor.

  *Example*   The area of a rectangle is 8 cm².
  The rectangle is enlarged by a scale factor of 3.
  What is the new area?

  Square of the scale factor is $3^2 = 9$
  New area = original area × square of the scale factor
  $= 8 \times 9$
  $= 72\,\text{cm}^2$

---

**1** Work out the areas of these shapes.

**a**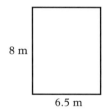

8 m

6.5 m

**d**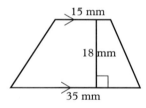

15 mm

18 mm

35 mm

**b**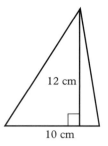

12 cm

10 cm

**e**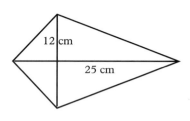

12 cm

25 cm

**c**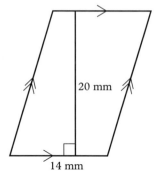

20 mm

14 mm

**f**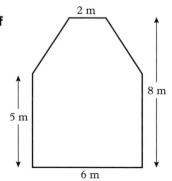

2 m

5 m

8 m

6 m

**2** Find the perimeter of shape **a** in question **1**.

**3** A shape has an area of 15 cm².
It is enlarged by a scale factor of 10.
What is the new area?

**4** Alan has enlarged a triangle by a scale factor of 2.
The new area is 48 cm².
What was the area of the triangle before the enlargement?

# Statistics: getting it together

**QUESTIONS**

**EXTENSION**

**SUMMARY**

**TEST YOURSELF**

## *Crazy Cricket Calculations*

Frank and Paul play for the same cricket team.

In the first half of the season, Frank averaged more runs per innings than Paul. He hoped he might win the trophy for the best batting average of the season.

Frank's average for the second half of the season was also better than Paul's.

Think how upset Frank was when he found out that Paul's average for the **whole** season was the best, so Paul won the trophy!

How could this happen?

## 1 Averages and range

◄◄REPLAY►

Year 8 pupils are in eight forms at Stanthorne High.
The forms do not all have the same number of pupils.
One form has 25 pupils, three have 27, two have 28 and two have 29.

| **Mean** | To find the **mean** of a set of data: |
|---|---|

(1) Find the total of all the data values.
(2) Divide by the number of data values.

*Example*    Find the mean number of pupils in a Year 8 form at Stanthorne High.

The total is:
$$25 + 27 + 27 + 27 + 28 + 28 + 29 + 29 = 220$$
The mean is $220 \div 8 = 27.5$

You cannot really have 27.5 people in a form! You must not round the mean to a whole number even if you think the answer is silly.

### Exercise 13:1

**1**  Stanthorne High has a school nurse. She counted the number of pupils with bad asthma every day for two weeks.
Here are her results:

    3    15    0    3    1    0    4    3    1    4

Work out the mean number of pupils with asthma.

**2**  Tony timed his journeys to and from school for a week.
Here are his times in minutes:

    25    21    24    26    21    24    26    27    21    27

Find the mean time for Tony's journeys.

**3** These are the monthly rainfall figures in millimetres for South Wales for one year.

| | | | | | | | |
|---|---|---|---|---|---|---|---|
| Jan | 115.8 | Apr | 63.5 | Jul | 85.4 | Oct | 114.3 |
| Feb | 76.2 | May | 76.2 | Aug | 99.1 | Nov | 116.8 |
| Mar | 58.4 | Jun | 55.8 | Sep | 91.4 | Dec | 109.1 |

**a** Work out the mean rainfall per month.
**b** Write down the months that had a rainfall lower than the mean.
**c** Write down the months that had a rainfall higher than the mean.

---

| **Mode** | The **mode** is the most common or the most popular data value. This is sometimes called the **modal value**. |
|---|---|

*Example*

Find the modal number of pupils in a Year 8 form at Stanthorne High.

The numbers in the forms are:
    25    27    27    27    28    28    29    29
The most common number is 27.

The modal value is 27 pupils.

---

**4** Here are the school nurse's results on bad asthma.
She wrote down the number of cases every day for two weeks.
    3    15    0    3    1    0    4    3    1    4
Write down the modal number of asthma cases.

**5** Here are Tony's times in minutes for his journeys to and from school.
    25    21    24    26    21    24    26    27    21    27
Write down the modal time for Tony's journeys.

**6** The mode does not have to be a number.
Here is a pie-chart of the ways 8M and their teacher come to school.
  **a** What is the mode?
  **b** Explain how you can find the mode from the pie-chart.
  **c** There are 30 people in this survey. Measure the angles of the pie-chart to find how many are in each category.

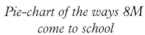
*Pie-chart of the ways 8M come to school*

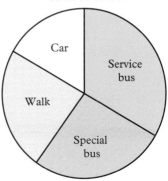

### Median

There is a third type of average called the **median**.
The median is the middle value of the data.
You must make sure that your data is in order from smallest to largest.

*Examples*

**1** These are the amounts that Manisha spent on her school lunches in one week.

75 p    92 p    95 p    88 p    98 p

Find the median amount Manisha spent.

Write the numbers in order:

75 p    88 p    92 p    95 p    98 p

The middle value is 92 p so this is the median.

**2** Find the median number of pupils in a Year 8 form at Stanthorne High.

The numbers in the forms are:

25    27    27    27    28    28    29    29

There are two middle values.

The median is $\dfrac{27 + 28}{2} = 27.5$

Like the mean, the median does not have to be one of the data values.

---

**7** Find the the median of each of these sets of numbers.

**a** 7    5    6    7    4    8    3

**b** 14    16    17    12    13

**8** Here are the school nurse's results on bad asthma.
She wrote down the number of cases every day for two weeks.

3    15    0    3    1    0    4    3    1    4

Work out the median.

**9** Here are Tony's times in minutes for his journeys to and from school.

25    21    24    26    21    24    26    27    21    27

Work out the median time for Tony's journeys.

| Range | For any set of data, the **range** is the biggest value take away the smallest value. |

*Example*

Find the range of the number of pupils in Year 8 forms at Stanthorne High.

The numbers in the forms are:

25    27    27    27    28    28    29    29

The range is $29 - 25 = 4$

## Exercise 13:2

**1** Here are the school nurse's results on bad asthma.
She wrote down the number of cases every day for two weeks.

3    15    0    3    1    0    4    3    1    4

Work out the range.

**2** Here are Tony's times in minutes for his journeys to and from school.

25    21    24    26    21    24    26    27    21    27

Work out the range for Tony's journeys.

### Choosing a sensible average

*Example*  Here are the numbers of pupils at chess club for ten weeks.

12    12    12    13    15    16    17    17    18    46

The three averages are: **mean 17.8, mode 12, median 15.5**
Which average is the most sensible to choose?

The mode is too small.
The mean is too large because of the 46 (the Christmas party).
The median is the most sensible.

### Using the range

The range tells us how the data is spread out around the mean.

*Example*  Here are the runs scored by two cricketers in their last six innings.

| Jack | 44 | 73 | 39 | 60 | 68 | 40 |
| Ian | 120 | 7 | 84 | 26 | 9 | 90 |

50 runs are needed to win.
Who is the best choice as batsman?

Jack has **mean 54** runs and **range 34** runs for his innings.
Ian has **mean 56** runs and **range 113** runs for his innings.
The mean scores are nearly the same but Ian's range is much larger than Jack's. Jack's scores are usually reliable, but Ian's vary more.
Jack is a better choice if 50 runs are needed to win.

## Exercise 13:3

**1** Look at this data. You have already found the three averages and
the range.

**a** The school nurse's daily numbers of pupils with bad asthma.

    3     15    0    3    1    0    4    3    1    4

**b** Tony's times in minutes for his journeys to and from school.

    25   21   24   26   21   24   26   27   21   27

For each set:

Write down the mean, mode and median.

Say which average or averages it is sensible to use.

**2** **a** Write down the mean and range of Tony's times from question **1**.

**b** Here are Tony's journey times for a different two weeks:

    26   22   20   28   24   18   27   19   28   30

Work out the mean and range for this second two weeks.

**c** Tony travels by bus. During the second two weeks the council tried
using different traffic lanes for buses.

Use your answers to **a** and **b** to decide which system is better for
getting the buses to run on time.

Explain how you chose your answer.

| Tally-table | When there is a lot of data we make a **tally-table**. We use tally marks. |
|---|---|
| Tally marks | **Tally marks** are done in groups of five. The fifth tally mark goes across the other four: ℍ |

## Exercise 13:4

**1** These are the numbers of pupils in each form for Years 7 to 11 at
Stanthorne High.

| | | | | | | | | |
|---|---|---|---|---|---|---|---|---|
| Year 7 | 30 | 27 | 26 | 28 | 29 | 30 | 28 | 29 |
| Year 8 | 25 | 27 | 28 | 27 | 29 | 27 | 28 | 29 |
| Year 9 | 28 | 27 | 29 | 27 | 26 | 29 | 25 | 27 |
| Year 10 | 28 | 24 | 27 | 28 | 26 | 27 | 28 | 27 |
| Year 11 | 25 | 26 | 27 | 29 | 27 | 28 | 26 | 28 |

**a** Find the range of the numbers of pupils in a form.

**b** Make a tally-table for the numbers of pupils in a form.

**c** Use the table to find the mode.

**2** The headteacher wants to know the mean number of pupils per form at Stanthorne High.
Use the data from question **1**.
Copy the table. Fill it in.
You can add an extra column to the table for question **1** if you prefer.
Add the numbers in the third column to find the total number of pupils.
Use the total to find the mean number of pupils per form.

| Number of pupils in a form | Number of forms | Total number of pupils |
|---|---|---|
| 24 | 1 | $24 \times 1 =$ |
| 25 | 3 | $25 \times 3 =$ |

**3** Some pupils at Stanthorne High come to school by car.
One morning 8F did a survey of how many pupils arrived in each car.
Here are their results:

| Number of pupils in a car | Tally | Total |
|---|---|---|
| 1 |卌 卌 卌 卌 卌 卌 卌 ||| | 38 |
| 2 | 卌 卌 卌 卌 卌 || | 27 |
| 3 | 卌 卌 || | 12 |
| 4 | ||| | 3 |
| | | Total  80 |

**a** Write down the mode.
**b** Work out the mean.
**c** Find the range of the number of pupils in a car.
**d** Find the median number of pupils in a car.

## 2 Grouping data

Children's books are often given a reading age.
This measures how difficult a book is to read.

There are a few ways of measuring reading age.
One way is to count the length of the words. Books for older children may have longer words.
Another way is to count the number of words in each sentence.

Word length and sentence length are examples of discrete data.

| Discrete data | When data can only be certain individual values it is called **discrete**. |
|---|---|
| *Example* | Shoe size is an example of discrete data. The values can only be 1, $1\frac{1}{2}$, 2, $2\frac{1}{2}$, etc. There are no shoe sizes in between these. |

### Exercise 13:5

**W 1 a** Look at the two pages from children's books. Copy this tally-table for Book A. Fill it in.

| Word length (letters) | Tally | Total |
|---|---|---|
| 1 | | |
| 2 | | |
| 3 | | |
| 4 | | |
| 5 | | |
| 6 | | |
| 7 | | |
| 8 | | |
| 9 | | |
| 10 | | |

**b** Now make a tally-table for Book B.

To compare the two books it is best to draw some diagrams.

**2**  **a**  Draw a bar-chart for Book A.
    **b**  Draw a bar-chart for Book B.

**3**  Use your two bar-charts to answer these questions.
    **a**  Which book has the most 3-letter words?
    **b**  Which book has the most 6-letter words?
    **c**  Which book do you think is easier to read?
        Explain your answer.

**4**  **a**  What is the modal word length for Book A.
    **b**  What is the modal word length for Book B.

**5**  **a**  Add a fourth column on to your tally-tables.

| Word length (letters) | Tally | Total | Total number of letters (= word length × total) |
|---|---|---|---|
| | | | |

   **b**  Fill in the fourth column.
        Add up the numbers in the column.
        This is the total number of letters.
   **c**  Divide your answer to **b** by the total number of words.
        This is the mean word length.
   **d**  Which book has the smallest mean word length?
   **e**  Does this match your answer to question **3c**? Explain.

· · · · · · · · · · · · · · · · · · · · · · · · · · · · · · · · · · · · · · · · · · · · · · · · · · · · · · ·

There is another way of measuring how difficult books are to read.
You can count the number of words in a sentence.
This is called the sentence length.

## Exercise 13:6

**1**  Go back to your page from Book A.
    Count the number of words in each sentence.
    Write down each sentence length.
    Tally the sentence lengths in a table like this.
    Add as many lines as you need.

| Length of sentence (words) | Tally | Total |
|---|---|---|
| 1–5 | | |
| 6–10 | | |
| 11–15 | | |

**2 a** Go back to your page from Book B.
Count the number of words in each sentence.
Write down each sentence length.

**b** Make a new tally-table.
Tally the sentence lengths from Book B.

**3 a** Use your tally-table for Book A to draw a bar-chart.
Don't leave gaps between the bars.

**b** Use your tally-table for Book B to draw another bar-chart.

**4 a** What is the modal sentence length for Book A?

**b** What is the modal sentence length for Book B?

**c** Think about your answers to **a** and **b**.
Which book do you think is easier to read?
Explain your answer.

**5** You can work out the mean sentence length.

**a** Write down the total number of words on the page from Book A.

**b** Write down the total number of sentences on the page from Book A.

**c** Copy and fill in:
mean sentence length = number of words ÷ number of sentences
= ... ÷ ...
= ...

**d** Write down the total number of words on the page from Book B.

**e** Write down the total number of sentences on the page from Book B.

**f** Work out the mean sentence length for Book B.

---

| **Continuous data** | Data is **continuous** when it can take *any* value in a certain range. |
|---|---|
| *Example* | The lengths of earthworms, the heights of pupils in Year 8, the weights of hamsters are all examples of continuous data. |

When you are grouping continuous data you need to think very carefully about the beginning and end of each group.

**Exercise 13:7**

**1** In a Science survey Howard measured the lengths of some earthworms in centimetres.
Here are his results to the nearest millimetre.

| 6.2 | 5.4 | 8.9 | 12.1 | 6.5 | 9.3 | 7.2 | 12.7 | 10.2 | 5.4 |
|------|------|------|------|------|------|------|------|------|------|
| 7.7 | 9.5 | 11.1 | 8.6 | 7.0 | 13.5 | 12.7 | 5.6 | 15.4 | 12.3 |
| 13.4 | 9.5 | 6.7 | 8.6 | 9.1 | 11.5 | 14.2 | 13.5 | 8.8 | 9.7 |

Howard put the data into groups like this:

| Length in cm | Tally | Total |
|---|---|---|
| 5 but less than 7 | | |
| 7 but less than 9 | | |
| 9 but less than 11 | | |
| 11 but less than 13 | | |
| 13 but less than 15 | | |
| 15 but less than 17 | | |

**a** Which group does 13.5 go into?
**b** Which group does 7.0 go into?
**c** Copy the tally-table.
Tally all the results in your table.
**d** Draw a bar-chart of this grouped data.
Don't leave gaps between the bars.

**2** Mariza used different groups.
**a** Copy this table.

| Length in cm | Tally | Total |
|---|---|---|
| 5 but less than 9 | | |
| 9 but less than 13 | | |
| 13 but less than 17 | | |

**b** Tally all the results from question **1** in your new table.
**c** Draw a bar-chart of your new table.
Don't leave gaps between the bars.
**d** Which bar-chart do you think is best for showing the data?
Explain your answer.

**3** These are the weights of 30 adults in kilograms.

| 47 | 65 | 52 | 43 | 58 | 69 | 71 | 49 | 56 | 60 |
| 82 | 54 | 91 | 54 | 70 | 56 | 95 | 47 | 82 | 86 |
| 75 | 79 | 96 | 99 | 100 | 57 | 98 | 63 | 80 | 92 |

**a** Copy this table. Add as many lines as you need.

| Weight in kg | Tally | Total |
|---|---|---|
| 40 but less than 50 | | |
| 50 but less than 60 | | |
| 60 but less than 70 | | |

**b** Which group does a weight of 100 kg go into?
**c** Which group does a weight of 80 kg go into?
**d** Tally all the results in your table.
**e** Draw a bar-chart of this grouped data.
  Don't leave gaps between the bars.

**4** Sian did a survey of how long her friends took to get to school.
Here are her results in minutes to the nearest minute.

| 8 | 13 | 21 | 5 | 16 | 24 | 9 | 14 | 16 | 17 |
| 7 | 5 | 25 | 31 | 14 | 17 | 19 | 23 | 5 | 12 |
| 8 | 12 | 16 | 19 | 21 | 24 | 5 | 2 | 33 | 4 |

**a** Choose sensible groups for this data.
**b** Make a tally-table for these groups.
  Fill it in.
**c** Draw a bar-chart of your table.

**5** Neil measured the weight of
crisps in 30 bags. The bags were
marked 'Average contents 25 g'.
He used a very accurate
electronic balance.

Here are his results in grams.

| 24.498 | 24.531 | 25.014 | 25.367 | 24.487 |
| 25.571 | 25.274 | 24.985 | 24.361 | 25.184 |
| 25.367 | 25.148 | 25.178 | 24.257 | 24.568 |
| 24.759 | 24.589 | 26.010 | 25.451 | 24.856 |
| 24.968 | 25.374 | 25.984 | 26.357 | 24.168 |
| 26.254 | 23.987 | 24.591 | 24.367 | 25.684 |

**a** Choose sensible groups for this data.
**b** Make a tally-table for these groups.
  Fill it in.
**c** Draw a bar-chart of your table.
**d** Is the average contents claim correct?

Once you have grouped your data, it is not so easy to work out averages.
Here are the boys' results in a Year 8 Maths test. They have been
grouped in tens.

| Mark | 31 to 40 | 41 to 50 | 51 to 60 | 61 to 70 | 71 to 80 | 81 to 90 | 91 to 100 |
|---|---|---|---|---|---|---|---|
| Number of boys | 5 | 14 | 28 | 35 | 24 | 16 | 9 |

Look at the first column.
We know that these boys scored between 31 and 40. But we do not
know *exactly* what each of them scored.

To work out an estimate for the mean, we have to assume that all 5 of
them scored the mark in the middle of the group.

This mid point is $\dfrac{31 + 40}{2} = 35.5$

In the same way we have to assume that the 14 boys in the second
column all scored the mark in the middle of that group.

This mid point is $\dfrac{41 + 50}{2} = 45.5$

If we work out all the mid points, we can make a new table like this:

| Mark (mid points) | 35.5 | 45.5 | 55.5 | 65.5 | 75.5 | 85.5 | 95.5 |
|---|---|---|---|---|---|---|---|
| Number of boys | 5 | 14 | 28 | 35 | 24 | 16 | 8 |

Now we can work out the mean as if these were the scores that
everybody got.

$$\text{Mean} = \frac{35.5 \times 5 + 45.5 \times 14 + 55.5 \times 28 + 65.5 \times 35 + 75.5 \times 24 + 85.5 \times 16 + 95.5 \times 8}{130}$$

$$= \frac{8050}{130}$$

$$= 61.9 \text{ (1dp)}$$

It is important to realise that this is only an **estimate** for the mean.
We assumed that all the boys in each group scored the middle mark in
each group.
This may not be true, so our mean may well be wrong!

## Exercise 13:8

**1** Here are the Year 8 girls' scores in the same Maths test.

| Mark | 31 to 40 | 41 to 50 | 51 to 60 | 61 to 70 | 71 to 80 | 81 to 90 | 91 to 100 |
|---|---|---|---|---|---|---|---|
| Number of girls | 4 | 17 | 23 | 26 | 21 | 19 | 10 |

**a** Copy this table.
Fill in the mid points for each group of marks.

| Mark (mid points) | 35.5 | | | | | | |
|---|---|---|---|---|---|---|---|
| Number of girls | 4 | 17 | 23 | 26 | 21 | 19 | 10 |

**b** Work out an estimate for the mean. Give your answer to 1 dp.

**2** Abbie did a survey in her class. She asked each person how much pocket money they received each week.
Here are her results.

| Amount | 0 p–99 p | £1–£1.99 | £2–£2.99 | £3–£3.99 | £4–£4.99 |
|---|---|---|---|---|---|
| Number of people | 6 | 5 | 8 | 6 | 5 |

**a** Copy this table.
Fill in the mid points for each group.

| Amount | | | | | |
|---|---|---|---|---|---|
| Number of people | 6 | 5 | 8 | 6 | 5 |

**b** Work out an estimate for the mean.
Give your answer to the nearest penny.

● **3** Go back to the data from Exercise **13:7**.
For each question work out an estimate for the mean using this method.
Then calculate the exact mean from the original data.
Write a sentence to describe the difference between the true value and the estimate.

# 3   Frequency polygons

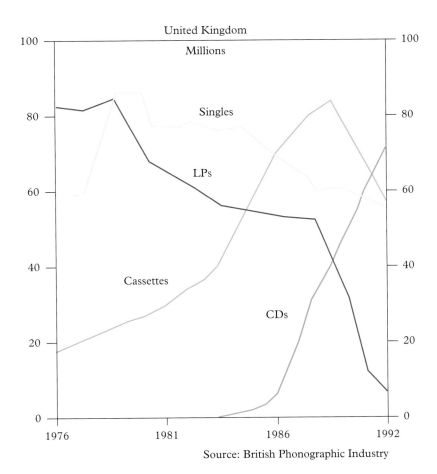

United Kingdom
Millions

Singles

LPs

Cassettes

CDs

Source: British Phonographic Industry

These frequency polygons show the sales of LPs, cassettes, CDs and singles since 1976.

| Frequency polygon | **Frequency polygons** are often used to compare two sets of data. |
|---|---|
| Trend | The points are joined together to show the **trend**. The trend shows how the data is changing. You do not read information from the lines in between the points. |

## Exercise 13:9

**1** Look at this table.
It shows the total number of goals scored in 40 football matches played one Saturday.

| Number of goals | 0 | 1 | 2 | 3 | 4 | 5 | 6 |
|---|---|---|---|---|---|---|---|
| Number of matches | 5 | 9 | 12 | 5 | 7 | 1 | 1 |

**a** Look at the figures in red.
How many matches had 2 goals in them?
**b** Look at the figures in green.
How many matches had 6 goals in them?
**c** Write down all the possible final scores that have 6 goals in them.
Start with 6–0, 5–1, 4–2, ...

Here is a frequency polygon showing this information.

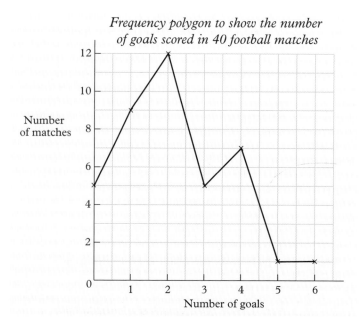

Frequency polygon to show the number of goals scored in 40 football matches

**d** How many matches had 5 goals in them?
Is this the same as in the table?
**e** How many matches had 2 goals in them?

**2** Look at this frequency polygon.
It shows the number of pupils in each year at a boys' secondary school.

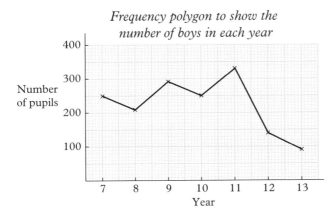

*Frequency polygon to show the
number of boys in each year*

Copy this table.

| Year | 7 | 8 | 9 | 10 | 11 | 12 | 13 |
|---|---|---|---|---|---|---|---|
| Number of pupils | | | | | | | |

Fill in the table. Get the information from the frequency polygon.

**3** This frequency polygon shows the number of pupils at the nearby girls' school.

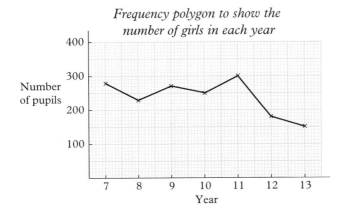

*Frequency polygon to show the
number of girls in each year*

Copy the table from question **2** again.
Fill it in. Get the information from the frequency polygon.

The frequency polygons from question **2** and question **3** can be drawn on the same diagram.
This makes them easier to compare.

**4** **a** Copy the frequency polygon from question **2** on to graph paper.
   **b** Copy the frequency polygon from question **3** on to the same set of axes.
   **c** Which school has the most Year 7 pupils?
   **d** Which school has more pupils in Year 9?
   **e** In which year do both schools have the same number of pupils?
   **f** How many more boys are there in Year 9 than girls?
   **g** How many more girls are there in Year 8 than boys?

**5** Look at these frequency polygons.
   They show the number of pupils at two schools.

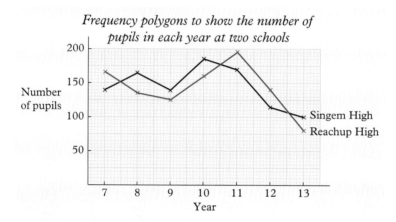

*Frequency polygons to show the number of pupils in each year at two schools*

   **a** Which school has the most Year 7 pupils?
   **b** Which school has the most Year 9 pupils?
      How many more Year 9 pupils has it got?
   **c** Make a list of the number of pupils in each year at Singem High.
      How many pupils does it have altogether?
   **d** How many pupils are there at Reachup High?

**6** 8P have been comparing two reading books. The books are for pupils in junior school.
   8P have counted the numbers of letters in the first 50 words of each book.
   Here are two tables showing their results.

| Number of letters in a word | 1 | 2 | 3 | 4 | 5 | 6 | 7 |
| --- | --- | --- | --- | --- | --- | --- | --- |
| Number of words in *Read for fun* | 3 | 5 | 14 | 17 | 6 | 4 | 1 |

| Number of letters in a word | 1 | 2 | 3 | 4 | 5 | 6 | 7 |
|---|---|---|---|---|---|---|---|
| Number of words in *Reading made easy* | 4 | 5 | 9 | 13 | 10 | 7 | 2 |

**a** Draw a frequency polygon for *Read for fun*.
**b** Draw a frequency polygon for *Reading made easy* on the same diagram.
Use a different colour.
**c** Which book do you think is easier to read? Explain your answer.

**7** Results are collected each year about casualties in traffic accidents. These are the numbers of school-age casualties in Derbyshire in one year.

| Age | 5 | 6 | 7 | 8 | 9 | 10 | 11 | 12 | 13 | 14 | 15 | 16 | 17 | 18 | 19 |
|---|---|---|---|---|---|---|---|---|---|---|---|---|---|---|---|
| Number | 37 | 35 | 42 | ? | 56 | 56 | 52 | 62 | 63 | 87 | 58 | 113 | 167 | 188 | 167 |

**a** Draw a frequency polygon to show this data.
Leave a gap between age 7 and age 9.
**b** Describe how the number of casualties changes as people get older.
**c** Do you think this trend will continue?
Explain your answer.
**d** Plot a point for the casualties aged 8.
Use the trend of the graph to estimate where you think it should go.
Write down the value you have chosen.

If the data is grouped then the points are plotted in the middle of each group.
This is like joining up the middle of the top of each bar on a bar-chart.

Here is a table of the casualty data from Exercise **13:9**.
The data has been grouped.

| Age | 5–7 | 8–10 | 11–13 | 14–16 | 17–19 |
|---|---|---|---|---|---|
| Number | 114 | 164 | 177 | 258 | 522 |

## Exercise 13:10

**1**  **a**  Draw a bar-chart of this grouped data. Use a pencil and draw it as lightly as possible.
   **b**  Put a small cross in the middle of the top of each bar.
   **c**  Join up your crosses with straight lines.
       You now have a frequency polygon.

**2**  Here is the casualty data for older age groups.

| Age | 20–22 | 23–25 | 26–28 | 29–31 | 32–34 |
|------|-------|-------|-------|-------|-------|
| Number | 485 | 406 | 359 | 292 | 246 |

   **a**  Draw a bar-chart for this data. Use a pencil and draw it lightly.
   **b**  Draw a frequency polygon over the top of your bar-chart.
   **c**  Describe the trend of the casualties as the people get older.
   **d**  Suggest why the trend is like this.

**3**  Here is a third set of casualty data for Derbyshire.

| Age | 41–43 | 44–46 | 47–49 | 50–52 | 53–55 |
|------|-------|-------|-------|-------|-------|
| Number | 158 | 166 | 156 | 130 | 98 |

   **a**  Plot all three sets of casualty data on one frequency polygon. Do NOT join up 33 to 42.
   **b**  By looking at the trend of the graph, suggest values for the groups that are missing: 35–37 and 38–40.

**1** Stanthorne High under-15 football team has played three matches.
The mean number of goals they have scored is two.
They play another match and score four goals.
What is the new mean?

**2** 8L collect 40 leaves from a tree.
They measure them in centimetres correct to the nearest millimetre.
Here are their results:

| | | | | | | | | | |
|---|---|---|---|---|---|---|---|---|---|
| 6.0 | 5.2 | 6.1 | 5.3 | 8.2 | 6.4 | 5.7 | 7.1 | 6.5 | 6.4 |
| 7.2 | 8.7 | 4.8 | 5.6 | 7.3 | 4.9 | 6.5 | 8.3 | 6.8 | 7.8 |
| 7.4 | 7.9 | 5.5 | 7.0 | 7.5 | 5.8 | 5.1 | 7.6 | 6.8 | 5.4 |
| 8.1 | 6.3 | 6.4 | 5.9 | 4.7 | 8.4 | 6.1 | 6.7 | 8.8 | 7.7 |

**a** Copy the table. Fill it in.

| Length of leaf in cm | Tally | Total |
|---|---|---|
| 4 but less than 5 | | |
| 5 but less than 6 | | |
| 6 but less than 7 | | |
| 7 but less than 8 | | |
| 8 but less than 9 | | |

**b** Draw a bar-chart of your table.
**c** Write down the modal group.
**d** Calculate the mean length of a leaf.
Take the mid points of the groups to be 4.5 cm, 5.5 cm, etc.

**3** Here is a table showing the numbers of pupils in two schools.

| Number of pupils | Year 7 | Year 8 | Year 9 | Year 10 | Year 11 |
|---|---|---|---|---|---|
| The Burton School | 170 | 160 | 180 | 200 | 150 |
| The Bravo School | 150 | 160 | 140 | 120 | 150 |

**a** Copy the axes on to
squared paper.
**b** Plot the points for
The Burton School.
Join them with straight lines.
**c** Plot the points for
The Bravo School.
Join them with straight lines.
Use a different colour.

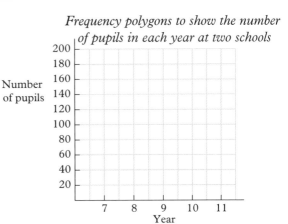

*Frequency polygons to show the number of pupils in each year at two schools*

291

**1** Bill recorded the number of
Super Jumbo ice creams he sold
each day for a month.
He drew this bar-chart of his
results to show to his friends.

Explain how you reach your
answers to parts **a–c**.

  **a** Jessie said that the graph
shows that Bill sold most
Super Jumbos at the
beginning of the month.
Is she right?

  **b** Jon said that he could see
the month for the graph had
only 30 days. Is he right?

  **c** Other friends used the
graph to estimate how many
Super Jumbos Bill sold
during the month.
Here are their estimates: 50, 100, 250, 500, 900.
Only one estimate can be correct.
Which estimate is it?

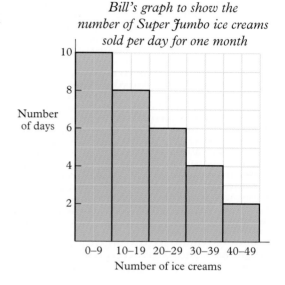

*Bill's graph to show the
number of Super Jumbo ice creams
sold per day for one month*

  **d** Copy the table and fill it in.

| Number of ice creams | 0–9 | 10–19 | 20–29 | 30–39 | 40–49 |
|---|---|---|---|---|---|
| Number of days | | | | | |

  **e** Calculate the mean number of ice creams sold per day, correct to 1 dp.

**2** Gemma and Kath have done a survey of two brands of carrots.
Both brands cost the same and the carrots are about the same size.
They have opened eight tins of each brand and counted the number
of carrots in each tin.
Here are their results:

| Brand A | 32 | 41 | 28 | 31 | 34 | 37 | 39 | 30 |
|---|---|---|---|---|---|---|---|---|
| Brand B | 32 | 34 | 36 | 30 | 32 | 35 | 33 | 32 |

  **a** Work out the mean number of carrots per tin for each brand.
Which brand looks better value?

  **b** Work out the range for each brand of carrots.
Explain what the range shows.
Which brand of carrots would you buy next time?

- **Mean**     To find the **mean** of a set of data:
  (1) Find the total of all the data values.
  (2) Divide by the number of data values.

  **Mode**     The **mode** is the most common or the most popular data value.

  **Median**     The **median** is the middle value when the data is in order from smallest to largest.

- **Range**     The **range** is the biggest value take away the smallest value.

- **Discrete data**     **Discrete data** can only be certain individual values.

  **Continuous data**     Data is **continuous** when it can take *any* value in a certain range.

- ### *Mean of grouped data*

  *Example*
  Here are the boys' results in a Year 8 Maths test.

  | Mark | 31 to 40 | 41 to 50 | 51 to 60 | 61 to 70 | 71 to 80 | 81 to 90 | 91 to 100 |
  |---|---|---|---|---|---|---|---|
  | Number of boys | 5 | 14 | 28 | 35 | 24 | 16 | 9 |

  We assume that all 5 boys in the first group scored the mark in the middle of the group.

  The mid point is $\dfrac{31 + 40}{2} = 35.5$

  If we work out all the mid points, we can make a new table like this:

  | Mark (mid points) | 35.5 | 45.5 | 55.5 | 65.5 | 75.5 | 85.5 | 95.5 |
  |---|---|---|---|---|---|---|---|
  | Number of boys | 5 | 14 | 28 | 35 | 24 | 16 | 8 |

  $$\text{Mean} = \frac{35.5 \times 5 + 45.5 \times 14 + 55.5 \times 28 + 65.5 \times 35 + 75.5 \times 24 + 85.5 \times 16 + 95.5 \times 8}{130}$$

  $$= \frac{8050}{130} = 61.9 \ (1 \text{ dp})$$

- **Frequency polygon**     **Frequency polygons** are often used to compare two sets of data.

  **Trend**     The points are joined together to show the **trend**.
  The trend shows how the data is changing.
  You do not read information from the lines in between the points.

**1**   Look at these numbers:

     7    6    9    0    3    4    7    6    4    7

   **a**   Work out the mean.

   **b**   Write down the mode.

   **c**   Find the median.

   **d**   Work out the range.

**2**   8J recorded the number of people in 50 cars passing the school. Here are their results:

| Number of people | 1 | 2 | 3 | 4 | 5 |
|---|---|---|---|---|---|
| Number of cars | 23 | 16 | 7 | 3 | 1 |

   **a**   Write down the mode.

   **b**   Work out the mean number of people per car.

   **c**   Draw a frequency polygon to show the data.

**3**   8F measured the heights of 40 seedlings four weeks after the seeds were planted.

Here are their results, given in centimetres correct to the nearest millimetre.

     2.8    10.3   3.6    6.3    8.1    7.2    4.7    7.1    4.3    8.2

     5.9    8.0    2.5    7.4    5.3    9.1    1.9    6.8    4.8    5.1

     9.4    7.3    3.8    7.9    9.0    8.7    5.5    8.4    3.6    8.5

     7.9    7.8    9.7    7.7    1.8    6.2    7.3    6.9    10.5   6.5

   **a**   Copy the table.

      Tally all the results in the table.

| Length in cm | Tally | Total |
|---|---|---|
| 0 but less than 2 | | |
| 2 but less than 4 | | |
| 4 but less than 6 | | |
| 6 but less than 8 | | |
| 8 but less than 10 | | |
| 10 but less than 12 | | |

   **b**   Write down the modal group.

   **c**   Draw a bar-chart of this grouped data.

   **d**   Draw a frequency polygon on your bar-chart.

   **e**   Calculate the mean height of a seedling.

      Take the mid points of the groups to be 1, 3, 5, etc

# 14 Volume: filling the space

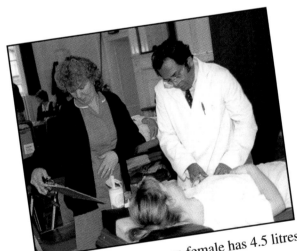

The average adult human female has 4.5 litres of blood in her body.

A male has slightly more.

If you give blood to the National Blood Service they take less than half a litre.

Altogether they collect 1.5 million litres each year.

This is the same as about 300 000 full bodies worth!

# 1 **Pack it in!**

The world record for the number of people in a phone box is 23.
This is a lot of people in a very small space!

---

| **Volume** | The amount of space that an object takes up is called its **volume**. |

---

### *Exercise 14:1*

**1** Look at these objects.

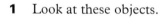

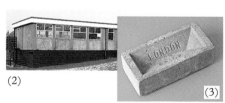

List the objects in order of volume. Start with the *smallest*.

| Capacity | The **capacity** of a hollow object is the volume of space inside it. |
|---|---|

**2** Look at these containers.

List the objects in order of capacity.
Start with the *biggest*.

## Units of volume

Volume is measured in cubic units.
These can be mm³, cm³ or m³

| **1 cm³** | **1 cm³** is the space taken up by a cube with all its edges 1 cm long. |
|---|---|

## Units of capacity

| **1 m*l*** | This cube is filled with water. The volume of water inside is **1 millilitre**. This is written **1 m*l*** **1 m*l*** is the same as **1 cm³** |
|---|---|

**3** Look at these containers.
  **a** Write down the volume of each drink in cm³
  **b** Calculate the volume of Coke that you get for 1 p for each container.
  **c** Which container gives the best value for money?

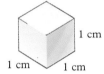

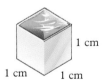

1500 m*l*
96 p

500 m*l*
55 p

330 m*l*
35 p

We measure large volumes in **litres**.
    1 litre = 1000 ml

This lemonade bottle holds 2 litres.
This petrol can holds 5 litres.
A petrol tanker holds 34 000 litres.

## Exercise 14:2

**1** Estimate the volume of these containers.
Write your answers in litres.

**a**

**c**

**e**

**b**

**d**

**2** Estimate the volume of these containers.
Write your answers in millilitres.

**3** Estimate the volume of these containers.
You need to choose millilitres or litres.

**a**

**b**

**c**

## 2  Stacking

Supermarkets stack their shelves so that you can see what they are selling.
They want to fit in as much as they can.
The shelf stackers need to work out how much they can fit in.

---

*Example*   Phil has to stack boxes of pizzas in the freezer.
He works out how many will fit in one layer.

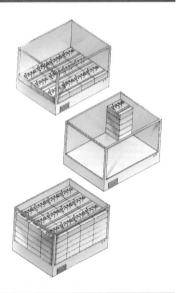

Then he works out how many layers he can fit in.
He multiplies the number in one layer by the number of layers.
This tells him the total number of pizzas he can fit in.

In this freezer he can fit 12 boxes in each layer and 5 layers.
He can fit $12 \times 5 = 60$ pizzas in altogether.

---

### Exercise 14:3

For each question work out:
a   The number of boxes in one layer.
b   The number of layers.
c   The total number of boxes in the stack.

**1**

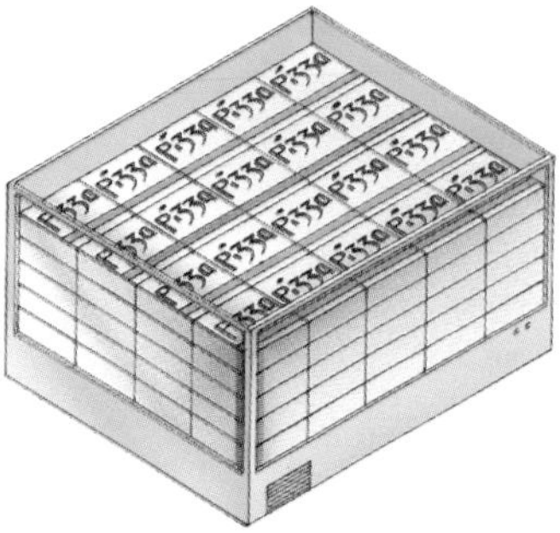

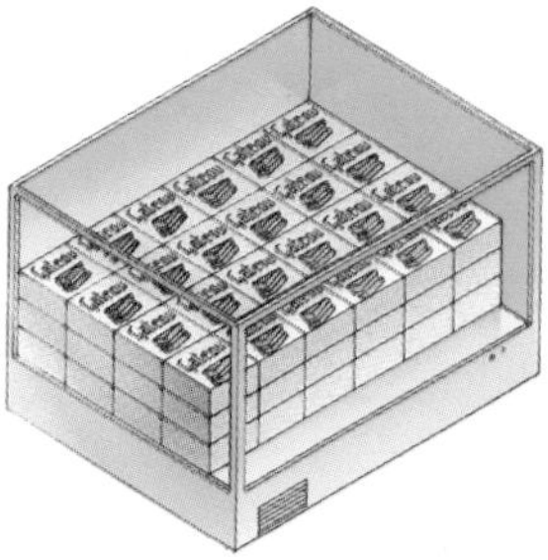

**4**

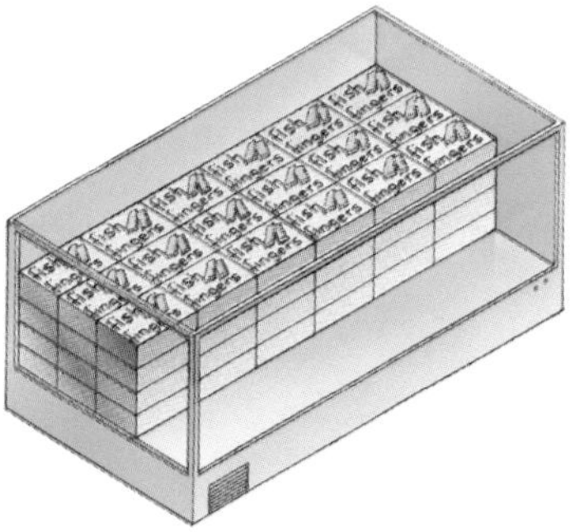

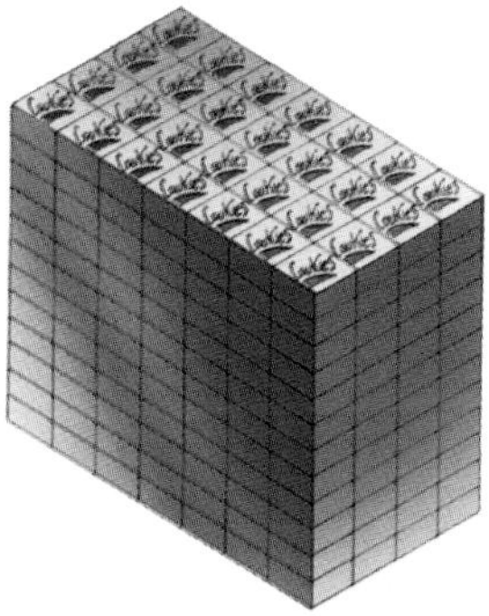

**2**

**5**

**3**

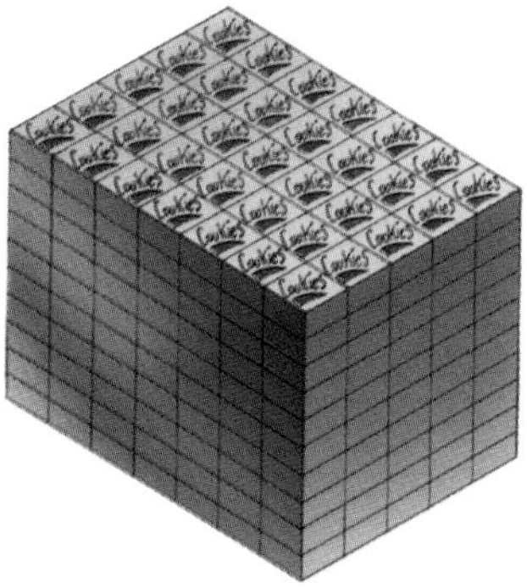

**6**

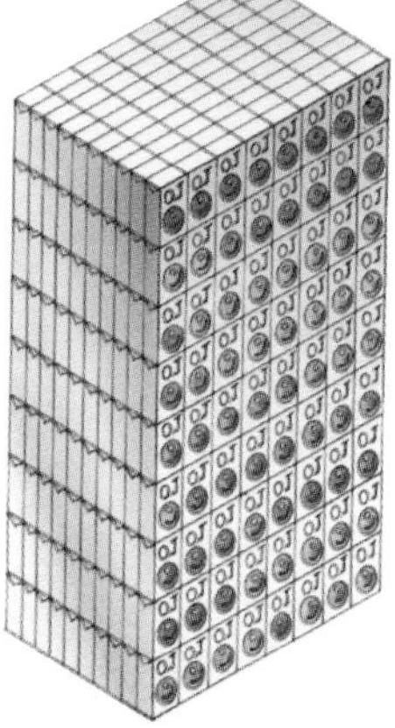

James is playing with wooden cubes.
He has learned to build them into towers.

## Exercise 14:4

For each question work out how many cubes James has altogether.

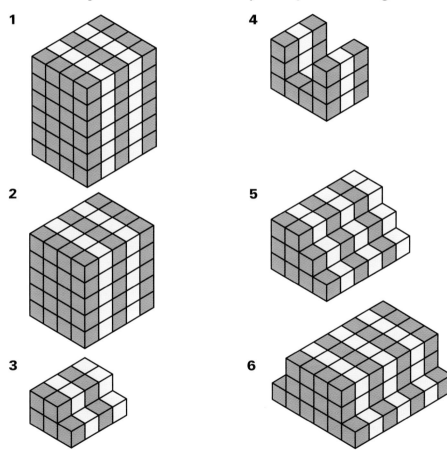

**1**

**2**

**3**

**4**

**5**

**6**

---

**1 cm³**

A cube that has sides of 1 cm is called a 1 cm cube.
We say that it has a volume of 1 cm cubed.
We write this as **1 cm³**

*Example*        This cuboid made of 1 cm cubes
has a volume of 24 cm³

## Exercise 14:5

Work out the volume of these shapes made from 1 cm cubes.
To do this:
**a** Work out the number of cubes in one layer.
**b** Multiply by the number of layers.

**1**

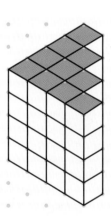

**3**

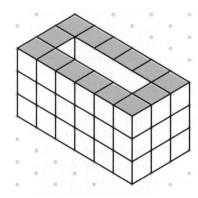

**2**

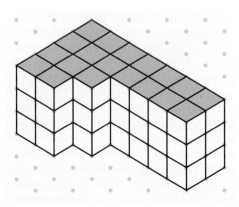

**4**

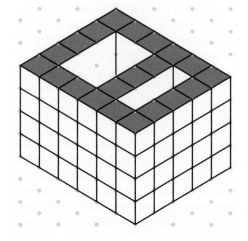

**5**

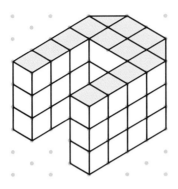

**7**

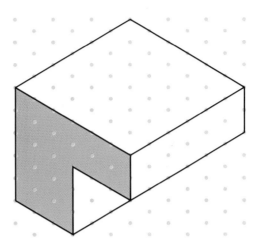

**6**

**8** Look at this solid. The yellow cubes go right through the shape.
   **a** Find the volume of the red cubes.
   **b** Find the volume of the yellow cubes.
   **c** Find the total volume of the shape.

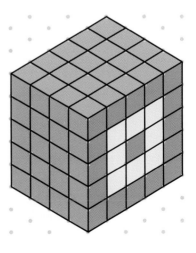

# 3   Prisms

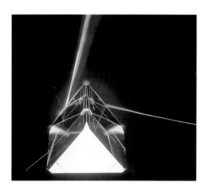

This is a picture of a triangular prism.

It is used to split white light into the colours of the rainbow.

| **Prism** | A **prism** is a solid which is exactly the same shape all the way through. Wherever you cut a slice through the shape it is the same size and shape. |
| --- | --- |
| **Cross section** | The shape of this slice is called the **cross section** of the solid. |

These shapes are prisms.

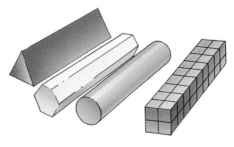

These shapes are not prisms.

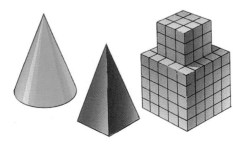

## Exercise 14:6

Look at these solids.
Write down the letters
of the prisms.

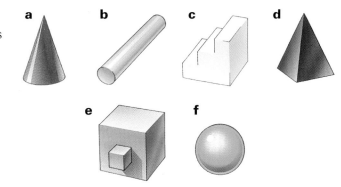

· · · · · · · · · · · · · · · · · · · · · · · · · · · · · · · · · · · · · · · · · · · · · · · · · · · · · · · · · · · · · ·

To find the volume of a prism:

(1) Find the number of cubes in one layer.

This is the same as the area of
the cross section.

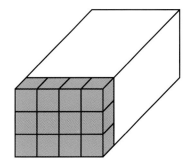

(2) Find the number of layers in the prism.

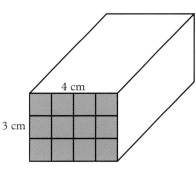

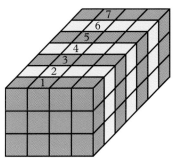

This is the same as the length of the prism.

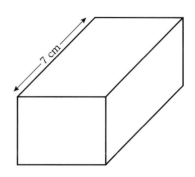

(3) Multiply the number of cubes in one layer by the number of layers. This is the same as multiplying the area of the cross section by the length.

---

**Volume of a prism**

The volume of a prism is **area of cross section × length**

If the prism is a cuboid this is the same as **length × width × height**

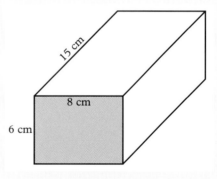

*Example*

Find the volume of this prism.

Area of cross section
$$= 6 \times 8$$
$$= 48 \text{ cm}^2$$

Volume $= 48 \times 15$
$$= 720 \text{ cm}^3$$

or    length × width × height $= 6 \times 8 \times 15 = 720 \text{ cm}^3$

---

## Exercise 14:7

Work out the volume of these prisms.

**1**

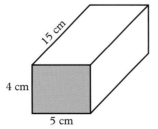

**2**

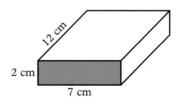

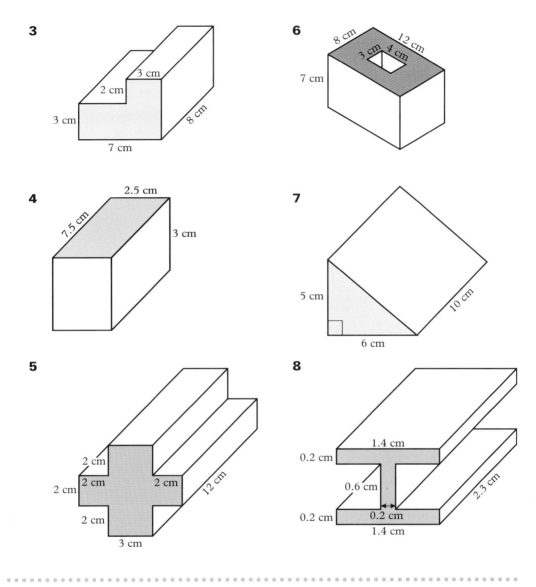

**3** 3 cm, 2 cm, 3 cm, 7 cm, 8 cm

**4** 2.5 cm, 7.5 cm, 3 cm

**5** 2 cm, 2 cm, 2 cm, 2 cm, 2 cm, 3 cm, 12 cm

**6** 8 cm, 3 cm, 4 cm, 12 cm, 7 cm

**7** 5 cm, 6 cm, 10 cm

**8** 1.4 cm, 0.2 cm, 0.6 cm, 2.3 cm, 0.2 cm, 0.2 cm, 1.4 cm

## Exercise 14:8

For each question:
**a** Sketch the shape.
Mark on the measurements.
**b** Colour the area of the cross section.
**c** Find the area of the cross section.
**d** Multiply the area of the cross section by the length to find the volume.

1 A cuboid with sides of length 5 cm, 8 cm and 3 cm.

2 A cube with sides 6 cm long.

3 A 750 g size cereal box has sides
of length 7 cm, 19 cm and 29 cm.

4 A 1 litre carton of juice is in the
shape of a cuboid.
It measures 5.9 cm by 9 cm by
19.5 cm.

5 A new type of tea is sold in a
T-shaped box.
The measurements are shown in
the diagram.

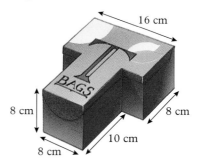

### Exercise 14:9

1 A 1 litre carton of milk is in the shape of a cuboid.
It measures 7 cm by 7 cm by 21 cm.
**a** Find the volume of the carton.
**b** 1 cm$^3$ takes up the same space as 1 m$l$.
How much space is left inside the carton when it has 1 $l$ of milk in it?

2 A Toberone box is in the shape of
a triangular prism.
The triangle has base of length
6 cm and height 5 cm.
The length of the box is 30 cm.
**a** Find the area of the cross section.
**b** Find the volume of the box.
**c** The triangular end is enlarged by
a scale factor of 2 but the length
is kept at 30 cm.
Find the volume of the new box.

**3** A trench is dug to lay some pipes.
The cross section of the trench is
in the shape of a trapezium.
It is 30 m long.

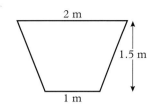

  **a** Find the area of the cross section of the trench.
  **b** Find the volume of earth dug out of the trench.
  **c** The earth is removed in skips. Each skip holds
    a volume of $12\,m^3$
    How many skips are needed to remove all of the earth?

**4** Saleem looks at two chocolate milkshake drinks.
One is in a bottle which has a capacity of 750 m*l*.
The other is in a carton which measures 8 cm by 6 cm by 15 cm.
Both containers are full.
Which one has the most milkshake in it?

**5** A bottle of fabric softener holds 1.5 litres.
The manufacturer wants to produce a carton to refill the bottle.
The carton must also hold 1.5 litres.
The base of the carton is a square with sides 8 cm.
How high does the carton need to be?
Give your answer to the nearest millimetre.

**6** A petrol tank in a car measures 60 cm by 50 cm by 30 cm.
  **a** Work out the volume of the tank in $cm^3$
  **b** Write your answer to part **a** in litres.
  **c** 1 gallon is about 4.5 litres.
    About how much petrol does the tank hold in gallons?

**7** **a** Hotchoc is sold in circular tins.
    The area of the end of the tin
    is $100\,cm^2$
    The tin is 15 cm high.
    Find the volume of the tin.
  **b** The Hotchoc company wants to
    change to rectangular tins.
    The new tin must have the same
    volume as the tin in part **a**.
    Suggest possible measurements
    for the new tin.

**8** Here is the cross section of a swimming pool.

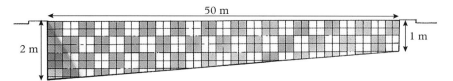

The pool is 15 m wide.
**a** Find the area of the cross section.
**b** Find the volume of the pool in m³
**c** Find the volume of the pool in litres. (1 m³ = 1000 *l*)
**d** The pool is filled at a rate of 10 litres each second.
How long does it take to fill the pool?

**9** A set of child's bricks contains 24 cubes with sides of 4 cm.
**a** Find the volume of each brick.
**b** Find the total volume of the whole set of bricks.
**c** The cubes are packed into a box.
Suggest possible measurements for the box.
**d** These boxes are to be packed into crates containing 100 boxes.
Find the volume of each crate.

**10** The cistern of Pauline's toilet is in
the shape of a cuboid.
The cistern measures 18 cm by
44 cm by 30 cm.
The cistern fills with water so that
it is three-quarters full.
**a** Find the volume of water in
the cistern in cm³.
**b** Write your answer to part **a** in litres.

Pauline puts a house brick into the
cistern so that it uses less water.
The brick measures 21 cm by 5 cm
by 10 cm.
**c** Find the volume of the brick.
**d** How many litres of water are now needed to fill the cistern to the
same level as before?
**e** What percentage saving of water is this?

## Exercise 14:10 Building a box

Get a piece of squared paper exactly 18 cm by 24 cm.

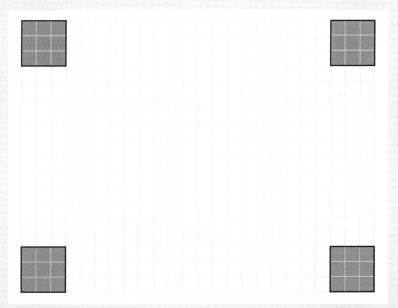

Cut squares out of each corner. This makes your paper into the net of a box.
Fold the paper to make the box.
Stick the corners with sticky tape.
The box will not have a lid.

Find the volume of the box.

Use more pieces of squared paper
18 cm by 24 cm to make more boxes.
Try changing the size of the squares
at the corners.

Find the volume of each box you make.
You will need to organise your results.

What is the biggest volume you can get?

Other things to try:
- The sides of the corner squares do not need to be a whole number of centimetres.
- You could make a box with a lid.
  How would this affect the volume?
- You could start with a piece of A4 paper.

Write a report on what you have found out.

**1** Estimate the volume of these containers.
You need to choose millilitres or litres.

**2** Find the volume of these blocks of cubes.
Write your answers in cm³

**a**

**b**

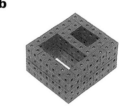

**3** Find the volume of these prisms.

**a**

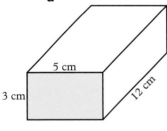

**c**

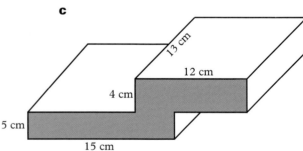

**b**

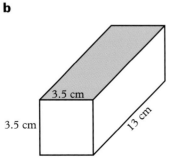

**d**

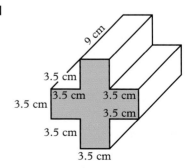

**4** For each question:
  (1) Sketch the shape.
    Mark on the measurements.
  (2) Colour the area of the cross section.
  (3) Find the area of the cross section.
  (4) Multiply the area of the cross section by the length to find
    the volume.
  **a** A box of computer discs which
    has sides of length 10 cm, 10 cm
    and 4.5 cm.
  **b** A CD case with sides of length
    14.2 cm, 12.4 cm and 1.1 cm.
  **c** This corner cabinet.

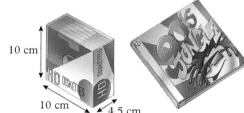

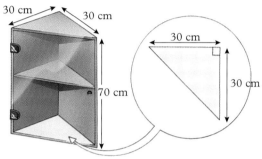

**5** **a** Find the volume of this piece of
    guttering in cm³. (Its total length
    is 5 m.)
  **b** How many litres of water will
    this guttering hold?

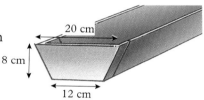

**6** This giant Toblerone box is in the
  shape of a triangular prism.
  The triangle has base of length
  15 cm and height 12.5 cm.
  The length of the box is 1 m.
  **a** Find the area of the cross section.
  **b** Find the volume of the box in cm³.
  This is a small Toblerone box.
  **c** How many times bigger are
    the lengths of the sides of the
    big box?
  **d** How many times more chocolate
    do you get in the big box?

313

**1** A corner unit is in the s
a prism.
This is the cross section

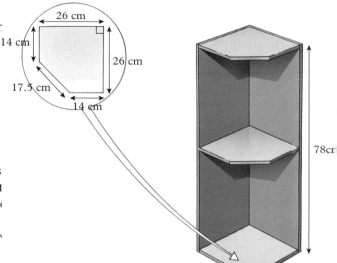

26 cm

14 cm

26 cm

17.5 cm

14 cm

78cr

**a** Find the volume ins
corner unit. Ignore t
The wood used to mak
1.5 cm thick.
**b** Find the volume of
to make the unit.

**2** This knife block is in
the shape of a prism.
Find the volume of
the knife block.

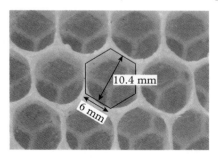

22 cm

12.5 cm

3.5 cm

8 cm

5 cm

19.5 cm

**3** Each cell in a honeycomb is a hexagonal prism about 12 mm deep.

10.4 mm

6 mm

**a** Find the volume of a cell in **cm³**
Every day the queen bee lays 3000 eggs.
Each egg is put in its own cell which is full
of honey.
**b** How many **litres** of honey are needed every week for the new eggs?

- **Volume**      The amount of space that an object takes up is called its **volume**.

- **Capacity**      The **capacity** of a hollow object is the volume of space inside it.

- **Units of volume**      Volume is measured in cubic units. These can be mm³, cm³ or m³

  **1 cm³**      **1 cm³** is the space taken up by a cube with all its edges 1 cm long.

  **Units of capacity**      This cube is filled with water. The volume of water inside is **1 millilitre**. This is written **1 ml**

  **1 ml**      **1 ml is the same as 1 cm³**

  We measure large volumes in litres.
  **1 litre = 1000 ml**

- **Prism**      A **prism** is a solid which is exactly the same shape all the way through.
  Wherever you cut a slice through the shape it is the same size and shape.

  **Cross section**      The shape of this slice is called the **cross section** of the solid.

- **Volume of a prism**      The volume of a prism is **area of cross section × length**

  If the prism is a cuboid this is the same as
  **length × width × height**

*Example*      Find the volume of this prism.

Area of cross section = $6 \times 8$
$$= 48 \text{ cm}^2$$

Volume = $48 \times 15$
$$= 720 \text{ cm}^3$$

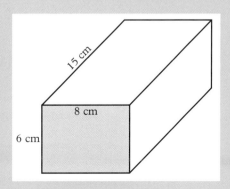

or    length × width × height = $6 \times 8 \times 15 = 720 \text{ cm}^3$

**1** Estimate the volume of these containers. You need to choose millilitres or litres.

**2** Find the volume of these prisms.

**a**

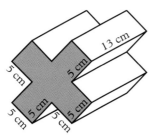

13 cm
5 cm
5 cm
5 cm
5 cm
5 cm
5 cm

**c**

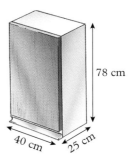

78 cm
40 cm
25 cm

**b**

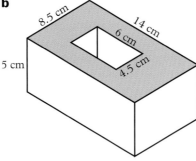

8.5 cm
14 cm
6 cm
5 cm
4.5 cm

**d**

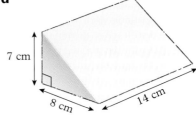

7 cm
8 cm
14 cm

**3** A water tank is in the shape of a cuboid.
The tank measures
1.2 m by 1.2 m by 0.8 m.
**a** Find the volume of the tank in **cm³**
The maximum depth of water in the tank is 0.7 m.
**b** How many litres of water are there in the tank when it is as full as possible?

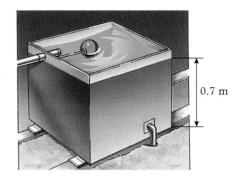

0.7 m

# 15 More or less?

A supertanker holds 300 000 tonnes of crude oil. This makes about 267 million litres of petrol.

A Mini covers about 13 km on 1 litre of petrol. The distance of the Sun from the Earth is about 150 million km.

So Bill could drive his car to the Sun and back more than 11 times!

# 1 Trial and improvement

◀◀**REPLAY**▶

Josie is practising her passing and shooting in hockey.
She sets up a target and tries to hit it.
If her ball goes to the right of the target she aims to the left next time.
If the ball goes to the left of the target she aims to the right next time.
She is getting closer to the target.

This happens in Maths.
You can solve equations by guessing different values. You then try to get closer to the right answer.

This method is called **trial and improvement**.

---

*Example*     Solve $12x - 35 = 163$

| Value of $x$ | Value of $12x - 35$ | |
|:---:|:---:|:---|
| 10 | 85 | too small |
| 20 | 205 | too big |
| 16 | 157 | too small |
| 17 | 169 | too big |
| 16.5 | 163 | correct |

Answer: $x = 16.5$

---

### Exercise 15:1

Solve these equations by trial and improvement.
For each question:
    copy the table
    fill it in
    add more rows until you find the answer.

**1**  $4x - 23 = 27$

| Value of $x$ | Value of $4x - 23$ | |
|---|---|---|
| 10 | | |
| 12 | | |
| 13 | | |

**2**  $8p + 25 = 221$     **3**  $25y - 124 = 356$

---

*Example*     Solve $x^2 = 1444$

| Value of $x$ | Value of $x^2$ | |
|---|---|---|
| 30 | 900 | too small |
| 40 | 1600 | too big |
| 38 | 1444 | correct |

Answer: $x = 38$

---

**4**  $x^2 + 25 = 2050$

| Value of $x$ | Value of $x^2 + 25$ | |
|---|---|---|
| 40 | | |

**5**  $x^2 - 253 = 3111$

| Value of $x$ | Value of $x^2 - 253$ | |
|---|---|---|
| | | |

**6**  $2x^2 = 2738$     *Remember: $2x^2$ means $2 \times x^2$*

**7**  $x^2 + x = 702$

**8**  $2x^2 - 3x + 35 = 1630$

Sometimes answers do not work out exactly.
When this happens you may have to give your answer correct to 1 dp.

*Example*     Solve $x^2 = 135$

| Value of $x$ | Value of $x^2$ | | |
|---|---|---|---|
| 11 | 121 | too small | |
| 12 | 144 | too big | $x$ is between 11 and 12 |
| 11.5 | 132.25 | too small | $x$ is between 11.5 and 12 |
| 11.6 | 134.56 | too small | $x$ is between 11.6 and 12 |
| 11.7 | 136.89 | too big | $x$ is between 11.6 and 11.7 |
| 11.65 | 135.7225 | too big | $x$ is between 11.6 and 11.65 |

11.6          11.65          11.7

$x$ must be somewhere in the green part of the number line. Any number in the green part rounds down to 11.6 to 1 dp.

Answer: $x = 11.6$ to 1 dp.

## Exercise 15:2

Solve these equations by trial and improvement.
Make a table to help you.
Give your answers to 1dp.

**1** $x^2 = 153$         **3** $x^2 = 456$         ● **5** $x(x + 1) = 259$

**2** $x^2 = 189$         **4** $x^2 + x = 153$      ● **6** $2x^2 + 5x = 1100$

**7** The area of this square is 559 cm².
Use trial and improvement to find the length of a side.
Give your answer to 1 dp.

$x$ | 559 cm²

$x$

**8** The length of this picture frame is
4 cm more than its width.
The area of the frame is 65 cm².
**a** Use trial and improvement to find
the width of the frame to 1 dp.
**b** Write down the length correct to 1 dp.

$x + 4$

$x$

**9**  The length of this garden is
three times its width.
The area is 45 m².
Find the width of the garden
using trial and improvement.
Give your answer to 1 dp.

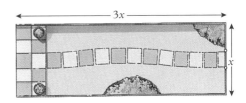

---

*Example*

You can give greater accuracy than 1 dp in your answer.
$x^2 = 135$ gives $x = 11.6$ to 1 dp but you can carry on to get
the answer to 2 dp.

| Value of $x$ | Value of $x^2$ | |
| --- | --- | --- |
| 11.6 | 134.56 | too small |
| 11.7 | 136.89 | too big |
| 11.65 | 135.7225 | too big |
| 11.61 | 134.7921 | too small |
| 11.62 | 135.0244 | too big |
| 11.615 | 134.908225 | too small |

$x$ is between 11.6 and 11.7
$x$ is between 11.6 and 11.65
$x$ is between 11.61 and 11.65
$x$ is between 11.61 and 11.62
$x$ is between 11.615 and 11.62

11.61     11.615     11.62

$x$ must be somewhere in the
green part of the number line.
Any number in the green part
rounds up to 11.62 to 2 dp.

Answer: $x = 11.62$ to 2 dp.

---

**10**  Solve the equations in questions **1–6**. Give your answers to 2 dp.

**11**  The area of this square carpet is 14 m².
Use trial and improvement to find the
length of a side correct to 2 dp.

● **12**  The area of a square carpet tile is 0.5 m².
Find the length of a side to the nearest centimetre.

● **13**  Solve the equations in questions **1–6**. Give your answers to 3 dp.

# 2  Inequalities

Mary wants to go on this ride.
She has to be at least 120 cm tall.
Her height must be greater than
or equal to 120 cm.
We write   height ⩾ 120
This is called an **inequality**.

---

**Number line**

We can show positive and negative numbers on a
**number line**.

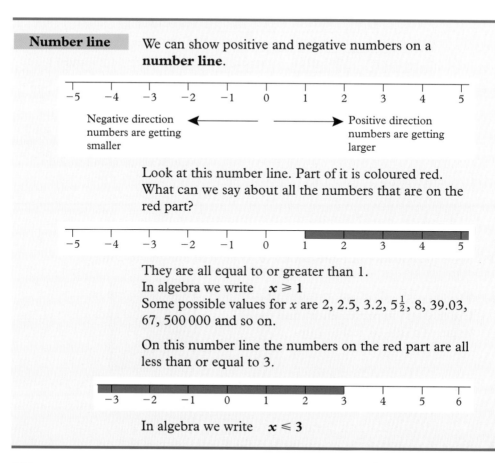

Look at this number line. Part of it is coloured red.
What can we say about all the numbers that are on the
red part?

They are all equal to or greater than 1.
In algebra we write   $x \geqslant 1$
Some possible values for $x$ are 2, 2.5, 3.2, $5\frac{1}{2}$, 8, 39.03,
67, 500 000 and so on.

On this number line the numbers on the red part are all
less than or equal to 3.

In algebra we write   $x \leqslant 3$

## Exercise 15:3

Use algebra to describe the numbers on the red part of the number line.

**1**

**2**

**3**

**4**

**5**

**6**

---

**Inequalities**   The signs $< \leqslant > \geqslant$ are all called inequality signs.

$x < 3$    $x \leqslant 5$    $x > 1$    $x \geqslant -2$ are called **inequalities**.

---

Draw a number line for each question.
Colour part of the number line to show the inequality.

**7**  $x \geqslant 2$        **9**  $x \geqslant 0$        **11**  $x \leqslant 1$

**8**  $x \geqslant -3$       **10**  $x \leqslant 3$       **12**  $x \leqslant -2$

---

*Examples*   **1**  Write down the possible values of $x$ if $x$ is a whole number and $x \geqslant 2$

The possible values of $x$ are 2, 3, 4, 5, 6, …
(… means that the numbers carry on in this way)

**2**  Write down the first five possible values of $x$ if $x$ is a whole number and $x > 2$

The first five possible values are 3, 4, 5, 6, 7

---

### Exercise 15:4

Write down the first five possible values of $x$ if $x$ is a whole number and:

**1**  $x \geqslant 4$      **4**  $x < 2$      **7**  $x \leqslant -2$

**2**  $x > -3$      **5**  $x \geqslant 0$      **8**  $x < -8$

**3**  $x \leqslant 5$      **6**  $x < 0$      **9**  $x \geqslant -7$

Sometimes you are asked to give just one of the possible values of $x$.
You can choose any one that you want.

Write down one possible value for $x$ if $x$ is a whole number and:

**10**  $x > 2$      **12**  $x < -1$      **14**  $x > -9$

**11**  $x \leqslant 3$      **13**  $x \geqslant 8$      **15**  $x \leqslant 1$

**16**  Write down one possible value for $x$ if $x > 2$ and $x$ is a square number.

In questions **17–20**, $x$ is a whole number.

**17**  Write down the highest value $x$ can have if $x < 5$

**18**  Write down the lowest value $x$ can have if $x > 2$

**19**  Write down the highest value $x$ can have if $x \leqslant -4$

**20**  Write down the lowest value $x$ can have if $x \geqslant -7$

**21**  Write down one possible value for $x$ if $x > 7$ and $x$ is a prime number.

**22**  Write down one possible value for $x$ if $x > -3$ and $x$ is a positive number.

---

Nathan wants to show $x > 1$ on a
number line.
He starts colouring the line. He doesn't
know how to show that 1 is not a
possible value.

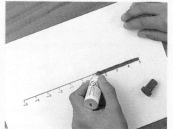

He draws a line above the number line
like this:

The circle above the 1 is not coloured in.
This shows that 1 is not a possible value of $x$.

Nathan shows $x \geqslant 1$ on a number line like this:

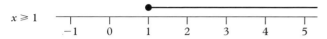

The circle above the 1 is coloured in. This shows that 1 is a possible value of $x$.

$x \leqslant 3$ on a number line is

$x < 3$ on a number line is

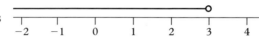

## Exercise 15:5

Show these inequalities on number lines.

**1**  $x \geqslant 2$        **4**  $x \geqslant -1$        **7**  $x < -3$

**2**  $x > 1$        **5**  $x \leqslant 3$        **8**  $x > -4$

**3**  $x < 4$        **6**  $x \leqslant -2$        **9**  $x \geqslant 0$

Write down the inequality shown on the number line.

**10**
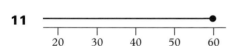

**11**

**12**
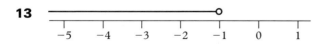

**13**

**14**

**15**

Michael wants to go on a fairground ride. He can only go on this ride if his height is at least 120 cm but less than 160 cm.

We write $h \geqslant 120$ and $h < 160$

We can show these on a number line.

$h \geqslant 120$

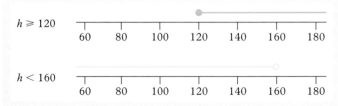

$h < 160$

Michael's height must fit both the inequalities. We look for the overlap of the lines.

In algebra we write $120 \leqslant h < 160$

We have made the two inequalities into one double inequality.

## Exercise 15:6

Show these inequalities on number lines.

**1** $2 \leqslant x < 4$     **3** $0 < x \leqslant 5$     **5** $-5 \leqslant x \leqslant -1$

**2** $1 \leqslant x \leqslant 6$     **4** $-4 \leqslant x < 3$     **6** $-3 < x < 0$

Write down the inequality shown on the number line.

**7** 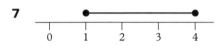    **10**

**8** 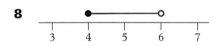    **11**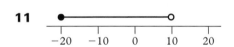

**9**     **12**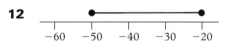

*Example*

Write down all the possible values of $x$ if $x$ is a whole number and $1 \leqslant x \leqslant 5$

$1 \leqslant x \leqslant 5$ on a number line is

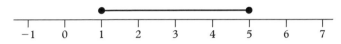

But $x$ can only be a whole number.
The possible values of $x$ are 1, 2, 3, 4, 5

Write down all the possible values of $x$ if $x$ is a whole number and:

**13**  $3 \leqslant x \leqslant 5$     **15**  $7 \leqslant x \leqslant 10$     **17**  $-7 \leqslant x \leqslant -3$

**14**  $0 \leqslant x \leqslant 4$     **16**  $-2 \leqslant x \leqslant 1$     **18**  $2 \leqslant x \leqslant 3$

*Example*

Write down all the possible values of $x$ if $x$ is a whole number and $2 \leqslant x < 4$

$2 \leqslant x < 4$ on a number line is

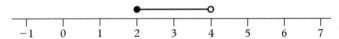

But $x$ can only be a whole number.
The possible values of $x$ are 2, 3
(4 is not a possible value because $x < 4$ means that 4 is not included.)

## Exercise 15:7

Write down all the possible values of $x$ if $x$ is a whole number and:

**1**  $1 \leqslant x < 6$     **3**  $3 < x \leqslant 7$     **5**  $7 < x < 13$

**2**  $-2 \leqslant x < 3$     **4**  $-6 < x \leqslant 0$     **6**  $-9 \leqslant x < -2$

Write down one possible value for $x$ if $x$ is a whole number and:

**7**  $5 \leqslant x < 8$     **9**  $3 < x < 5$     **11**  $-7 < x < -5$

**8**  $-1 < x \leqslant 2$     **10**  $0 \leqslant x < 5$     **12**  $0 \leqslant x \leqslant 2$

# 3 Solving simple linear inequalities

The lift cable will break if there are too many people in the lift.
The cable is safe if the total weight of the lift and people is
less than or equal to 1400 kg.

$$w\text{eight of people} + \text{weight of lift} \leqslant 1400$$

The weight of the lift is 824 kg.

$$w + 824 \leqslant 1400$$

---

We need to solve the inequality to find the maximum safe weight of people.
We do this in the same way as we solved equations.
We use inverses.

$$w + 824 \leqslant 1400$$

The inverse of $+824$ is $-824$

$$w + 824 - 824 \leqslant 1400 - 824$$
$$w \leqslant 576$$

We have solved the inequality.
The maximum safe weight of people is 576 kg.

---

### Exercise 15:8

Solve these inequalities using inverses.

**1** $x + 3 \geqslant 5$      **2** $x + 6 \leqslant 9$      **3** $x + 2 < 6$

*Example*
Solve the inequality $x - 3 < 7$
Show the answer on a number line.

$$x - 3 + 3 < 7 + 3$$
$$x < 10$$

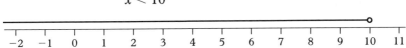

Solve these inequalities.
Show the answers on number lines.

**4** $x + 1 < 2$     **6** $x - 1 \leq 3$     **8** $x - 6 > 1$

**5** $x - 2 \geq 7$     **7** $x + 4 \leq 6$     **9** $x - 5 \leq 4$

**10** Bill's small van cannot carry more than 1000 kg.
This includes Bill's weight.

weight of boxes + Bill's weight $\leq 1000$

Bill weighs 85 kg.
What is the greatest weight of boxes that Bill can put in the van?

Write down the first five possible values for $x$ if $x$ is a whole number and:

**11** $x + 1 \leq 5$     **13** $x - 5 \geq 3$     **15** $x - 1 \leq 1$

**12** $x - 3 > 2$     **14** $x + 6 < 7$     **16** $x - 3 < 0$

Write down one possible value for $x$ if $x$ is a whole number and:

**17** $x - 2 > 12$     **19** $x + 7 < 20$     **21** $x + 9 > 1$

**18** $x + 6 \leq 5$     **20** $x - 8 \geq 2$     **22** $x + 5 \geq 0$

*Example*
Solve the inequality $3x \geq 12$

$3x$ means that $x$ is multiplied by 3.
The inverse of $\times 3$ is $\div 3$

$$\frac{3x}{3} \geq \frac{12}{3}$$     *Remember:* $\frac{12}{3}$ means $12 \div 3$

$$x \geq 4$$

## Exercise 15:9

Solve these inequalities.

**1** $5x > 25$             **4** $3x < 21$

**2** $2x \leqslant 8$             **5** $10x \geqslant 40$

**3** $4x \geqslant 12$             **6** $6x \leqslant 18$

---

*Example*

Solve the inequality $\frac{x}{4} \geqslant 2$

$\frac{x}{4}$ means that $x$ is divided by 4.

The inverse of $\div 4$ is $\times 4$

$\frac{x}{4} \times 4 \geqslant 2 \times 4$

$x \geqslant 8$

---

Solve these inequalities.

**7** $\frac{x}{2} < 6$             **10** $\frac{x}{8} \geqslant 5$

**8** $\frac{x}{5} \geqslant 3$             **11** $\frac{x}{3} > 7$

**9** $\frac{x}{7} \leqslant 10$             **12** $\frac{x}{9} \leqslant 11$

**13** A chef cuts a large cheesecake into
24 slices.
Each slice must weigh at least 150 g.

$$\frac{\text{weight of cheesecake}}{24} \geqslant 150$$

Solve this inequality to find the
minimum weight of the cheesecake.

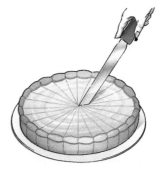

*Example*

Solve the inequality $4x + 3 \geqslant 19$

$4x + 3$ means that
  (1) $x$ is multiplied by 4
  (2) then 3 is added

The inverse of this process is:
  (1) take away 3
$$4x + 3 - 3 \geqslant 19 - 3$$
$$4x \geqslant 16$$
  (2) divide by 4
$$\frac{4x}{4} \geqslant \frac{16}{4}$$
$$x \geqslant 4$$

## Exercise 15:10

Solve these inequalities.

**1**   $2x + 3 > 15$     **3**   $5x + 12 \geqslant 7$     • **5**   $4x + 45 \geqslant 55$

**2**   $4x - 5 < 19$     **4**   $6x + 34 \leqslant 22$     • **6**   $30x - 345 < 63$

*Example*

Solve $15 < 4x + 7 < 19$

This is a double inequality (two inequalities written together)
$$15 < 4x + 7 \text{ and } 4x + 7 < 19$$

Solve each inequality in turn.

$$\begin{array}{ll} 15 < 4x + 7 & 4x + 7 < 19 \\ 15 - 7 < 4x + 7 - 7 & 4x + 7 - 7 < 19 - 7 \\ 8 < 4x & 4x < 12 \\ \dfrac{8}{4} < \dfrac{4x}{4} & \dfrac{4x}{4} < \dfrac{12}{4} \\ 2 < x & x < 3 \end{array}$$

Then put the two parts back together.
Answer: $2 < x < 3$

Solve these double inequalities.

**7**   $35 < 3x + 8 < 44$         **10**   $-35 < 12x + 13 < -11$

**8**   $36 \leqslant 6x - 42 \leqslant 54$       • **11**   $23 < 8x + 7 \leqslant 35$

**9**   $-7 \leqslant 3x - 1 \leqslant 32$       • **12**   $-40 < 34x - 57 < 28$

## Exercise 15:11

Find all the possible values of $x$ if $x$ is a whole number and:

**1**  $4 < 2x - 4 < 8$

**4**  $27 < 12x - 9 \leqslant 51$

**2**  $13 \leqslant 4x + 5 \leqslant 29$

● **5**  $32 < 20x - 18 < 92$

**3**  $12 \leqslant 3x + 9 < 24$

● **6**  $55 \leqslant 3x + 1 < 64$

---

Some people solve double inequalities like this:

*Example*

$$\text{Solve} \quad 25 < \quad 6x + 7 \quad < 31$$
$$25 - 7 < 6x + 7 - 7 < 31 - 7$$
$$18 < \quad 6x \quad < 24$$
$$\frac{18}{6} < \quad \frac{6x}{6} \quad < \frac{24}{6}$$
$$3 < \quad x \quad < 4$$

This is the same as before but the two parts are done at the same time.

---

## Exercise 15:12

Use the method in the last example to solve these inequalities. Show the answers on number lines.

**1**  $15 < 3x + 9 < 45$

**5**  $-35 \leqslant 4x + 7 < 29$

**2**  $22 \leqslant 5x - 8 < 37$

**6**  $183 < 42x + 78 < 351$

**3**  $51 \leqslant 8x + 19 \leqslant 59$

● **7**  $5 < \frac{x}{4} + 1 \leqslant 13$

**4**  $-26 < 4x - 18 \leqslant -22$

● **8**  $-3 \leqslant \frac{x}{3} + 2 \leqslant 0$

**1**  Solve $x^2 + x = 153$ by trial and improvement.
Copy this table to help you.
Give your answer correct to 1 dp.

| Value of $x$ | Value of $x^2 + x$ | |
|---|---|---|
| | | |

**2**  Solve $2x^2 + x = 271$ by trial and improvement.
Copy this table to help you.
Give your answer correct to 1 dp.

| Value of $x$ | Value of $2x^2 + x$ | |
|---|---|---|
| | | |

**3**  Show these inequalities on number lines.

  **a**  $x < 5$        **c**  $x \leqslant -3$        **e**  $x \leqslant 1$

  **b**  $x \geqslant -4$        **d**  $x > 0$        **f**  $x > -6$

**4**  Write down the inequality shown on the number line.

**a**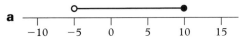

**b**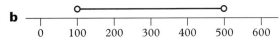

**c**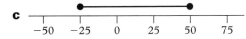

**d**

**5**  Solve these inequalities.

  **a**  $x + 4 \geqslant 9$        **d**  $5x \leqslant 35$        **g**  $4x - 3 > 17$

  **b**  $x - 3 < 7$        **e**  $\dfrac{x}{4} > 6$        **h**  $5 \leqslant 2x - 13 < 17$

  **c**  $2x \geqslant 12$        **f**  $\dfrac{x}{7} \leqslant 12$        **i**  $27 < 5x + 7 \leqslant 42$

**1** **a** Solve these equations by trial and improvement.
Give your answers correct to 1 dp.
(1) $x^3 = 120$
(2) $3^x = 15$
(3) $x^3 + \sqrt{x} = 35$

**b** Solve this equation by trial and improvement.
$$x^2 - 14x = 10$$
One solution is between 10 and 20 and the other is negative.
Find both solutions correct to 1 dp.

**2** **a** Write down all the possible values of $x$ if $x$ is a whole number and $1 \leqslant x \leqslant 7$

**b** These inequalities give the same possible values of $x$ as part **a**.
Copy and fill in the gaps:
$\ldots < x \leqslant 7$          $\ldots < x < \ldots$          $\ldots \leqslant x < \ldots$

In questions **3–6**, $x$ is a whole number.

**3** Write down the four inequalities that have 5, 6, 7, 8, 9 as the possible values of $x$.

**4** Write down the four inequalities that have $-4, -3, -2, -1$ as the possible values of $x$.

**5** What inequalities have 10 as the only possible value of $x$?

**6** What inequalities have $-4$ as the only possible value of $x$?

**7** Look at these facts:

If $x = 4$ then $x^2 = 4 \times 4$          If $x = -4$ then $x^2 = -4 \times -4$

$= 16$          $= 16$

**a** Investigate which values of $x$ satisfy the inequality $x^2 > 16$
*Hint:* Some answers are positive and some are negative.

**b** Investigate which values of $x$ satisfy the inequality $x^2 < 1$
*Hint:* Again some answers are positive and some are negative.

**8** Solve these inequalities.

| | | |
|---|---|---|
| **a** $x^2 < 9$ | **d** $x^2 < 100$ | **g** $x^3 > 27$ |
| **b** $x^2 \geqslant 25$ | **e** $x^2 \leqslant 4$ | **h** $x^3 \leqslant 125$ |
| **c** $x^2 > 36$ | **f** $x^2 > 121$ | **i** $x^4 \geqslant 16$ |

**9** Which values of $x$ satisfy the inequality $x^2 < x$?

- ## *Trial and improvement*

*Example*    Solve $x^2 = 135$

| Value of $x$ | Value of $x^2$ | |
|---|---|---|
| 11 | 121 | too small |
| 12 | 144 | too big |
| 11.5 | 132.25 | too small |
| 11.6 | 134.56 | too small |
| 11.7 | 136.89 | too big |
| 11.65 | 135.7225 | too big |

$x$ is between 11 and 12
$x$ is between 11.5 and 12
$x$ is between 11.6 and 12
$x$ is between 11.6 and 11.7
$x$ is between 11.6 and 11.65

Answer: $x = 11.6$ to 1 dp.

$x$ must be somewhere in the green part of the number line. Any number in the green part rounds down to 11.6 to 1 dp.

- *Example*    Write down all the possible values of $x$ if $x$ is a whole number and $2 \leqslant x < 4$

  The possible values of $x$ are 2, 3
  (4 is not a possible value because $x < 4$ means that 4 is not included.)

- *Example*    Solve the inequality $4x + 3 \geqslant 19$

$$4x + 3 - 3 \geqslant 19 - 3$$
$$4x \geqslant 16$$
$$\frac{4x}{4} \geqslant \frac{16}{4}$$
$$x \geqslant 4$$

- *Example*    Solve $15 < 4x + 7 < 19$

$$15 < 4x + 7 \qquad\qquad 4x + 7 < 19$$
$$15 - 7 < 4x + 7 - 7 \qquad 4x + 7 - 7 < 19 - 7$$
$$8 < 4x \qquad\qquad 4x < 12$$
$$\frac{8}{4} < \frac{4x}{4} \qquad\qquad \frac{4x}{4} < \frac{12}{4}$$
$$2 < x \qquad\qquad x < 3$$

Then put the two parts back together.
Answer: $2 < x < 3$

**1** Solve $x^2 + 56 = 622$ by trial and improvement.
Copy this table. Fill it in.
Add more rows until you have found $x$ correct to 1 dp.

| Value of $x$ | Value of $x^2 + 56$ | |
|:---:|:---:|:---:|
| 20 | | |

**2** Show these inequalities on number lines.
**a** $x \geqslant -1$        **c** $x < 4$
**b** $3 < x \leqslant 6$        **d** $-1 \leqslant x < 2$

**3** Write down the possible value of $x$ if $x$ is a square number and
$12 \leqslant x < 19$

**4** Write down all the possible values of $x$ if $x$ is a whole number and
$7 \leqslant x < 11$

**5** Write down the highest value $x$ can have if $x < 7$ and $x$ is a
whole number.

**6** Write down the lowest value $x$ can have if $x \geqslant 8$ and $x$ is a
whole number.

**7** Solve these inequalities.
Show the answers on number lines.
**a** $x + 3 < 7$        **b** $x - 4 \geqslant 1$

**8** Solve these inequalities.
**a** $3x \geqslant 18$        **c** $4x - 7 < 13$

**b** $\dfrac{x}{4} \leqslant 2$        **d** $7 \leqslant 3x - 2 < 22$

**9** Write down the inequality shown on the number line.

**a** 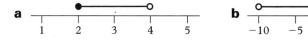    **b**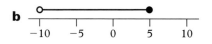

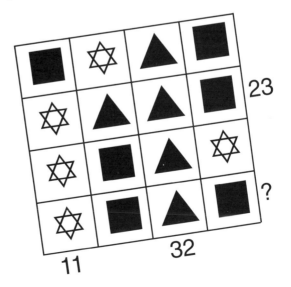

# 16 The crossing point

Each symbol in the diagram has a value. The total values are placed alongside some rows and columns. What number should replace the question mark to give the value of the bottom row?

# 1   Intersecting lines

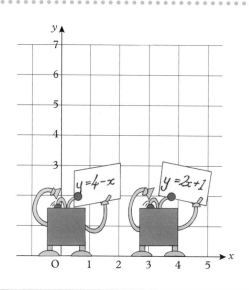

**◄◄REPLAY►**

*Example*

The robot has to draw the line
$y = 2x + 1$
He uses the $x$ values 1, 2, 3

He can use screens:

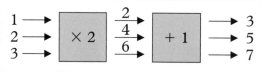

or he can use a table:

| $x$ | 1 | 2 | 3 |
|---|---|---|---|
| $y$ | 3 | 5 | 7 |

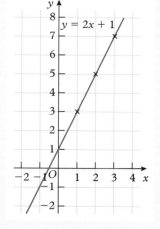

He plots the points (1, 3) (2, 5) (3, 7)
He joins them with a ruler.
He labels his line with its equation $y = 2x + 1$

You only need two points to draw a straight line.
The third point acts as a check.

## Exercise 16:1

**1** Copy the axes from the example.
Use the $x$ values 1, 2, 3 in **a** and **b**.
  **a** Draw the line $y = x + 2$
    Label your line.
  **b** On the same set of axes draw the line $y = 3x - 2$
    Label your line.
  **c** Write down the co-ordinates of the point where the two lines cross.
    *Remember:* this is called a **point of intersection**.

Make a table for each of these lines. Do not draw the lines.
Use the $x$ values 1, 2, 3.

**2** $y = 4x + 1$       **5** $y = 3x - 7$       **8** $y = 10 - 2x$

**3** $y = 5x - 3$       **6** $y = 4x - 8$       **9** $y = 4 - 3x$

**4** $y = 4 + 2x$       **7** $y = 6 - x$       **10** $y = 1 - 5x$

**11** Copy the axes from question **1**.
  **a** Draw and label the line $y = 2x - 1$
  **b** Draw and label the line $y = 7 - 2x$
  **c** Write down the co-ordinates of the point of intersection of the lines.

- - - - - - - - - - - - - - - - - - - - - - - - - - - - - - - - - - - - - - - - - - - - - - - - - - - - - - - -

Sometimes equations of lines are written in a different way.

*Example*    Draw the line $x + 2y = 4$

We do not use $x = 1$, 2 and 3 for this
type of equation.
It is easier to find points when $x = 0$
and when $y = 0$

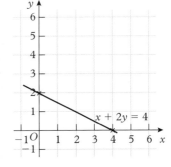

When $x = 0$       When $y = 0$
   $0 + 2y = 4$      $x + 2 \times 0 = 4$
     $2y = 4$         $x + 0 = 4$
      $y = 2$           $x = 4$
This gives $(0, 2)$   This gives $(4, 0)$

It can be difficult to find a third point. We will just use two.

## Exercise 16:2

**1**  Copy the axes on to squared paper.

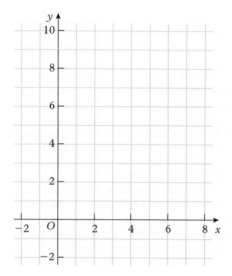

**a**  Find the co-ordinates of two points on the line $x + 3y = 6$

**b**  Plot the points.
Draw and label the line $x + 3y = 6$

**2**  Repeat question **1** for these lines.
Plot all the lines on the same diagram.
Label each line.

$x + y = 7$        $2x + y = 8$
$5x + y = 10$      $3x + y = 9$

**3**  Repeat question **2** for these lines.

$x + 4y = 8$        $x - y = 2$
$4x + 3y = 24$     $5x + 3y = 30$

# 2   Solving problems with lines

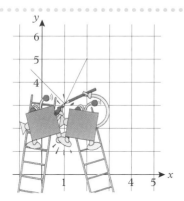

You can use graphs of intersecting lines to solve problems.

*Example*   Charlotte and Brendan are buying presents.
Charlotte buys one *perfume* spray and one bottle of *aftershave* for £5.
Brendan buys three *perfume* sprays and two bottles of *aftershave* for £12.
Find the cost of a perfume spray and the cost of a bottle of aftershave.

Charlotte's equation is $p + a = 5$
Two points on this line are $(0, 5)$
and $(5, 0)$

Brendan's equation is $3p + 2a = 12$
Two points on this line are $(0, 6)$
and $(4, 0)$

The lines intersect at $(2, 3)$
This means that $p = 2$ and $a = 3$

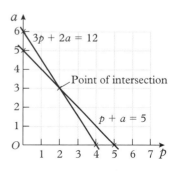

So a perfume spray costs £2 and a bottle of aftershave costs £3.

*Check:*   We can check the answer.

Charlotte buys one perfume spray and one bottle of aftershave.
They cost £2 + £3, which is £5.

Brendan buys three perfume sprays and two bottles of aftershave.
They cost $3 \times £2 + 2 \times £3$, which is £12.

**Simultaneous equations**   Equations we solve at the same time like this are called **simultaneous equations**.

### Exercise 16:3

Check your answers in the original problem each time.

**1** A shop is having a sale of CDs and
games.
Sonya buys one **CD** and
one **g**ame for £10.
Jamie buys three **CD**s and
two **g**ames for £24.
Find the cost of one CD and the
cost of one game.

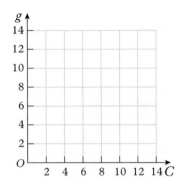

**2** The Smith family and the Patel
family go to the theatre together.
The Smiths buy one **a**dult ticket
and four **children**'s tickets at
a cost of £12.
The Patels buy two **a**dult tickets and
one **child**'s ticket at a cost of £10.
Find the cost of an adult ticket and
the cost of a child's ticket.

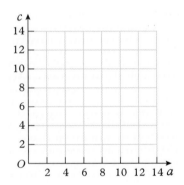

**3**

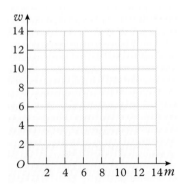

Denis is going fishing. He uses maggots and worms as bait for the fish.
Ten **m**aggots and four **w**orms cost 40 p.
One **m**aggot and one **w**orm cost 7 p.
Find the cost of one maggot and the cost of one worm.

**4**

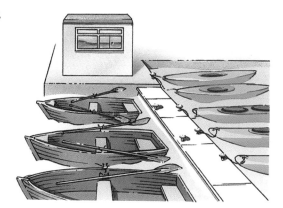

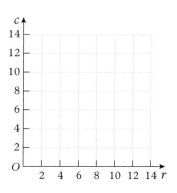

Emma hires out boats.
Her charges are for one hour's hire of a rowing boat or canoe.
One Saturday morning she hires out one **r**owing boat and
two **c**anoes during the first hour.
She takes £10 for these.
During the second hour she hires out three **r**owing boats and
four **c**anoes and takes £24.
Find the cost of an hour's hire of a rowing boat and the cost of
an hour's hire of a canoe.

**5** Stanthorne High is having a
school fair.
At the cake stall Henry buys two
**b**uns and five pieces of **f**lapjack
for 50 p.
His friend Wasim is less greedy.
Wasim only buys one **b**un and
one piece of **f**lapjack for 13 p.
Find the cost of one bun and the
cost of one piece of flapjack.

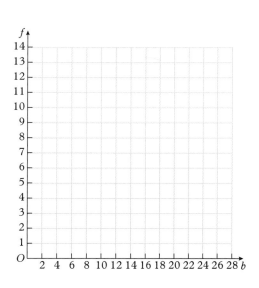

**6** Mrs Evans is buying a train set for her son Owen.
She pays £60 for one **e**ngine and one **c**arriage.
An **e**ngine costs three times as much as a **c**arriage.
Find the cost of an engine and the cost of a carriage.

*Example*  Find two points on the line $5x - 3y = 15$

| When $x = 0$ | When $y = 0$ |
|---|---|
| $5 \times 0 - 3y = 15$ | $5x - 3 \times 0 = 15$ |
| $-3y = 15$ | $5x = 15$ |
| $3y = -15$ | $x = 3$ |
| $y = -5$ | This gives (3, 0) |
| This gives (0, $-5$) | |

We use these two points to draw a graph.

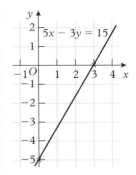

## Exercise 16:4

Find two points on each of these lines. Do not draw the lines.

**1**  $3y - 2x = 12$   **4**  $2x - 5y = 20$   **7**  $5x - 4y = 80$

**2**  $7y - 4x = 28$   **5**  $6x - 2y = 36$   **8**  $9y - 4x = 72$

**3**  $3x + 4y = 12$   **6**  $5y + 2x = 30$   **9**  $13x + 2y = 26$

**10**  Draw an $s$ axis from $-3$ to 7 and a $t$ axis from $-2$ to 10.
At the Stanthorne High school fair, a school enterprise company is selling scarves and ties.
The headteacher buys five *scarves* and three *ties* for £30.
A *tie* costs £2 more than a *scarf*.
Find the cost of a scarf and the cost of a tie.

● **11**  A group of friends have a Chinese meal.
They have eight portions of *curried chicken* and two portions of *sweet and sour king prawns*.
The *sweet and sour king prawns* costs £3 more than the *curried chicken*.
The bill comes to £32.
Find the cost of a portion of curried chicken and the cost of a portion of sweet and sour king prawns.

# 3  Using algebra

Kate has found a puzzle in a newspaper.
She has to find the value of each shape.

*Exercise 16:5*

**1**  Here is Kate's newspaper problem.
The shapes add up to the numbers shown.
Kate has to find the value of each shape.

She sees that four squares add up to 16.
One square must have value 4.

| | | | | |
|---|---|---|---|---|
| ▲ | ▲ | ● | ● | 10 |
| ▲ | ▲ | ● | ■ | 12 |
| ■ | ■ | ■ | ■ | 16 |

Two *c*ircles and two *t*riangles add up to 10.
One circle, two triangles and one square add up to 12.
One *c*ircle and two *t*riangles must add up to 8.

$$2t + 2c = 10$$

$$2t + c = 8$$

Find the value of a circle and the value of a triangle.

Solve these picture puzzles.

**2**

| | | | | |
|---|---|---|---|---|
| ♥ | ♣ | ♥ | ♥ | 9 |
| ♦ | ♦ | ♦ | ♦ | 20 |
| ♦ | ♦ | ♥ | ♣ | 15 |

**3**

| | | | | |
|---|---|---|---|---|
| B | A | A | C | 16 |
| B | A | B | A | 14 |
| C | C | C | C | 32 |

We can solve simultaneous equations using algebra.

---

*Example*

Solve this pair of simultaneous equations $5x + y = 25$
$$3x + y = 17$$

Number the equations

(1) $5x + y = 25$
(2) $3x + y = 17$

Subtract to get rid of $y$

Subtract $2x \quad = 8$

This finds $x$

$x = 4$

Use equation (1) to find $y$

Put $x = 4$ in equation (1)
$$5 \times 4 + y = 25$$
$$20 + y = 25$$
$$y = 5$$

The answer is $x = 4$, $y = 5$

Use equation (2) to check your answer $\quad 3x + y = 17$

Check: $\quad 12 + 5 = 17$ ✓ Correct

---

### Exercise 16:6

Solve these pairs of simultaneous equations.
Start by subtracting the equations each time.

**1** $4x + y = 13$
$x + y = 4$

**4** $4x + 2y = 34$
$x + 2y = 22$

**2** $7x + y = 44$
$4x + y = 26$

**5** $5x + 3y = 29$
$2x + 3y = 17$

**3** $5x + 2y = 45$
$3x + 2y = 35$

**6** $2x + 5y = 57$
$x + 5y = 46$

*Example*  Solve this pair of simultaneous equations  $2x + y = 16$
$$x - y = 2$$

Number the equations

(1) $2x + y = 16$
(2) $\underline{x - y = 2}$

We add to get rid of $y$  Add  $3x \quad = 18$

This finds $x$  $x = 6$

Use equation (1) to find $y$  Put $x = 6$ in equation (1)
$$2 \times 6 + y = 16$$
$$12 + y = 16$$
$$y = 4$$

The answer is $x = 6$, $y = 4$

Use equation (2) to check your answer  $x - y = 2$
Check:  $6 - 4 = 2 \checkmark$ Correct

## Exercise 16:7

Solve these pairs of simultaneous equations.
Start by adding the equations each time.

**1** $4x + y = 23$
$x - y = 2$

**4** $4x + 2y = 42$
$3x - 2y = 14$

**2** $3x + y = 13$
$x - y = 3$

**5** $2x + 3y = 21$
$4x - 3y = 15$

**3** $x + 2y = 11$
$3x - 2y = 17$

**6** $5x + 3y = 45$
$4x - 3y = 36$

## Exercise 16:8

Solve these pairs of simultaneous equations.
You need to decide whether to add or subtract the equations.

**1** $3x + y = 22$
$4x - y = 20$

**4** $4x - 3y = 12$
$x + 3y = 18$

**2** $5x + y = 17$
$3x + y = 11$

**5** $5x + 2y = 56$
$2x - 2y = 14$

**3** $4x + 2y = 22$
$3x + 2y = 17$

**6** $7x + 4y = 86$
$3x + 4y = 62$

You don't always need lines to solve puzzles.
Here are some puzzles to solve without lines.

### Exercise 16:9

1 The numbers in ◯ and ◯ add up to the number in ▢ like this:

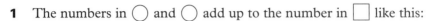

**a** Copy these.
Fill in the missing numbers.

(1) 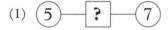   (3)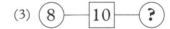

(2)    (4)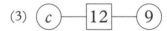

**b** Write down the value of each letter:

(1) (2)—[ a ]—(3)   (3) ( c )—[12]—(9)

(2) (10)—[ b ]—(5)   (4) (15)—[20]—( d )

2 The numbers in △ and △ are multiplied to give the number in ▢ like this:

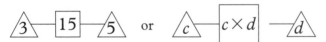

**a** Copy these.
Fill in the missing numbers.

(1) 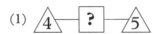   (3)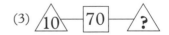

(2) 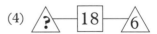   (4)

**b** Write down the value of each letter.

(1) 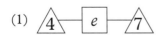   (3)

(2)    (4)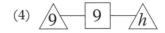

**1**  **a**  Copy the axes on to squared paper.
   **b**  (1) Make a table for $y = x + 5$
       (2) Draw and label the line $y = x + 5$
   **c**  (1) Make a table for $y = 4x - 4$
       (2) Draw and label the line $y = 4x - 4$
   **d**  Write down the co-ordinates of the
       point of intersection of the lines.

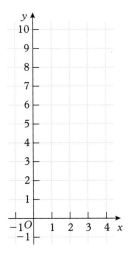

**2**  Find two points on each of these lines. Do not draw the lines.
   **a**  $9x + y = 18$          **c**  $2x + 4y = 16$
   **b**  $3x + y = 30$          **d**  $3x + 2y = 18$

**3**  Draw a $c$ axis from 0 to 12 and an $a$ axis from 0 to 30.
   Two families go out ten-pin bowling together.
   The Morley family pay £24 for two *a*dults and one *c*hild.
   The Pleavin family pay £27 for one *a*dult and three *c*hildren.
   Find the cost of a child's ticket and the cost of an adult's ticket.

   Solve these pairs of simultaneous equations using algebra.
   You need to decide whether to add or subtract the equations.

**4**   $x + 2y = 17$              **6**   $2x - y = 10$
    $3x - 2y = 27$                   $3x + y = 25$

**5**   $2x + 3y = 23$             **7**   $5x + 4y = 30$
    $4x + 3y = 31$                   $3x + 4y = 18$

**8**  Solve this puzzle.

| P | P | P | P | P | 30 |
|---|---|---|---|---|----|
| B | B | B | A | A | 18 |
| P | P | B | A | A | 22 |

**1 a** Three points on this line are marked ×.
Write down their co-ordinates.
These three points lie on the line with
the equation …$x$ + …$y$ = 12
Find the missing numbers in the
equation.

**b** These points lie on the line.
Use your answer to **a** to find the missing
co-ordinates.
(−3, …)   (…, −10)

**c** The point (4, 5) is above the line.
Look at these points:
(4, 0)   (2, 5)   (−1, −5)   (−2, 6)
Which of these points are above the line?
Explain your answer.

**d** The point (…, 20) is above the line.
Write down a possible $x$ co-ordinate for the point.

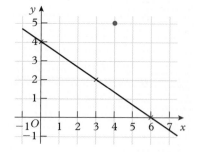

**2** Copy the axes on to squared paper.
**a** Draw and label the line $y = 2x - 1$
**b** Draw and label the line $y = 2 - x$
This is the first parallel line.
**c** Draw and label the second
parallel line $y = 5 - x$
**d** Draw and label the third
parallel line $y = 8 - x$
**e** Write down the equation of the
next parallel line in the pattern.
**f** Write down the co-ordinates of the
points of intersection of the first
three parallel lines with the line
$y = 2x - 1$
**g** Look at your answer to **f**.
Write down the co-ordinates of the
point of intersection of the fourth
parallel line with the line $y = 2x - 1$
**h** Where will the tenth parallel line cross $y = 2x - 1$?
**i** Write down the equation of the 15th parallel line.

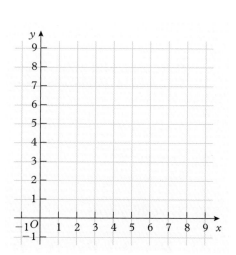

- *Example*

The robot has to draw the line $y = 2x + 1$
He uses the $x$ values 1, 2, 3
He can use screens or he can use a table:

| $x$ | 1 | 2 | 3 |
|---|---|---|---|
| $y$ | 3 | 5 | 7 |

He plots the points (1, 3) (2, 5) (3, 7)

- *Example*

Draw the line $5x - 3y = 15$

We do not use $x = 1$, 2 and 3 for this type of equation.
It is easier to find points when $x = 0$ and when $y = 0$

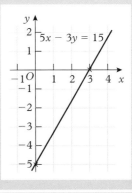

| When $x = 0$ | When $y = 0$ |
|---|---|
| $5 \times 0 - 3y = 15$ | $5x - 3 \times 0 = 15$ |
| $-3y = 15$ | $5x = 15$ |
| $3y = -15$ | $x = 3$ |
| $y = -5$ | This gives (3, 0) |
| This gives (0, −5) | |

- *Example*

Solve this pair of simultaneous equations $\quad 5x + y = 25$
$\phantom{Solve this pair of simultaneous equations \quad} 3x + y = 17$

Number the equations
$\qquad$ (1) $5x + y = 25$
$\qquad$ (2) $3x + y = 17$

Subtract to get rid of $y$ $\qquad$ Subtract $\quad 2x \quad = 8$
This finds $x$ $\qquad\qquad\qquad\qquad\qquad x = 4$
Use equation (1) to find $y$ $\qquad$ Put $x = 4$ in equation (1)
$\qquad\qquad\qquad\qquad\qquad 5 \times 4 + y = 25$
$\qquad\qquad\qquad\qquad\qquad 20 + y = 25$
$\qquad\qquad\qquad\qquad\qquad y = 5$

The answer is $x = 4$, $y = 5$
Use equation (2) to check your answer $\quad 3x + y = 17$
$\qquad\qquad\qquad$ Check: $\quad 12 + 5 = 17$ ✓ Correct

**1**  Copy the axes on to squared paper.
   **a**  (1) Make a table for $y = x + 1$
         Use the $x$ values 1, 2, 3.
      (2) Draw and label the line $y = x + 1$
   **b**  (1) Make a table for $y = 2x - 3$
      (2) Draw and label the line $y = 2x - 3$
   **c**  Write down the co-ordinates of the
      point of intersection of the lines.

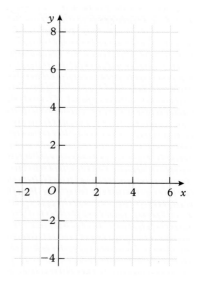

**2**  Copy the axes from question **1** again.
Find *three* points on each of these lines.
Plot each set of points to check that they lie on a straight line.
   **a**  $x + y = 7$         **c**  $x + 3y = 6$
   **b**  $2x + y = 4$       **d**  $3x + 2y = 12$

**3**  Find *two* points on each of these lines. Do not draw the lines.
   **a**  $3x - 4y = 12$      **c**  $6x - 5y = 30$
   **b**  $5x + 7y = 35$      **d**  $7x - 2y = 14$

**4**  Steven buys two chicken and chips and three sausage and chips for £12.
Keeley buys four chicken and chips and two sausage and chips for £16.
   **a**  Write the things that Keeley and Steven buy as two equations.
   **b**  Draw a $c$ axis from 0 to 8 and an $s$ axis from 0 to 10.
   **c**  Solve the two equations by plotting lines.
      Write down the cost of one chicken and chips and
      one sausage and chips.

**5**  Solve these pairs of simultaneous equations using algebra.
In each case, check to see that the solution is correct.
   **a**  $4x + 3y = 19$        **b**  $3x + y = 10$
      $x + 3y = 16$          $5x - y = 6$

# Help yourself

# 1 Multiplying

When we are adding lots of the same number it is quicker to multiply.

*Example*

```
  3 1
  3 1   is the same as
  3 1
  3 1
+ 3 1
  1 5 5
```

```
    3 1
×    5
  1 5 5
```

To do
```
    3 1
×    5
```
first do  $5 \times 1$
```
    3 1
×    5
     5
```

then do  $5 \times 3$
```
    3 1
×    5
  1 5 5
```

Remember to keep your numbers in columns.

Here are some more examples:

```
  6 2
×  4
2 4 8
```

```
  5 1
×  9
4 5 9
```

## Exercise 1

**1**
```
  2 3
×  2
```

**2**
```
  2 1 3
×    3
```

**3**  $42 \times 4$

**4**  $423 \times 3$

Sometimes we need to carry.

*Example*

```
  2 6
×  3
   8
   1
```
→
```
  2 6
×  3
 7 8
   1
```

$3 \times 2 = 6$
Then add the 1 to give 7

## Exercise 2

**1**
```
    3 7
×    2
```

**2**
```
    4 5
×    2
```

**3**  $46 \times 4$

**7**  $146 \times 9$

**4**  $124 \times 3$

**8**  $178 \times 9$

**5**  $259 \times 2$

**9**  $357 \times 5$

**6**  $637 \times 5$

**10**  $803 \times 4$

## Other words

These words can also mean **multiply**.

**times**     **product**     **of**

*Examples*

Find 24 **times** 16
Find the **product** of 24 and 16
Find one half **of** 24

# 2 Multiplying by 10

When we multiply by 10, all the digits move across **one** column to the **left**. This makes the number 10 times bigger.
We can use the headings **Th H T U** to help.
They mean **Th**ousands, **H**undreds, **T**ens and **U**nits. Units is another way of saying 'ones'.

*Example*

$23 \times 10 = 230$

```
 H   T   U
     2   3
 2   3   0
```

Here are some more examples:

Th  H  T  U

    4  6        46 × 10 = 460
  4  6  0

    2  5  3      253 × 10 = 2530
  2  5  3  0

---

## Exercise 3

Multiply each of these numbers by 10.

**1**  39        **3**  756        **5**  5000

**2**  45        **4**  684        **6**  8007

## 3  Multiplying by 100, 1000, …

When we multiply by 100, all the digits move across **two** columns to the **left**.
This makes the number 100 times bigger.
This is because 100 = 10 × 10.
So multiplying by 100 is like multiplying by 10 twice.

*Example*

74 × 100 = 7400

Th  H  T  U

      7  4
  7  4  0  0

When we multiply by 1000 all the numbers move across three columns to the left.

This is because 1000 = 10 × 10 × 10.
This means that multiplying by 1000 is like multiplying by 10 three times.

*Example*

74 × 1000 = 74 000

TTh  Th  H  T  U

              7  4
  7  4  0  0  0

---

## Exercise 4

Write down the answers to these.

**1**  75 × 100                **7**  5243 × 100

**2**  82 × 100                **8**  800 × 1000

**3**  36 × 1000               **9**  5004 × 1000

**4**  178 × 100               **10**  815 × 10 000

**5**  3190 × 100              **11**  302 × 10 000

**6**  420 × 1000              **12**  835 × 100 000

## 4  Multiplying by 20, 30, …

When we multiply by 20 it is like multiplying by 2 then by 10. This is because 20 = 2 × 10.

*Example*

To do 18 × 20:
first do
$$\begin{array}{r} 18 \\ \times\ \ 2 \\ \hline 3\,6 \\ \tiny 1 \end{array}$$

Then do        36 × 10 = 360

So             18 × 20 = 360

In the same way multiplying by 30 is the same as multiplying by 3 and then multiplying by 10.

*Example*

To do $26 \times 30$:

first do

$$
\begin{array}{r}
2\,6 \\
\times\ \ 3 \\
\hline
7\,8 \\
{\scriptstyle 1}
\end{array}
$$

Then do $\quad 78 \times 10 = 780$

So $\quad\quad\ \ 26 \times 30 = 780$

## Exercise 5

Work these out.

| | | | |
|---|---|---|---|
| **1** | $28 \times 20$ | **7** | $83 \times 40$ |
| **2** | $36 \times 20$ | **8** | $45 \times 50$ |
| **3** | $27 \times 30$ | **9** | $62 \times 50$ |
| **4** | $34 \times 30$ | **10** | $213 \times 20$ |
| **5** | $58 \times 30$ | **11** | $371 \times 30$ |
| **6** | $26 \times 40$ | **12** | $425 \times 70$ |

## 5 Multiplying decimals by 10

We can multiply decimals by 10 in the same way.

*Example 1*

$41.5 \times 10$

$$
\text{H}\quad \text{T}\quad \text{U}\ .\ \tfrac{1}{10}
$$

$41.5 \times 10 = 415$

*Example 2*

$56.87 \times 10$

$$
\text{H}\quad \text{T}\quad \text{U}\ .\ \tfrac{1}{10}\quad \tfrac{1}{100}
$$

$56.87 \times 10$
$= 568.7$

## Exercise 6

Multiply these decimals by 10.

| | | | |
|---|---|---|---|
| **1** | 9.5 | **4** | 86.31 |
| **2** | 28.2 | **5** | 10.7 |
| **3** | 17.83 | **6** | 0.9 |

## 6 Multiplying decimals by 100

When we multiply by 100, all the digits move across **two** columns to the **left**.

*Example 1*

$27.65 \times 100$

$$
\text{Th}\quad \text{H}\quad \text{T}\quad \text{U}\ .\ \tfrac{1}{10}\quad \tfrac{1}{100}
$$

$27.65 \times 100$
$= 2765$

*Example 2*

$96.5 \times 100$

$$
\text{Th}\quad \text{H}\quad \text{T}\quad \text{U}\ .\ \tfrac{1}{10}
$$

$96.5 \times 100$
$= 9650$

## Exercise 7

Multiply these decimals by 100.

| | | | |
|---|---|---|---|
| **1** | 42.91 | **4** | 137.4 |
| **2** | 57.04 | **5** | 60.59 |
| **3** | 71.6 | **6** | 7.08 |

# 7 Long multiplication

When we want to multiply two quite large numbers we have to do it in stages.
Here are two methods. You only have to know one of them.

## Method 1

*Example*
146 × 24

First do  146 × 4

```
   146
 ×   4
  584
  1 2
```

Then do 146 × 20

```
   146
 ×   2
  292
    1
```

292 × 10 = 2920

Now add the two answers together.

```
    584
 + 2920
   3504
```

Usually the working out looks like this:

```
    146
 ×   24
    584
   2920
   3504
```

Here is another example.

```
    223
 ×   36
   1338 ← (223 × 6)
   6690 ← (223 × 30)
   8028
   1 1
```

## Method 2

*Example*
125 × 23

First set out the numbers with boxes,
like this:

Now draw in the diagonals like this:

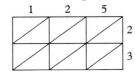

Fill in like a table square then add
along the diagonals like this:

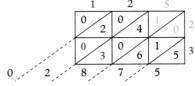

1 × 3 = 3

Notice the 0 in the
top box when the
answer is a single
digit.

So 125 × 23 = **2875**

Here is another example.
When the diagonal adds up to more
than 10, we carry into the next one.

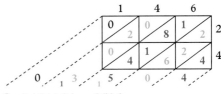

So 146 × 24 = **3504**

357

Use the method you prefer to work these out.

| | | | |
|---|---|---|---|
| **1** | $34 \times 25$ | **7** | $391 \times 43$ |
| **2** | $63 \times 34$ | **8** | $172 \times 84$ |
| **3** | $123 \times 42$ | **9** | $545 \times 33$ |
| **4** | $314 \times 26$ | **10** | $612 \times 65$ |
| **5** | $271 \times 35$ | **11** | $754 \times 61$ |
| **6** | $257 \times 53$ | **12** | $989 \times 98$ |

# 8 Dividing

*Example*

$68 \div 2$

$$2\overline{)68}$$

First work out $6 \div 2 = 3$. Put the 3 above the 6:

$$\begin{array}{r} 3 \\ 2\overline{)68} \end{array}$$

Now work out $8 \div 2 = 4$. Put the 4 above the 8:

$$\begin{array}{r} 34 \\ 2\overline{)68} \end{array}$$

So $68 \div 2 = 34$

Here is another example:    $84 \div 4$

$$\begin{array}{r} 21 \\ 4\overline{)84} \end{array}$$

So $84 \div 4 = 21$

*Exercise 9*

Work these out.

| | | | |
|---|---|---|---|
| **1** | $2\overline{)84}$ | **4** | $96 \div 3$ |
| **2** | $3\overline{)93}$ | **5** | $64 \div 2$ |
| **3** | $5\overline{)55}$ | **6** | $884 \div 4$ |

Sometimes we need to 'carry'. This happens when a number does not divide exactly.

*Example*

$72 \div 4$

$$4\overline{)72}$$

First do $7 \div 4$. This is 1 with 3 left over.
Put the 1 above the 7 and carry the 3 like this.

$$\begin{array}{r} 1 \\ 4\overline{)7\,^32} \end{array}$$

Now do $32 \div 4$. This is 8. Put the 8 above the $^32$ like this

$$\begin{array}{r} 18 \\ 4\overline{)7\,^32} \end{array}$$

So $72 \div 4 = 18$

Here is another example:    $85 \div 5$

$$\begin{array}{r} 17 \\ 5\overline{)8\,^35} \end{array}$$

So $85 \div 5 = 17$

## Exercise 10

Work these out.

**1** $2\overline{)58}$      **7** $96 \div 6$

**2** $3\overline{)54}$      **8** $128 \div 8$

**3** $72 \div 4$      **9** $424 \div 4$

**4** $64 \div 4$      **10** $276 \div 2$

**5** $84 \div 7$      **11** $621 \div 3$

**6** $76 \div 4$      **12** $364 \div 7$

---

Sometimes there is a remainder left at the end.

*Example*

$58 \div 4$

$$4\overline{)5^18} \quad \text{remainder } 2$$
$$\phantom{4)}1\,4$$

We carry the 2 by putting in the decimal point and extra zeros.

$$4\overline{)5^18\,.\,0}$$
$$\phantom{4)}1\,4$$

Now we can finish it off.

$$4\overline{)5^18\,.\,{}^20}$$
$$\phantom{4)}1\,4\,.\,5$$

So $58 \div 4 = 14.5$

---

## Exercise 11

Work these out.

**1** $84 \div 8$      **5** $223 \div 5$

**2** $138 \div 4$      **6** $354 \div 5$

**3** $147 \div 4$      **7** $257 \div 8$

**4** $162 \div 8$      **8** $387 \div 8$

# 9 Long Division

Sometimes we need to do long division. This is usually when we are dividing by a number bigger than 10.

*Example*

$468 \div 12$

$$12\overline{)468}$$

12 will not go into 4 so

first do $46 \div 12$

We need to find out how many times 12 goes into 46.

$$12 \times 2 = 24$$
$$12 \times 3 = 36 \leftarrow$$
$$12 \times 4 = 48$$

12 will go in 3 times.
Put the 3 above the 6.

$$12\overline{)468}$$
$$\phantom{12)}3$$

Work out $3 \times 12$ and put the answer under the 46.

$$12\overline{)468}$$
$$\phantom{12)}3$$
$$\phantom{12)}36$$

Now subtract the 36 from the 46.

$$12\overline{)468}$$
$$\phantom{12)}3$$
$$\phantom{12)}36$$
$$\phantom{12)}10$$

The 10 is the carry.
We don't put it with the 8.
Instead we bring the 8 down to the 10.

$$12\overline{)468}$$
$$\phantom{12)}3$$
$$\phantom{12)}36\downarrow$$
$$\phantom{12)}108$$

Now do $108 \div 12$

$$12 \times 8 = 96$$
$$12 \times 9 = 108 \leftarrow$$

12 will go in 9 times exactly.
Put the 9 after the 3.

$$
\begin{array}{r}
39 \\
12\overline{)468} \\
36 \\
\hline
108
\end{array}
$$

Work out $9 \times 12$ and put the answer under the 108.

When you subtract this time there is no remainder.

You have finished!

$$
\begin{array}{r}
39 \\
12\overline{)468} \\
36 \\
\hline
108 \\
108 \\
\hline
-
\end{array}
$$

So $468 \div 12 = 39$

## Exercise 12

Work these out.

| | | | |
|---|---|---|---|
| **1** | $516 \div 12$ | **7** | $782 \div 23$ |
| **2** | $754 \div 13$ | **8** | $806 \div 26$ |
| **3** | $924 \div 14$ | **9** | $864 \div 32$ |
| **4** | $630 \div 15$ | **10** | $594 \div 27$ |
| **5** | $660 \div 12$ | **11** | $1072 \div 16$ |
| **6** | $522 \div 18$ | **12** | $1764 \div 18$ |

Sometimes there is a remainder left at the end.

*Example*

$383 \div 14$

$$
\begin{array}{r}
27 \\
14\overline{)383} \\
28 \\
\hline
103 \\
98 \\
\hline
5
\end{array}
$$

We could carry on and divide the 5 by the 14 to get a decimal.

It is easier to leave it as a fraction.

$5 \div 14$ is the fraction $\frac{5}{14}$

So $383 \div 14 = 27\frac{5}{14}$

## Exercise 13

Work these out.

| | | | |
|---|---|---|---|
| **1** | $697 \div 12$ | **7** | $211 \div 14$ |
| **2** | $588 \div 13$ | **8** | $417 \div 17$ |
| **3** | $759 \div 16$ | **9** | $406 \div 13$ |
| **4** | $911 \div 22$ | **10** | $309 \div 18$ |
| **5** | $870 \div 24$ | **11** | $3214 \div 14$ |
| **6** | $776 \div 32$ | **12** | $4236 \div 15$ |

# 10 Dividing by 10

When we divide by 10, all the digits move across **one** column to the **right**. This makes the number smaller.

*Example*

$230 \div 10 = 23$

| H | T | U |
|---|---|---|
| 2 | 3 | 0 |

$\phantom{x}$2$\phantom{xx}$3

Here are some more examples.

| Th | H | T | U |
|----|---|---|---|
|    | 5 | 8 | 0 |

$580 \div 10 = 58$

$\phantom{xxx}$5$\phantom{xx}$8

| | 2 | 4 | 6 | 0 |
|---|---|---|---|---|

$2460 \div 10 = 246$

$\phantom{x}$2$\phantom{xx}$4$\phantom{xx}$6

## Exercise 14

Divide these numbers by 10.

**1** 740
**2** 80
**3** 5960
**4** 830
**5** 9040
**6** 7200
**7** 5000
**8** 700 000

# 11 Dividing by 100, 1000, …

When we divide by 100, all the digits move across **two** columns to the **right**. This is because $100 = 10 \times 10$. So dividing by 100 is like dividing by 10 twice.

*Example*

$7400 \div 100 = 74$

| Th | H | T | U |
|----|---|---|---|
| 7  | 4 | 0 | 0 |

$\phantom{xxxx}$7$\phantom{xx}$4

When we divide by 1000, all the numbers move across **three** columns to the **right**.

*Example*

$74\,000 \div 1000 = 74$

| TTh | Th | H | T | U |
|-----|----|---|---|---|
| 7   | 4  | 0 | 0 | 0 |

$\phantom{xxxxx}$7$\phantom{xx}$4

## Exercise 15

Work these out.

**1** $7800 \div 100$
**2** $5300 \div 100$
**3** $6400 \div 100$
**4** $42\,000 \div 1000$
**5** $78\,000 \div 100$
**6** $78\,000 \div 1000$
**7** $200\,000 \div 1000$
**8** $200\,000 \div 10\,000$

# 12 Dividing by 20, 30, …

When we divide by 20, it is like dividing by 2 then by 10. This is because $20 = 2 \times 10$.

*Example*

To do $360 \div 20$

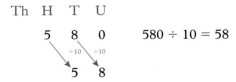

first do
$$\begin{array}{r} 1\,8\,0 \\ 2\,\overline{)3^{1}6\,0} \end{array}$$

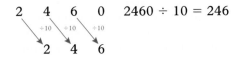

Then do $\phantom{x}180 \div 10 = 18$

So $\phantom{xxxxx}360 \div 20 = 18$

In the same way dividing by 30 is the same as dividing by 3 then by 10.

*Example*

To do 780 ÷ 30

first do

$$3{\overline{\smash{)}7^18\,0}} \quad 260$$

Then do     260 ÷ 10 = 26

So          780 ÷ 30 = 26

### Exercise 16

Work these out.

| | | | |
|---|---|---|---|
| **1** | 640 ÷ 20 | **5** | 7540 ÷ 20 |
| **2** | 240 ÷ 30 | **6** | 2820 ÷ 30 |
| **3** | 5680 ÷ 40 | **7** | 1890 ÷ 90 |
| **4** | 2350 ÷ 50 | **8** | 24 240 ÷ 80 |

## 13 Dividing decimals by 10

We can divide decimals by 10 in the same way.

*Example 1*

47.1 ÷ 10

47.1 ÷ 10 = 4.71

*Example 2*

2.9 ÷ 10

2.9 ÷ 10 = 0.29

### Exercise 17

Divide these decimals by 10.

| | | | | | |
|---|---|---|---|---|---|
| **1** | 51.7 | **3** | 4.3 | **5** | 4.02 |
| **2** | 86.2 | **4** | 5.69 | **6** | 10.5 |

## 14 Dividing decimals by 100

When we divide by 100, all the digits move across **two** columns to the **right**.

*Example 1*

257.1 ÷ 100

257.1 ÷ 100 = 2.571

*Example 2*

52.3 ÷ 100

52.3 ÷ 100 = 0.523

### Exercise 18

Divide these decimals by 100.

| | | | | | |
|---|---|---|---|---|---|
| **1** | 193.4 | **3** | 38.5 | **5** | 10.6 |
| **2** | 362.8 | **4** | 16.9 | **6** | 27.04 |

### Other words

These words can also mean **divide**.

**share**          **quotient**

*Examples*

**Share** 240 by 12
Find the **quotient**      }  both mean
of 240 and 12                   240 ÷ 12

# 15 Adding fractions

To add fractions, the bottom numbers (denominators) **must** be the same.

*Examples*

$\frac{2}{7} + \frac{3}{7} = \frac{5}{7}$

| two sevenths | + | three sevenths | = | five sevenths |

$\frac{3}{5} + \frac{3}{5} = \frac{6}{5} = 1\frac{1}{5}$

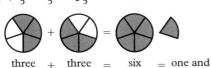

| three fifths | + | three fifths | = | six fifths | = one and one fifth |

## Exercise 19

Work these out.

**1** $\frac{2}{9} + \frac{5}{9}$     **3** $\frac{8}{12} + \frac{5}{12}$     **5** $\frac{6}{8} + \frac{5}{8}$

**2** $\frac{5}{12} + \frac{4}{12}$     **4** $\frac{4}{5} + \frac{3}{5}$     **6** $\frac{9}{11} + \frac{5}{11}$

Sometimes the two bottom numbers are different. Before we can add the fractions we **must** make them the same.

*Example*

$\frac{2}{3} + \frac{1}{6}$

We need to find a number that 3 and 6 both divide into exactly.

Numbers that 3 goes into:
3 ⑥ 9 12 ...
Numbers that 6 goes into:
⑥ 12 18 ...

The first number that is in both lists is 6. The 6 is called the common denominator.

Now write the fractions with 6 as the bottom number:

$\frac{2}{3} = \frac{?}{6}$ so $\frac{2}{3} \overset{\times 2}{=} \frac{4}{6}$ so $\frac{2}{3} = \frac{4}{6}$.

We can see this in a diagram.

The $\frac{1}{6}$ does not need changing.

So $\frac{2}{3} + \frac{1}{6} = \frac{4}{6} + \frac{1}{6} = \frac{5}{6}$

Here is another example

$\frac{2}{3} + \frac{1}{4}$

Numbers that 3 goes into:
3 6 9 ⑫ 15 ...

Numbers that 4 goes into:
4 8 ⑫ 16 ...

We need to change both fractions to twelfths. 12 is the common denominator.

$\frac{2}{3} = \frac{?}{12}$    $\frac{2}{3} \overset{\times 4}{=} \frac{8}{12}$

$\frac{1}{4} = \frac{?}{12}$    $\frac{1}{4} \overset{\times 3}{=} \frac{3}{12}$

So $\frac{2}{3} + \frac{1}{4} = \frac{8}{12} + \frac{3}{12} = \frac{11}{12}$

## Exercise 20

Work these out.

**1** $\frac{1}{4} + \frac{1}{2}$      **7** $\frac{1}{3} + \frac{1}{5}$

**2** $\frac{1}{5} + \frac{1}{10}$      **8** $\frac{2}{7} + \frac{1}{2}$

**3** $\frac{2}{5} + \frac{3}{10}$      **9** $\frac{2}{5} + \frac{1}{3}$

**4** $\frac{5}{8} + \frac{1}{4}$      **10** $\frac{1}{7} + \frac{4}{5}$

**5** $\frac{5}{12} + \frac{1}{6}$      **11** $\frac{1}{8} + \frac{3}{7}$

**6** $\frac{5}{9} + \frac{1}{3}$      **12** $\frac{1}{2} + \frac{1}{3} + \frac{1}{4}$

# 16 Subtracting fractions

This works just like adding fractions.

*Example*

$\frac{3}{5} - \frac{2}{5} = \frac{1}{5}$

The two bottom numbers must still be the same.

*Example*

$\frac{3}{8} - \frac{1}{4}$

Numbers that 8 goes into:
⑧ 16 24 ...
Numbers that 4 goes into:
4 ⑧ 12 16 ...

$\frac{1}{4} = \frac{?}{8} \quad \overset{\times 2}{\frac{1}{4}} = \frac{2}{8}$

The $\frac{3}{8}$ does not need changing.

So $\frac{3}{8} - \frac{1}{4} = \frac{3}{8} - \frac{2}{8} = \frac{1}{8}$

# 17 Simplifying fractions

This is also known as **cancelling**.

We look for a number that divides exactly into both the top and bottom numbers.

*Example 1*

Simplify $\frac{6}{15}$

3 goes into both 6 and 15 exactly

$\overset{\div 3}{\frac{6}{15}} = \frac{2}{5}$

We can divide by more than one number.

*Example 2*

Simplify $\frac{18}{24}$

$\overset{\div 2}{\frac{18}{24}} = \overset{\div 3}{\frac{9}{12}} = \frac{3}{4}$

## Exercise 21

Work these out.

1  $\frac{7}{8} - \frac{2}{8}$    7  $\frac{1}{4} - \frac{1}{5}$

2  $\frac{2}{5} - \frac{1}{5}$    8  $\frac{3}{6} - \frac{1}{3}$

3  $\frac{7}{11} - \frac{3}{11}$    9  $\frac{6}{7} - \frac{2}{3}$

4  $\frac{3}{5} - \frac{1}{10}$    10  $\frac{3}{4} - \frac{2}{3}$

5  $\frac{5}{8} - \frac{1}{4}$    11  $\frac{5}{8} - \frac{2}{5}$

6  $\frac{11}{12} - \frac{2}{3}$    12  $\frac{10}{11} - \frac{5}{8}$

## Exercise 22

Simplify these.

1  $\frac{3}{6}$    7  $\frac{12}{18}$

2  $\frac{4}{6}$    8  $\frac{16}{24}$

3  $\frac{10}{15}$    9  $\frac{24}{36}$

4  $\frac{14}{21}$    10  $\frac{18}{30}$

5  $\frac{8}{12}$    11  $\frac{15}{45}$

6  $\frac{20}{50}$    12  $\frac{28}{70}$

## CHAPTER 1

**1  a**  DM10 = £5          **b**  DM13 = £6.50          **c**  £3.50 = DM7

**2  a**

| Number of hours | 1 | 2 | 3 | 4 | 5 |
|---|---|---|---|---|---|
| Wages £ | 5 | 10 | 15 | 20 | 25 |

**b**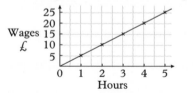

*Graph to show Alison's wages*

**3**  midnight − 19 30 = 4 hours 30 minutes
4 h 30 min + 16 h 48 min = 21 h 18 min

**4  a**  Stopped from 7.50 to 8.00 which is 10 minutes.          **b**  35 km
  **c**  (1)  Mohammed travelled faster in the first part.
      (2)  The graph is steeper from 7.30 to 7.50.
  **d**  15 km in 30 minutes is a speed of 30 km per hour.

## CHAPTER 2

**1  a**  289                    **b**  12.96                    **c**  0.0064

**2  a**  25          **b**  2.81 (2 dp)          **c**  111.11 (2 dp)          **d**  0.11

**3  a**  16 807          **b**  28 561          **c**  592.704          **d**  0.000 064

**4  a**  5          **b**  2          **c**  1.416 (3 dp)          **d**  0.3

**5  a**  193          **c**  34          **e**  304          **g**  4
  **b**  83          **d**  19          **f**  144          **h**  6.8

**6  a**  73.5          **b**  0.069          **c**  6.90          **d**  0.0304

**7  a**  (1)  estimate 300 + 600 = 900          (3)  estimate 6 × 3 = 18
      (2)  estimate 1000 − 900 = 100          (4)  estimate 500 ÷ 20 = 25
  **b**  (1)  916          (2)  327          (3)  17.92          (4)  28
All the estimates are quite close to the correct answers, except for part (2). In
this case, rounding to one significant figure is very inaccurate.

**8  a**  6 × 90 = 540                    **b**  £5 + £8 + £22 + £9 = £44
                              all rounded to the nearest £.

**9  a**  $\sqrt{25}$ = 5, $\sqrt{36}$ = 6, $\sqrt{30}$ is about 5.5

  **b**  $\sqrt{49}$ = 7, $\sqrt{64}$ = 8, $\sqrt{61}$ is about 7.8

  **c**  $\sqrt{64}$ = 8, $\sqrt{81}$ = 9, $\sqrt{80}$ is about 8.9

  **d**  $\sqrt{16}$ = 4, $\sqrt{25}$ = 5, $\sqrt{17}$ is about 4.1

As all these are estimates, allow yourself any answer which is close to them.

## CHAPTER 3

**1** **a** groups: 1–5, 6–10, 11–15, 16–20, 21–25, 26–30

**b**

| Time taken (min) | Tally | Total |
|---|---|---|
| 1–5 | ЖІ І | 6 |
| 6–10 | ЖІ ЖІ | 10 |
| 11–15 | ІІІ | 3 |
| 16–20 | ІІІІ | 4 |
| 21–25 | ЖІ | 5 |
| 26–30 | ІІ | 2 |

**c**

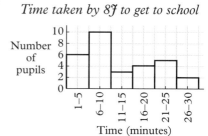

*Time taken by 8J to get to school*

**2**  10 + 4 + 9 + 7 = 30 pupils   360° ÷ 30 = 12°

|  | Number of of pupils | Working | Angle |
|---|---|---|---|
| Radio 1 | 10 | 10 × 12 | 120° |
| Radio 2 | 4 | 4 × 12 | 48° |
| Radio 5 Live | 9 | 9 × 12 | 108° |
| Atlantic 252 | 7 | 7 × 12 | 84° |
| **Total** | 30 |  | 360° |

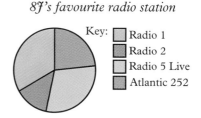

*8J's favourite radio station*

Key: Radio 1, Radio 2, Radio 5 Live, Atlantic 252

**3**

|  | Number of of pupils | Working | Angle |
|---|---|---|---|
| Radio 1 | 11 | 360 ÷ 28 × 11 = | 141° |
| Radio 2 | 3 | 360 ÷ 28 × 3 = | 39° |
| Radio 5 Live | 8 | 360 ÷ 28 × 8 = | 103° |
| Atlantic 252 | 6 | 360 ÷ 28 × 6 = | 77° |
| **Total** | 28 |  | 360° |

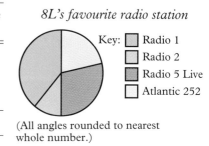

*8L's favourite radio station*

Key: Radio 1, Radio 2, Radio 5 Live, Atlantic 252

(All angles rounded to nearest whole number.)

**4** **a** (1) is biased    (2) can give many answers
   (3) is unclear    (4) is nothing to do with the survey.

  **b** (1) Read the following statement:
      'Discipline in schools is not as good as it used to be.'
      Circle one number: strongly agree  1  2  3  4  5  strongly disagree
   (2) How would you describe the behaviour of children in your
      community:
      ☐ very good   ☐ acceptable   ☐ poor   ☐ very poor?
   (3) Read the following statement:
      'Children have too little freedom to make their own decisions'.
      Circle one number: strongly agree  1  2  3  4  5  strongly disagree
   (4) Do you think the amount of work children get in school is:
      ☐ too much   ☐ about right   ☐ too little   ☐ don't know?

## CHAPTER 4

**1** **a**

| Number of blue tiles | 1 | 2 | 3 | 4 | 5 |
|---|---|---|---|---|---|
| Number of white tiles | 5 | 8 | 11 | 14 | 17 |

**b** 3 white tiles
**c** number of white tiles = 3 × number of blue tiles
**d** add 2
**e** number of *w*hite tiles = 3 × number of *b*lue tiles + 2
**f** $3 \times 17 + 2 = 51 + 2 = 53$

**g** $\longrightarrow$ ⬛ × 3 ⬛ $\longrightarrow$ ⬛ + 2 ⬛ $\longrightarrow$

**h** $\longleftarrow$ ⬛ ÷ 3 ⬛ $\longleftarrow$ ⬛ − 2 ⬛ $\longleftarrow$

**i** $20 \longleftarrow$ ⬛ ÷ 3 ⬛ $\overset{60}{\longleftarrow}$ ⬛ − 2 ⬛ $\longleftarrow$ 62, 20 blue tiles

**2** term 1: $4 \times 1 + 3 = 7$      term 2: $4 \times 2 + 3 = 11$      term 3: $4 \times 3 + 3 = 15$

**3** **a** $2 \times 2 + 10 = 14$    **c** $7 \times 7 = 49$      **e** $2 \times 5 \times 5 = 50$
    **b** $2 \times 5 + 7 = 14$    **d** $5 \times 5 \times 5 = 125$    **f** $(2 \times 5)^2 = 10 \times 10 = 100$

**4** **a** $4x + 5 = 3x + 12$             **b** $7x - 10 = 3x + 2$
       $4x = 3x + 7$                 $7x = 3x + 12$
          $x = 7$                     $4x = 12$
                                $x = 3$

## CHAPTER 5

**1** **a**

**b**

**2** **a** 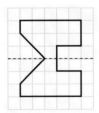    **b** 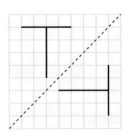    **c**

**3** **a**       **b**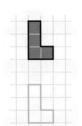

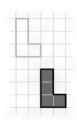

**4**

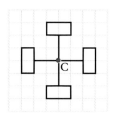

**5**  **a**

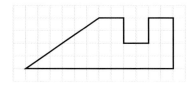

**b**

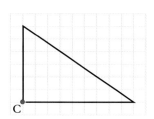

## CHAPTER 6

**1**  $-5\,°C, -3\,°C, -1\,°C, 0\,°C, 1\,°C, 2\,°C, 6\,°C$

**2**  **a**  $5\,°C > 3\,°C$  **b**  $-6\,°C > -8°C$  **c**  $-4°C < 0\,°C$

**3**  The difference between $-9\,°C$ and $43\,°C$ is $52°$.

**4**  **a**  6  **b**  $-6$  **c**  $-9$  **d**  1

**5**  **a**  10  **c**  $-4$  **e**  $-15$  **g**  $-60$
    **b**  $-7$  **d**  $-8$  **f**  8  **h**  5

**6**  **a**  $-1736$  **c**  $-17$  **e**  20
    **b**  $-7$  **d**  23  **f**  1035

**7**  **a**  $r = 68 - 25 = 43$  **c**  $r = 35 - 25 = -60$
    **b**  $r = 12 - 25 = -13$

**8**  **a**  $v = 5 \times 6 - 12 = 18$  **c**  $v = 5 \times 4 - 12 = -32$
    **b**  $v = 5 \times 2 - 12 = -2$

**9**  **a**  $-2 \times -2 = 4$  **c**  $8 \times -2 \times -2 \times -2 = -64$
    **b**  $5 \times -2 \times -2 = 20$

**10**  **a**  $E = 5 \times 3 \times 3 = 45$  **c**  $E = 5 \times -5 \times -5 = 125$
    **b**  $E = 5 \times 1 \times 1 = 5$

## CHAPTER 7

**1**  **a**  $a = 180° - 71° - 41° = 68°$  **d**  isosceles triangle: $f = 34°$
    **b**  $b = 360° - 107° - 90° = 163°$      $g = 180° - (2 \times 34°) = 112°$
    **c**  $c = 180° - 32° = 148°$,
        $d = 32°$ (opposite angles),
        $e = 148°$ (opposite angles)

**2**  **a**  $g = 48°$, $h = 132°$, $i = 48°$     **b**  $m = 72°$, $n = 108°$
$j = 132°$, $k = 48°$     $p = 108°$, $q = 72°$
$l = 132°$     $r = 108°$, $s = 72°$,

**3**  **a**  $s = 112°$ (corresponding)   **b**  $t = 57°$ (alternate)   **c**  $u = 99°$ (interior)

**4**  **a**  Octagon can be divided into 6 triangles.
So interior angle sum $= 6 \times 180° = 1080°$
  **b**  One interior angle $= 1080° \div 8 = 135°$

**5**  **a**  $240° - 180° = 60°$
Bearing of A from B $= 60°$
  **b**  $115° + 180° = 295°$
Bearing of A from B $= 295°$
  **c**  $77° + 180° = 255°$
Bearing of A from B $= 255°$

## CHAPTER 8

**1**  There are 14 sweets in the bag.
  **a**  $\frac{4}{14} = \frac{2}{7}$     **b**  $\frac{10}{14} = \frac{5}{7}$

**2**  There are 15 pencils in the case.
  **a**  (1)  $3 \times 2 = 6$     (2)  $5 \times 2 = 10$     (3)  $7 \times 2 = 14$
  **b**  (1)  $3 \times 6 = 18$     (2)  $5 \times 6 = 30$     (3)  $7 \times 6 = 42$

**3**  $1 - \frac{2}{5} = \frac{3}{5}$

**4**  $\frac{1}{6} + \frac{7}{12} = \frac{2}{12} + \frac{7}{12} = \frac{9}{12}$
$1 - \frac{9}{12} = \frac{3}{12} = \frac{1}{4}$

The probability that it will last for more than 20 minutes is $\frac{1}{4}$.

**5**  **a**  $P(A) = \frac{3}{6} = \frac{1}{2}$     **b**  $P(A') = 1 - P(A) = 1 - \frac{1}{2} = \frac{1}{2}$

**6**  **a**

|  |  | Second bag | | | | | | |
|---|---|---|---|---|---|---|---|---|
|  |  | R | R | B | B | B | Y | Y |
| First bag | R | R,R | R,R | R,B | R,B | R,B | R,Y | R,Y |
|  | R | R,R | R,R | R,B | R,B | R,B | R,Y | R,Y |
|  | R | R,R | R,R | R,B | R,B | R,B | R,Y | R,Y |
|  | B | B,R | B,R | B,B | B,B | B,B | B,Y | B,Y |
|  | Y | Y,R | Y,R | Y,B | Y,B | Y,B | Y,Y | Y,Y |

  **b**  There are 35 possible outcomes.
  (1)  $\frac{2}{35}$ (▢)     (2)  $\frac{11}{35}$ (◯)     (3)  $\frac{19}{35}$ (◇)

## CHAPTER 9

**1** 12 out of 50 is the same as 24 out of 100, which is 24%

**2 a** 10% of £9.50 = 95 p      **b** 10% of £12.50 = £1.25

**3 a** 10% of £400 = £40
  **b** 40% of £400 = $4 \times$ £40 = £160
  **c** 50% of £340 = £170, so 25% is £170 ÷ 2 = £85

**4 a** 48% of 6700 = 0.48 × 6700 = 3216 people
  **b** 7% of 1327 = 0.07 × 1327 = £92.89
  **c** $67\frac{1}{2}$% of 750 = 0.675 × 750 = 506.25 g
  **d** $38\frac{1}{4}$% of 1200 = 0.3825 × 1200 = 459 cm

**5 a** $17\frac{1}{2}$% of 30 = 0.175 × 30 = £5.25

  **b** $17\frac{1}{2}$% of 40 = 0.175 × 40 = £7

**6** $\frac{26}{40}$ = 26 ÷ 40 = 0.65 = 65%

**7** Total cars sold = 2400 + 3600 = 6000
$\frac{2400}{6000}$ = 24 ÷ 60 = 0.4 = 40%
Percentage sold in August is 40%

**8 a** $\frac{1}{7}$ of 28 = 28 ÷ 7 = 4, so $\frac{2}{7}$ is 8 teeth
  **b** $1 - \frac{2}{7} = \frac{5}{7}$ are not filled

**9 a** Total cakes sold = 24 + 28 + 28 + 36 + 44 = 160
    Fraction sold on Monday = $\frac{24}{160} = \frac{3}{20}$
    Fraction sold on Tuesday = $\frac{28}{160} = \frac{7}{40}$
    Fraction sold on Wednesday = $\frac{28}{160} = \frac{7}{40}$
    Fraction sold on Thursday = $\frac{36}{160} = \frac{9}{40}$
    Fraction sold on Friday = $\frac{44}{160} = \frac{11}{40}$

  **b** Monday 3 ÷ 20 = 0.15 = 15%
    Tuesday 7 ÷ 40 = 0.175 = $17\frac{1}{2}$%
    Wednesday 7 ÷ 40 = 0.175 = $17\frac{1}{2}$%
    Thursday 9 ÷ 40 = 0.225 = $22\frac{1}{2}$%
    Friday 11 ÷ 40 = $27\frac{1}{2}$%

## CHAPTER 10

**1 a** $x = 5$      **b** $y = 4$      **c** $y = -3$      **d** $x = -2$

**2** $x = 5$, $y = 3$

**3 a** $y = 5x + 1$ is the steepest      **b** $y = x + 7$ is the least steep

**4**    **a**   the lines are parallel

      **b**   $y = x + 7$ crosses the $y$ axis at 7

      **c**   $y = x + 7$ is highest up the grid

      **d**   $y = x$ is lowest on the grid

      **e**   $y = x + 2$ would be between $y = x$ and $y = x + 4$

**5**    $y = 2 \times 4 - 2$

       $= 8 - 2$

       $= 6$

The point $(4, 6)$ lies on the line $y = 2x - 2$.

**6**    $y = 3 \times 4 - 2$        $y = 3 \times 0 - 2$        $16 = 3 \times x - 2$

       $= 12 - 2$           $= 0 - 2$            $18 = 3 \times x$

       $= 10$               $= -2$              $6 = x$

       $(4, 10)$            $(0, -2)$           $(6, 16)$

**7**    **a**   $y = 2x + 4$

      **b**   $y = 1 - x$

## CHAPTER 11

**1**    **a**   $300\,\text{cm} = 300 \div 100\,\text{m} = 3\,\text{m}$        **e**   $7.2\,\text{kg} = 7.2 \times 1000\,\text{g} = 7200\,\text{g}$

      **b**   $7\,\text{km} = 7 \times 1000\,\text{m} = 7000\,\text{m}$        **f**   $0.4\,\text{t} = 0.4 \times 1000\,\text{kg} = 400\,\text{kg}$

      **c**   $8.6\,\text{m} = 8.6 \times 100\,\text{cm} = 860\,\text{cm}$        **g**   $3000\,\text{m}l = 3000 \div 1000\,l = 3\,l$

      **d**   $4500\,\text{g} = 4500 \div 1000\,\text{kg} = 4.5\,\text{kg}$        **h**   $4.8\,l = 4.8 \times 1000\,\text{m}l = 480\,\text{m}l$

**2**    **a**   $2 \times 3 = 6$

          $\frac{1}{2}$ of $3 = 1\frac{1}{2}$

      **b**   3 inches is $6 + 1\frac{1}{2} = 7\frac{1}{2}\,\text{cm}$

          177 yd is a bit less than 177 m, about $160 - 170\,\text{m}$

      **c**   $\frac{1}{2}$ of 30 is 15, $30 + 15 = 45$

          30 miles per hour is a bit more than 45 km per hour, about 48 km per hour

      **d**   4 ounces is about $4 \times 30\,\text{g} = 120\,\text{g}$

      **e**   165 pounds is a bit less than half of 165, 82.5 kg. It is about 75 kg.

      **f**   3 gallons is a bit less than $3 \times 5$ or $15\,l$

      **g**   1 pint is a bit more than $\frac{1}{2}\,l$

**3**    **a**   $3\,\text{in} = 3 \times 2.5\,\text{cm} = 7.5\,\text{cm}$

      **b**   $177\,\text{yd} = 177 \times 0.9\,\text{m} = 159.3\,\text{m}$

      **c**   30 miles an hour $= 30 \times 1.6\,\text{km}$ an hour $= 48\,\text{km}$ an hour

      **d**   4 ounces $= 4 \times 28\,\text{g} = 112\,\text{g}$

      **e**   165 pounds $= 165 \times 0.45\,\text{kg} = 74.25\,\text{kg}$

      **f**   3 gallons $= 3 \times 4.5\,l = 13.5\,l$

      **g**   1 pint $= 0.57\,l$

**4**  **a**  6 years : 18 years = 6 : 18 = 1 : 3

   **b**  £60 shared in the ratio 1 : 3

      1 + 3 = 4 shares are needed.

      One share is 60 ÷ 4 = £15

      So Melanie gets £15, Keith gets 3 × 15 = £45.

**5**  **a**  You add  3 × 250 ml = 750 ml of water

   **b**  750 + 250 = 1000 ml = 1 l of orange drink is made

**6**  **a**  $12 : 20 = \frac{12}{4} : \frac{10}{5} = 3 : 5$          **c**  $50 : 45 = \frac{50}{5} : \frac{45}{5} = 10 : 9$

   **b**  $15 : 10 = \frac{15}{5} : \frac{10}{5} = 3 : 2$        **d**  $10 : 1000 = \frac{10}{10} : \frac{1000}{10} = 1 : 100$

**7**  **a**  5 cm : 1 km = 5 : 100 000 = 20 000     **b**  7 : 20 = 0.35 : 1

**8**  **a**  24 ÷ 4 = 6 km

   **b**  2.5 × 4 = 10 cm

**9**  **a**  300 m = 300 × 100 cm = 30 000 cm

      On the model 30 000 cm is 30 000 ÷ 500 = 60 cm

   **b**  15 cm × 500 = 7500 cm

                   = 7500 ÷ 100 m

                   = 75 m

## CHAPTER 12

**1**  **a**  Area = length × width = 6.5 × 8 = 52 m²

   **b**  Area $= \dfrac{\text{base} \times \text{height}}{2} = \dfrac{10 \times 12}{2} = 60$ cm²

   **c**  Area = base × height = 14 × 20 = 280 mm²

   **d**  Area $= \dfrac{a + b}{2} \times h = \dfrac{15 + 35}{2} \times 18 = \dfrac{50}{2} \times 18 = 450$ mm²

   **e**  Area $= \dfrac{\text{product of diagonals}}{2} = \dfrac{12 \times 25}{2} = 150$ cm²

   **f**

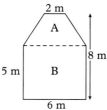

      Area of A $\;= \dfrac{a + b}{2} \times h$

                   $= \dfrac{6 + 2}{2} \times 3$

                   = 4 × 3 = 12 m²

      Area of B $\;= 6 \times 5 = 30$ m²

      Total Area = 12 + 30

                   = 42 m²

**2** Perimeter $= 8 + 6.5 + 8 + 6.5 = 29\,\text{m}$

**3** New area $= 15 \times 10^2 = 1500\,\text{cm}^2$

**4** New area $\quad=$ original area $\times 2^2$
Original area $=$ new area $\div 2^2 = 48 \div 4$
$\qquad\qquad\qquad = 12\,\text{cm}^2$

## CHAPTER 13

**1** **a** Mean $= \dfrac{7 + 6 + 9 + 0 + 3 + 4 + 7 + 6 + 4 + 7}{10}$

$\qquad\quad = 53 \div 10 = 5.3$

**b** Mode is the most common number $= 7$

**c** Writing the numbers in order: $0\quad 3\quad 4\quad 4\quad \boxed{6\quad 6}\quad 7\quad 7\quad 7\quad 9$
Median is the mean of the two middle numbers $= 6$

**d** Range $=$ biggest number $-$ smallest number
$\qquad\quad = 9 - 0 = 9$

**2** **a** Mode is the most common number of people in cars $= 1$

**b**

| Number of people | Number of cars | Total number of people |
|---|---|---|
| 1 | 23 | $1 \times 23 = 23$ |
| 2 | 16 | $2 \times 16 = 32$ |
| 3 | 7 | $3 \times 7 = 21$ |
| 4 | 3 | $4 \times 3 = 12$ |
| 5 | 1 | $5 \times 1 = 5$ |
| Total | 50 | 93 |

Mean number of people
per car $= 93 \div 50 = 1.86$

**c**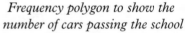

*Frequency polygon to show the number of cars passing the school*

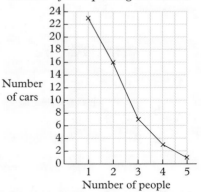

**3** **a**

| Length in cm | Tally | Total |
|---|---|---|
| 0 but less than 3 | IIII | 4 |
| 3 but less than 6 | ЖН ЖН | 10 |
| 6 but less than 9 | ЖН ЖН ЖН ЖН | 20 |
| 9 but less than 12 | ЖН I | 6 |

**b** Modal group is 6 but less than 9 because it has the most seedlings in it.

**c, d**

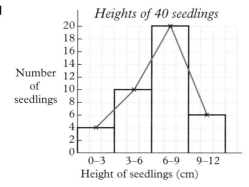

*Heights of 40 seedlings*

**e**

| Length in cm (mid-points) | 1.5 | 4.5 | 7.5 | 10.5 |
|---|---|---|---|---|
| Number of seedlings | 4 | 10 | 20 | 6 |

$$\text{Estimate for the mean} = \frac{(4 \times 1.5) + (10 \times 4.5) + (20 \times 7.5) + (6 \times 10.5)}{40}$$

$$= \frac{264}{40} = 6.6$$

## CHAPTER 14

**1**  **a**  1 litre          **b**  60 m$l$          **c**  2 litres
As all of these are estimates allow yourself any answer that is close to them.

**2**  **a**  Area of cross section = 5 × 5 × 5
                = 125 cm²
      Volume of prism      = 125 × 13 = 1625 cm³

  **b**  Area of cross section = (8.5 × 14) − (4.5 × 6)
                = 92 cm²
      Volume of prism      = 92 × 5
                = 460 cm³

  **c**  Volume = 78 × 40 × 25
            = 78 000 cm³

  **d**  Area of cross section = $\frac{1}{2}$ × 8 × 7
                = 28 cm²
      Volume of prism      = 28 × 14
                = 392 cm³

**3**  **a**  Tank measures 120 cm by 120 cm by 80 cm
      Volume of tank       = 1 152 000 cm³
  **b**  Volume of water      = 120 × 120 × 70
                = 1 008 000 cm³
                = 1008 litres

## CHAPTER 15

**1**

| Value of $x$ | Value of $x^2 + 56$ | |
|---|---|---|
| 20 | 456 | too small |
| 30 | 956 | too big |
| 25 | 681 | too big |
| 24 | 632 | too big |
| 23 | 585 | too small |
| 23.8 | 622.44 | too big |
| 23.7 | 617.69 | too small |
| 23.75 | 620.0625 | too big |

$x$ is between 23.7 and 23.75

Answer: $x = 23.7$ to 1 d.p.

**2** **a**

**b**

**c**

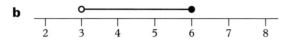

**d**

**3** The only square number between 12 and 19 is 16 which is $4^2$

**4** For $7 \leqslant x < 11$, $x$ can be 7, 8, 9, 10.

**5** For $x < 7$, the highest whole number value of $x$ is 6.

**6** For $x \geqslant 8$, the lowest whole number value of $x$ is 8.

**7** **a**
$$x + 3 < 7$$
$$x + 3 - 3 < 7 - 3$$
$$x < 4$$

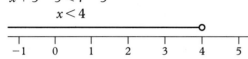

**b**
$$x - 4 \geqslant 1$$
$$x - 4 + 4 \geqslant 1 + 4$$
$$x \geqslant 5$$

**8**  **a**  $3x \geqslant 18$

$\frac{3x}{3} \geqslant \frac{18}{3}$

$x \geqslant 6$

**c**  $4x - 7 < 13$

$4x - 7 + 7 < 13 + 7$

$4x < 20$

$\frac{4x}{4} < \frac{20}{4}$

$x < 5$

**b**  $\frac{x}{4} \leqslant 2$

$\frac{x}{4} \times 4 \leqslant 2 \times 4$

$x \leqslant 8$

**d**  $7 \leqslant 3x - 2 < 22$

$7 + 2 \leqslant 3x - 2 + 2 < 22 + 2$

$9 \leqslant 3x < 24$

$\frac{9}{3} \leqslant \frac{3x}{3} < \frac{24}{3}$

$3 \leqslant x < 8$

**9**  **a**  $2 \leqslant x < 4$

**b**  $-10 < x \leqslant 5$

## CHAPTER 16

**1**

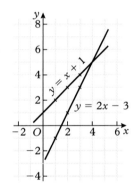

**a**  (1)

| $x$ | 1 | 2 | 3 |
|---|---|---|---|
| $y$ | 2 | 3 | 4 |

**b**  (1)

| $x$ | 1 | 2 | 3 |
|---|---|---|---|
| $y$ | $-1$ | 1 | 3 |

**c**  (1)  The coordinates of the point of intersection are $(4, 5)$

**2**  **a**  $0 + y = 7$       $x + 0 = 7$

$\quad\quad\quad y = 7$       $\quad\quad x = 7$

$\quad\quad\quad (0, 7)$       $\quad\quad (7, 0)$

**d**  $0 + 2y = 12$       $3x + 0 = 12$

$\quad\quad\quad y = 6$       $\quad\quad\quad x = 4$

$\quad\quad (0, 6)$       $\quad\quad\quad (4, 0)$

**b**  $0 + y = 4$       $2x + 0 = 4$

$\quad\quad\quad y = 4$       $\quad\quad x = 2$

$\quad\quad\quad (0, 4)$       $\quad\quad (2, 0)$

**e**  $0 - 5y = 30$       $6x - 0 = 30$

$\quad\quad\quad y = -6$       $\quad\quad\quad x = 5$

$\quad\quad (0, -6)$       $\quad\quad\quad (5, 0)$

**c**  $0 + 3y = 6$       $x + 0 = 6$

$\quad\quad\quad y = 2$       $\quad\quad x = 6$

$\quad\quad\quad (0, 2)$       $\quad\quad (6, 0)$

**f**  $0 - 2y = 14$       $7x - 0 = 14$

$\quad\quad\quad y = -7$       $\quad\quad\quad x = 2$

$\quad\quad (0, -7)$       $\quad\quad\quad (2, 0)$

**3**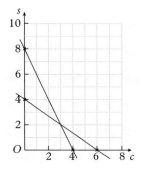

**b** $2c + 3s = 12$
$4c + 2s = 16$

**c**  $2c + 3s = 12$
When $c = 0$                              When $s = 0$
$2 \times 0 + 3s = 12$                     $2c + 3 \times 0 = 12$
$3s = 12$                                  $2c = 12$
$s = 4$                                    $c = 6$
This gives $(0, 4)$                        This gives $(6, 0)$

$4c + 2s = 16$
When $c = 0$                              When $s = 0$
$4 \times 0 + 2s = 16$                     $4c + 0 = 16$
$2s = 16$                                  $4c = 16$
$s = 8$                                    $c = 4$
This gives $(0, 8)$                        This gives $(4, 0)$

The point of intersection is $(3, 2)$. This means that $c = 3$ and $s = 2$.
So chicken and chips cost £3, sausage and chips £2.

**d** If $c = 3$ and $s = 2$, Steven will buy two chicken and chips at $2 \times 3 = £6$ and
three sausage and chips at $3 \times 2 = £6$ making a total of £12, Keeley will
buy four chicken and chips at $4 \times 3 = £12$ and two sausage and chips at
$2 \times 2 = £4$ making a total of £16.

**4  a**              $4x + 3y = 19$                    **b**              $3x + y = 10$
$x + 3y = 16$                                           $5x - y = 6$
Subtract $3x \quad = 3$                        Add $8x \quad = 16$
$x = 1$                                                 $x = 2$
Put $x = 1$ in equation (1):                   Put $x = 2$ in equation (1):
$4 + 3y = 19$                                           $6 + y = 10$
$3y = 15$                                               $y = 4$
$y = 5$                                         The answer is $x = 2, y = 4$
Check: $x = 1, y = 5$ in equation (2)          Check: put $x = 2, y = 4$ in equation (2)
$1 + 15 = 16$ ✓ correct                        $10 - 4 = 6$ ✓ correct

378

## Exercise 1

**1** 46    **2** 639    **3** 168    **4** 1269

## Exercise 2

**1** 74           **6** 3185
**2** 90           **7** 1314
**3** 184          **8** 1602
**4** 372          **9** 1785
**5** 518          **10** 3212

## Exercise 3

**1** 390    **3** 7560    **5** 50 000
**2** 450    **4** 6840    **6** 80 070

## Exercise 4

**1** 7500         **7** 524 300
**2** 8200         **8** 800 000
**3** 36 000       **9** 5 004 000
**4** 17 800       **10** 8 150 000
**5** 319 000      **11** 3 020 000
**6** 420 000      **12** 83 500 000

## Exercise 5

**1** 560    **5** 1740    **9** 3100
**2** 720    **6** 1040    **10** 4260
**3** 810    **7** 3320    **11** 11 130
**4** 1020   **8** 2250    **12** 29 750

## Exercise 6

**1** 95     **3** 178.3   **5** 107
**2** 282    **4** 863.1   **6** 9

## Exercise 7

**1** 4291   **3** 7160    **5** 6059
**2** 5704   **4** 13 740   **6** 708

## Exercise 8

**1** 850    **5** 9485    **9** 17 985
**2** 2142   **6** 13 621   **10** 39 780
**3** 5166   **7** 16 813   **11** 45 994
**4** 8164   **8** 14 448   **12** 96 922

## Exercise 9

**1** 42     **3** 11      **5** 32
**2** 31     **4** 32      **6** 221

## Exercise 10

**1** 29     **5** 12      **9** 106
**2** 18     **6** 19      **10** 138
**3** 18     **7** 16      **11** 207
**4** 16     **8** 16      **12** 52

## Exercise 11

**1** 10.5       **5** 44.6
**2** 34.5       **6** 70.8
**3** 36.75      **7** 32.125
**4** 20.25      **8** 48.375

## Exercise 12

**1** 43     **5** 55      **9** 27
**2** 58     **6** 29      **10** 22
**3** 66     **7** 34      **11** 67
**4** 42     **8** 31      **12** 98

## Exercise 13

**1** $58\frac{1}{12}$  **7** $15\frac{1}{14}$

**2** $45\frac{3}{13}$  **8** $24\frac{9}{17}$

**3** $47\frac{7}{16}$  **9** $31\frac{3}{13}$

**4** $41\frac{9}{22}$  **10** $17\frac{3}{18} = 17\frac{1}{6}$

**5** $36\frac{6}{24} = 36\frac{1}{4}$  **11** $229\frac{8}{14} = 229\frac{4}{7}$

**6** $24\frac{8}{32} = 24\frac{1}{4}$  **12** $282\frac{6}{15} = 282\frac{2}{5}$

## Exercise 14

**1** 74  **5** 904

**2** 8  **6** 720

**3** 596  **7** 500

**4** 83  **8** 70 000

## Exercise 15

**1** 78  **5** 780

**2** 53  **6** 78

**3** 64  **7** 200

**4** 42  **8** 20

## Exercise 16

**1** 32  **5** 377

**2** 8  **6** 94

**3** 142  **7** 21

**4** 47  **8** 303

## Exercise 17

**1** 5.17  **3** 0.43  **5** 0.402

**2** 8.62  **4** 0.569  **6** 1.05

## Exercise 18

**1** 1.934  **3** 0.385  **5** 0.106

**2** 3.628  **4** 0.169  **6** 0.2704

## Exercise 19

**1** $\frac{7}{9}$  **4** $1\frac{2}{5}$

**2** $\frac{9}{12} = \frac{3}{4}$  **5** $1\frac{3}{8}$

**3** $1\frac{1}{12}$  **6** $1\frac{3}{11}$

## Exercise 20

**1** $\frac{3}{4}$  **5** $\frac{7}{12}$  **9** $\frac{11}{15}$

**2** $\frac{3}{10}$  **6** $\frac{8}{9}$  **10** $\frac{33}{35}$

**3** $\frac{7}{10}$  **7** $\frac{8}{15}$  **11** $\frac{31}{56}$

**4** $\frac{7}{8}$  **8** $\frac{11}{14}$  **12** $1\frac{1}{12}$

## Exercise 21

**1** $\frac{5}{8}$  **5** $\frac{3}{8}$  **9** $\frac{4}{21}$

**2** $\frac{1}{5}$  **6** $\frac{3}{12} = \frac{1}{4}$  **10** $\frac{1}{12}$

**3** $\frac{4}{11}$  **7** $\frac{1}{20}$  **11** $\frac{9}{40}$

**4** $\frac{5}{10} = \frac{1}{2}$  **8** $\frac{1}{6}$  **12** $\frac{25}{88}$

## Exercise 22

**1** $\frac{1}{2}$  **5** $\frac{2}{3}$  **9** $\frac{2}{3}$

**2** $\frac{2}{3}$  **6** $\frac{2}{5}$  **10** $\frac{3}{5}$

**3** $\frac{2}{3}$  **7** $\frac{2}{3}$  **11** $\frac{1}{3}$

**4** $\frac{2}{3}$  **8** $\frac{2}{3}$  **12** $\frac{2}{5}$